EMERGING GOVERNANCE OF A GREEN ECONOMY

The idea of building an economy, which supports sustainable development without degrading the environment has been widely debated and broadly embraced by politicians, civil servants, the media, academics and the public alike for several decades. This book explores the measures being trialled at various levels of governance in the European region to reduce the adverse impacts of human behaviour on the environment whilst simultaneously addressing society's economic and social needs as part of the intended shift towards a 'green' economy. It includes European case studies that scrutinise the efforts being undertaken at subnational, national and regional tiers of governance to facilitate the transition to a low carbon economy. This book will be of interest to graduate students, researchers, practitioners, and policy-makers working in environmental governance, European studies, environmental studies, political science and management studies.

JENNY M. FAIRBRASS is an associate professor at the University of East Anglia. She is a multi- and trans-disciplinary researcher with almost thirty years' experience in investigating the European Union. Her research combines political science, environmental studies and management studies. She has led several large international research teams and has published widely in the areas of environmental policy, energy policy and corporate social responsibility.

NICHOLAS VASILAKOS is a lecturer in International Business at the University of East Anglia, faculty member of the Centre for Competition Policy and the Tyndall Centre for Climate Change Research. Nicholas Vasilakos is one of the two recipients of the 2012 Campbell Watkins award by the International Association for Energy Economics.

EMERGING GOVERNANCE OF A GREEN ECONOMY

Cases of European Implementation

Edited by

JENNY M. FAIRBRASS
University of East Anglia

NICHOLAS VASILAKOS
University of East Anglia

CAMBRIDGE
UNIVERSITY PRESS

CAMBRIDGE
UNIVERSITY PRESS

University Printing House, Cambridge CB2 8BS, United Kingdom

One Liberty Plaza, 20th Floor, New York, NY 10006, USA

477 Williamstown Road, Port Melbourne, VIC 3207, Australia

314–321, 3rd Floor, Plot 3, Splendor Forum, Jasola District Centre, New Delhi – 110025, India

79 Anson Road, #06–04/06, Singapore 079906

Cambridge University Press is part of the University of Cambridge.

It furthers the University's mission by disseminating knowledge in the pursuit of education, learning, and research at the highest international levels of excellence.

www.cambridge.org
Information on this title: www.cambridge.org/9781108490436
DOI: 10.1017/9781108780933

First published 2021

A catalogue record for this publication is available from the British Library.

ISBN 978-1-108-49043-6 Hardback

Contents

Figures and Tables

Figures

Chart

Tables

Contributors

Alejandro Agafonow
Department of Management and Corporate Environment, ESSCA School of Management (Ecole Supérieure des Sciences Commerciales d'Angers), France

Amanar Akhabbar
Department of Management and Corporate Environment, ESSCA School of Management (Ecole Supérieure des Sciences Commerciales d'Angers), France

David Benson
Environment and Sustainability Institute, University of Exeter, UK

Simona Davidescu
EU-Asia Institute, ESSCA School of Management (Ecole Supérieure des Sciences Commerciales d'Angers), France
Department of Politics, University of York, UK

Pauline Deutz
Department of Geography, Geology and Environment, University of Hull, UK

Will Eadson
Centre for Regional Economic and Social Research, Sheffield Hallam University, UK

Jenny M. Fairbrass
Norwich Business School, University of East Anglia, UK

Rosa Maria Fernandez
Department of Social and Political Science, University of Chester, UK

Thomas Hoerber
EU-Asia Institute, ESSCA School of Management (Ecole Supérieure des Sciences Commerciales d'Angers), France

Andrew Jonas
Department of Geography, Geology and Environment, University of Hull, UK

Irene Lorenzoni
School of Environmental Sciences, University of East Anglia, UK

Jeremy Moulton
Department of Politics, University of York, UK

Tim O'Riordan
School of Environmental Sciences, University of East Anglia, UK

Winfried Osthorst
Faculty of Social Sciences, University of Applied Sciences, Bremen, Germany

Jaap Rozema
Formerly School of Environmental Sciences, University of East Anglia, UK
Independent Scholar, Netherlands

Duncan Russel
Department of Politics, University of Exeter, UK

Nicholas Vasilakos
Norwich Business School, University of East Anglia, UK

Aidan While
Department of Urban Studies and Planning, University of Sheffield, UK

Rüdiger Wurzel
Department of Politics, University of Hull, UK

Preface

This edited volume has had a long gestation period. The contributions assembled represent the culmination of more than a dozen years of collaborative research work undertaken by a community of scholars. Some of the origins of the book can be traced back to the work of two consecutive research groups funded by the University Association for Contemporary European Studies (UACES). The first was established in 2006, operated for two years, and focused on 'European Union (EU) Environmental Policy'. The second commenced its work in 2009 and ran for three years, focusing on the 'Governance of Sustainability in the EU'. Typically, during the life of the UACES-funded research groups, a series of workshops (normally three during the funded period) would be held at which original research work would be presented and debated by scholars and practitioners. Ideas relating to the topic of greening an economy were then further developed through an Economic and Social Research Council (ESRC)-funded seminar series, entitled 'Constructing the Green Economy: Integrating Sustainability for Governance', that operated during 2013–2014. The ESRC-funded seminar series comprised four workshops held over a two-year period, in London, in Bradford and in Norwich (at the University of East Anglia). Building on that earlier work, the debate was then continued via a subsequent Society for the Advancement of Management Studies (SAMS)-funded two-day workshop held at the University of East Anglia's Norwich Business School in July 2015. Finally, the contents of the edited book were further refined, shaped and decided at another UACES-funded event held at the University of East Anglia's business school in July 2019. Most importantly, all the contributors present at the final UACES-funded workshop in 2019 were specifically invited to participate because of their proven track records and acknowledged expertise in the chosen field of the 'green economy', established over the course of several years. As a result, the chapters gathered in this edited book represent the best of the papers from more than a decade of research work.

Crucially, continuity for the work was provided by the presence of one lead academic, who co-convened all of the various research groups and workshops mentioned above, usually in harness with an evolving but overlapping community of collaborators. Additionally, further important links were formed and strengthened through the participation of a number of scholars and practitioners who were involved in (all or more than one of) the events. These contributors helped to build, shape and maintain the threads and themes of the emerging debate. In effect, the development of this edited volume took the form of a sustained discussion over the course of several years. It is also worth highlighting that the various events and partnerships mentioned above brought together a variety of participants, ranging from established, eminent academics and leading practitioners to PhD students and early career researchers. Significantly, the workshops and seminars drew on inter- and multi-disciplinary approaches, combining concepts and approaches from a range of disciplines such as political science, geography, economics, environmental studies and law and management studies. In sum, an army of academics, practitioners and support staff were mobilised to see this project through to completion.

Our thanks go to the many participants of the UACES-funded workshops and conferences over the past decade and a half, the ESRC seminars, and the SAMS workshop. It is these participants along with the key staff at Cambridge University Press, namely Emma Kiddle and Sarah Lambert, who have made such a major contribution to the volume. We are deeply in your debt. We thank everyone for their commitment, patience and stamina in seeing this work through to publication.

Book Synopsis

This edited volume represents part of the collective research output of an established group of scholars, based on the work they have undertaken during the past dozen or more years. The book begins with an introductory chapter that sets out the research agenda, closes with a chapter that responds to the core research questions that underpin the scholarship, and sandwiched in between, provides eight case studies. All of the case study chapters are directly concerned with the processes of 'greening' of the European economy, analysed through the lens of governance or multi-level governance (MLG). They furnish examples of the ways in which the idea of a 'green economy' can be understood and is (or can be) enacted in the real world. It is against this background, of the real-world events and debates, that this edited volume reflects on what it means to speak of a 'green economy' in a European context. As a collection, the book also contemplates the actions that may be required (or should or must be taken) to implement 'green' ideas and considers which actors can and need to act (or interact) in realising such a green economy. Various case studies contained in the volume also offer an evaluation of various green policies advocated in Europe and the measures that have been taken in bringing about (or not) a shift towards a green European economy.

Our overriding ambition in assembling this volume is to provoke further, informed debate about constituting a green economy, pose important questions about how such an economy could or should be realised in practice and offer some potential answers or solutions to the problems surrounding the realisation of a green European economy.

Jenny M. Fairbrass and Nicholas Vasilakos

Acknowledgements

The group of scholars who have contributed to this collection wish to acknowledge the support of a number of funding bodies. In chronological order, they are UACES for funding two research networks (2006–2008 and 2009–2012); an ESRC for funding seminar series (2013–2014); the Society for the Advancement of Management Studies for a grant that enabled a workshop in 2015; and, finally, UACES for a further grant that supported the final book-writing workshop in 2018.

Nicholas Vasilakos also acknowledges financial support towards this project from the European Union's Horizon 2020 research and innovation programme under grant agreement 776868.

Abbreviations

ABPs	Associated British Ports
ACER	Agency for the Cooperation of Energy Regulators
AGMA	Association of Greater Manchester Authorities
ARRA	American Recovery and Reinvestment Act
ATC	Average Total Cost
BEIS	Department for Business, Energy and Industrial Strategy
BIS	Bremerhavener Gesellschaft für Investitionsförderung
BRIC	Brazil-Russia-India-China
CC	Climate Change
CEC	Commission of the European Communities
CSR	Corporate Social Responsibility
DEFRA	Department for Environment, Food and Rural Affairs
DG	Directorate General
DGECCSD	Department of Green Economy, Climate Change and Sustainable Development
EAPs	Environmental Action Programmes
EDP	Energias de Portugal
EEC	European Economic Community
EEG	Erneuerbare Energien Gesetz
EFSI	European Fund for Strategic Investment
EIB	European Investment Bank
EM	Ecological Modernisation
ENTSO-E	European Network of Transmission System Operators for Electricity
ESRC	Economic and Social Research Council
ETS	Emission Trading System
EU	European Union
FiT	Feed-in-Tariff

FoE	Friends of the Earth
GCs	Green Certificates
GDP	Gross Domestic Product
GE	Green Economy
GGGI	Global Green Growth Institute
GHG	Green House Gases
GND	Green New Deal
GVA	Gross Value Added
HECA	Home Energy Conservation Act
ICN	International Competition Network
ILO	International Labour Organisation
IMF	International Monetary Fund
IWES	Institute for Wind Energy and Energy System Technology
K-ETS	Korea Emissions Trading Scheme
KW/H	Kilo Watt per Hour
LCGES	Low Carbon and Environmental Goods and Services
LDO	Local Development Order
LEPs	Local Enterprise Partnerships
MC	Marginal Cost
MEWF	Ministry of Environment, Waters and Forests
MLG	Multi-level governance
MR	Marginal Revenue
NEF	New Economics Foundation
NEPUD	New Environmental Protection Politics
NGOs	Non-governmental organisations
OECD	Organisation for Economic Co-operation and Development
OEMs	Original Equipment Manufacturers
OJEU	*Official Journal of the European Union*
OTB	Offshore Terminal Bremerhaven
OWE	Offshore Wind Energy
PCGG	Presidential Committee on Green Growth
R & D	Research and Development
RES	Renewable Energy Sources
RWEA	Romanian Wind Energy Association
SAMS	Society of Advanced Management Studies
SAP	Standard Assessment Procedure
SBI	Social Business Initiative
SCC	Social Cost of Carbon
SD	Sustainable Development
SDCs	Sustainable Development Cities

SDS	Sustainable Development Strategy
SPD	Social Democratic Party
UACES	University Association of Contemporary European Studies
UK	United Kingdom
UN	United Nations
UNDESA	United Nations' Department of Economic and Social Affairs
UNEP	United Nations Environment Programme
UNFCCC	United Nations Framework Convention on Climate
WAB	Wind Energy Agency Bremerhaven/Bremen
WCED	World Commission on Environment and Development
WSSD	World Summit on Sustainable Development

1

The Green Economy

Setting Out the Agenda

JENNY M. FAIRBRASS AND NICHOLAS VASILAKOS

1.1 Introduction

This chapter provides an introduction to the collection of eight case studies presented in this edited volume, all of which are concerned with the processes of 'greening' of the European economy, analysed through the lens of governance or multi-level governance (MLG). In doing so, the main aims are to briefly outline the following: the notion of a 'green' economy; the academic origins of the book and the rationale for the volume, and the choice of case studies; the chosen conceptual framework and the research questions; and, finally, the structure of the book. However, before turning specifically to the idea of a 'green economy', the chapter first sets the scene by examining the real-world context that has triggered and surrounds the debate.

Even the most cursory review of events of recent months and years reveals and highlights the magnitude, scope and urgency of the sustainability issues facing humanity. At local, national, international and global levels of governance, human populations (and other species) face mounting existential and interconnected challenges associated with, inter alia, climate change, food and water supply, energy security and declining biodiversity linked to habitat loss and ecosystem degradation. For example, at the time of writing (late 2019, early 2020), it is clear that 'extreme weather events' are occurring with growing frequency and are having a major impact across the globe.[1] Whilst some parts of the world have suffered exceptionally high levels of rainfall leading to flooding, other places have been subjected to sustained and abnormally high temperatures with lower than average rainfall levels resulting in drought and major fires. These actual episodes, and the

[1] For example, during 2019 Indonesia and parts of Europe were subject to major flooding events and in late 2019, early 2020, several parts of Australia were experiencing their worst bush fires for many years. Both types of events have led to loss of life (both human and other species) and had a devastating impact on the environment. At the time of writing the long-term impacts are unknown but are expected to be highly damaging to life on earth.

forecasts about their attendant longer-term trends, have captured the attention of private individuals, community groups,[2] business actors and public policy-makers alike, and, arguably, have focused minds on the need to take urgent corrective action. There appears to be an intensifying recognition and appreciation that a failure to act swiftly and decisively could be catastrophic for humans and other species. Crucially, however, whilst such understanding is a critical first step towards addressing the prevailing threats; such thinking does need to be translated into real and effective remedial action. To date, such action has not entirely been forthcoming, and those measures that have been taken could be described as 'too little and too late'.

Unsurprisingly, in the absence of significant and impactful practical and definitive strides to address the sustainability challenges referred to immediately above, one typical response tends to be yet another 'call for action' to create or develop a 'green' or 'greener' economy. In other words, members of the public, politicians, civil servants, the media, business organisations and certain interest groups reiterate demands for a greater commitment to and re-doubled efforts geared towards shifting to a low(er)-carbon economy. Amongst those who have issued such a clarion call is the European Union (EU). In its vision of a 'green' economy, entitled 'The European Green Deal' (Commission of the European Communities (CEC), 2019), the EU has very recently repeated its plea for sustainable transport systems, environmentally friendly and energy-efficient food production, cleaner and more affordable secure energy supplies coupled with improved efficiency of use and the means for preserving and restoring ecosystems and biodiversity. Appeals of this type have been issued for a number of years until now but with limited effect to date.

It is against the background of the real-world events and debates briefly mentioned above that this edited volume ponders what it means to speak of a 'green economy' in a European context. As a collection, the book also reflects on what actions may be required (or should or must be taken) to implement 'green' ideas and considers which actors can and need to act (or interact) in realising such a green economy. The various case studies contained in the volume also permit an evaluation of the various green policies advocated and measures taken in shifting (or not) towards a green economy in Europe.

1.2 The Green Economy: Terminology and Definitions

Clearly, the notion of the 'green economy' is not a new idea. Taking a long-term view, its antecedents are discernible in many previous discussions and debates. Its

[2] For example, as reflected in the media attention to Greta Thunberg and as manifested in the high-profile actions of Extinction Rebellion.

origins may be traced over several decades (if not centuries), although different terms have been favoured or fashionable at different points in time and this has somewhat obfuscated deliberations (see Chapter 2 which follows and traces the development of the idea over time). In the past, for example, some governmental bodies, business actors and other non-government organisational actors (NGOs) have deliberately opted to adopt terms such as 'sustainable development', and more recently, 'sustainability' labels that reflect their underpinning bias or approach to the issue. Equally, alternative phrases such as 'low-carbon economy' or a 'circular economy' are also in use now. Furthermore, adding to the fog surrounding this topic, currently, there are now a number of substitute phrases in use that include the word 'green' as an adjective in conjunction with other terms such as 'jobs', 'collar' and 'economy', often used as a direct proxy for 'sustainability'. These patterns signal that over time, notions such as 'sustainability' have been repackaged or rebranded as a 'green economy' by some, partly in an effort to make the idea more appealing and palatable to a wider audience. Business actors, for example, seem to be more comfortable with the term 'green economy' than the other preceding alternative labels and their undertones.

Despite the changes in the use of terminology outlined above, the elements that would typically be thought to comprise the earlier concepts of 'sustainable development' or 'sustainability' are also to be found contained within the notion of the 'green economy', although the nuances and emphases may vary between the different sobriquets or tags. In other words, the 'green economy' can be viewed as one in which various actors seek to address and meet sustainability goals such as those identified in the European Commission's 'Green Deal' document mentioned above and represented by Figure 1.1 taken from that policy document.

What is significant for the purposes of contemporary debates and this edited volume is that the term 'green economy' re-emerged and found favour about a decade ago, used notably as a buzzword in inconclusive discussions across the globe amongst politicians, civil servants, business, NGOs, community interest groups, the media and academics at that point in time. Some of those actors would undoubtedly have argued that by offering the possibility of integrating economic priorities with more ecologically sensitive and socially just forms of overall progress, the concept of a green economy could outwardly provide some direction in terms of the efforts to attain long-term sustainability goals and ambitions across a range of tiers of governance and in different types of economy. Unfortunately, it is likely that for as long as a range of terms can be employed, each conveying different subtexts, the actual words and notion of the 'green economy' (and its synonyms) will remain elusive, deeply disputed, often poorly understood and unevenly applied. Whilst those circumstances prevail, there is every danger that the notion will remain both unworkable and marginalised.

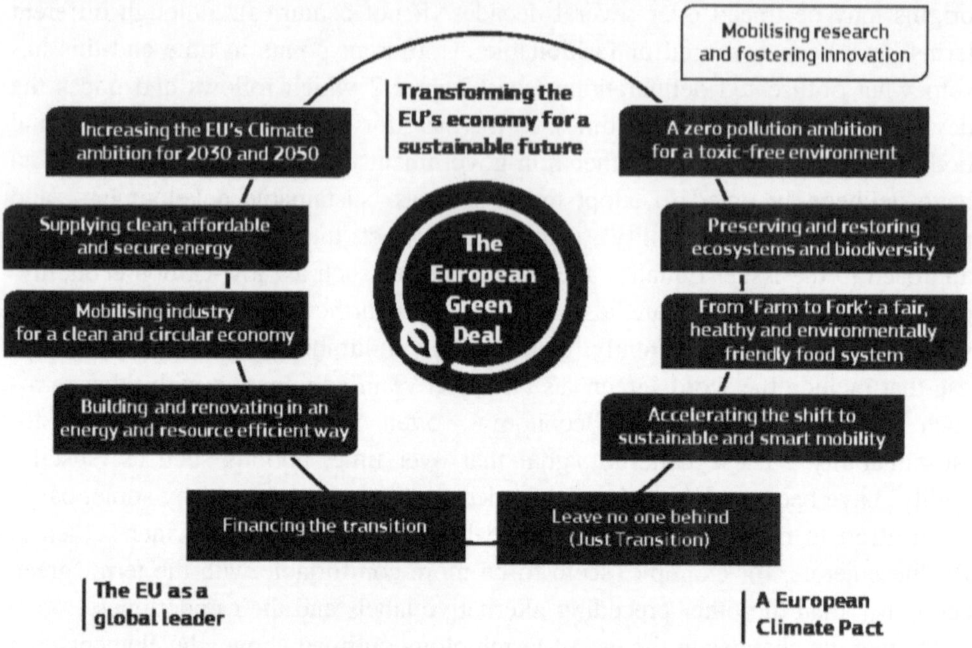

Figure 1.1. The European Green Deal.
Source: European Commission (2019, p. 3)

1.3 Origins and Rationale

1.3.1 Origins of the Collection

The contributions assembled for this edited book represent the culmination of more than a dozen years of collaborative research work. Some of the origins of the book can be traced back to the work of two consecutive University Association for Contemporary European Studies (UACES) – funded research groups.[3] The first was established in 2006, operated for two years, and focused on 'EU Environmental Policy'. The second UACES-funded group commenced its work in 2009 and ran for three years, focusing on the 'Governance of Sustainability in the EU'. Ideas were then further developed through an ESRC-funded seminar series,[4] entitled 'Constructing the green economy: integrating sustainability for governance' that operated during 2013–2014. Additionally, this edited collection draws on a subsequent Society for the Advancement of Management Studies (SAMS) funded a two-day workshop, held at the University of East Anglia – Norwich Business School in July 2015. Finally, the shape and contents of the

[3] Typically, during the life of the UACES-funded research groups, a series of at least three workshops was held at which original research work would be presented by scholars and/or practitioners.
[4] The ESRC-funded seminar series held four workshops during a two-year period.

edited book were decided at another UACES-funded event held at the University of East Anglia – Norwich Business School in July 2019.[5] Crucially, continuity for the work was provided by the continual involvement of one academic[6] in all of these research groups and workshops and the fact that a number of the scholars and practitioners were also involved in, or were present at, all or more than one of the research groups or workshops. In effect, the development of this edited volume took the form of a sustained discussion over several years.

It is also worth highlighting the point that the various events brought together a variety of participants, ranging from established, eminent academics and leading practitioners to PhD students and early career researchers. The workshops and seminars drew on inter- and multi-disciplinary approaches, combining ideas from disciplines such as management studies, economics, political science, geography and environmental studies and law.

1.3.2 Motivations for Assembling the Collection

We had several reasons for undertaking the research that has led to the subsequent construction of this edited collection. Firstly, for the editors and contributors of this edited volume, the burgeoning debate surrounding the topic of the 'green economy' and the variety of terms and meanings in use, provided one of the main reasons for undertaking the project. By assembling this edited book, we aimed to remove, or at least reduce, some of the miasma surrounding the subject and bring some clarity and greater precision to the debate. Secondly, we were inspired by awareness that the issue of the 'transition to a green economy' is especially important at this point in time. This is primarily because it has come to the forefront of public and private agendas and concerns, partly as a result of the real-world events and trends alluded to earlier in this chapter. Thirdly, we were propelled to publish the research accumulated because of the intrinsic importance of the 'green' European economy. As scholars (and citizens) we recognise the critical significance of the potential benefits to humanity of a 'green economy', as well as the dangers of failing to create one. Finally, we were motivated by the

[5] Most importantly, all the contributors present at the UACES-funded workshop in July 2019 were specifically invited to participate because of their proven track-records and acknowledged expertise in the chosen field of the 'Green Economy', established over the course of several years. As a result, the papers gathered for this edited book represent the best of the papers developed during roughly a dozen or more years of research work.

[6] Jenny M. Fairbrass was the common factor. She co-convened all of the research groups named above but on each occasion worked in harness with different colleagues. In the first instance, Jenny M. Fairbrass co-convened the UACES study group with Charlotte Burns who was then at Leeds University. For the second UACES research group, Jenny was joined by Simon Lightfoot (University of Leeds) and Thomas Hoerber (ESSCA). The ERSC seminar series was led by David Benson, Duncan Russel, Tim O'Riordan, Irene Lorenzoni, Camy Adelle and Jenny M. Fairbrass (all associated with the University of East Anglia at one point in time or another). The SAMS workshop in 2015 and the UACES-funded workshop in 2019 were both co-convened by Jenny M. Fairbrass and Nicholas Vasilakos (both at the University of East Anglia), the joint editors of this volume.

desire to create a volume that would have relevance for both scholars and practitioners, and for that reasons, both types of individuals participated in the seminars and workshops that have led to the preparation of this book. As a result, we contend that the book is germane to both categories of readers. Overall, we see this collection as timely and pertinent, and one that addresses a number of significant aims.

1.3.3 Case Study Selection

The case studies selected for this collection were those that best illustrated the emergence of the European 'green' economy from among the papers that were delivered during the development of this edited book (more than twenty-five papers over the course of several years as outlined above), particularly when viewed as an MLG system. Here, it is important to underscore the point that we selected 'Europe' as our focal point and geographical boundary for the book because that region perceives itself to be a 'leader' in this field. As a regional actor that places such a heavy weighting on the formation of a 'green economy', we anticipated that by scrutinising it, we would be able to uncover some vital insights and lessons.

Additionally, in terms of the choices made when assembling the book, we would argue that although this collection is essentially about the very broad topic of 'greening' the European economy, we decided to give greater prominence to energy transitions. Several of the chosen case studies focus on energy and particularly on renewable energy (see Chapters 4–7). That choice was based on the grounds that energy forms an important element of the most characterisations of a green economy. Notably, the EU's 'Green Deal' gives prominence to energy. In addition, energy is not only an important aspect of a 'green economy' in its own right but also has close connections to other dimensions or provides the foundations for other green goals (such as climate change, creating a toxic-free, zero pollution environment and sustainable transport systems). Having outlined the motivations and rationale for this collection and the case studies that it contains, we now turn to the underpinning conceptual frameworks and research questions selected.

1.4 Conceptual Framework Adopted and Research Questions

1.4.1 Literature and Underpinning Concepts

The contributing case study authors were all asked to adopt the same conceptual framework(s) so that the edited collection would have coherence and a shared approach. The notions of 'governance' and 'MLG' were selected as the central, underpinning, common frameworks for the debates contained in this collected volume. Crucially, both concepts have a long and well-developed track record in the context of EU studies and whilst they have both been criticised (and to a certain extent been discarded in recent years), they do still provide a useful, shared point of entry into a discussion about EU public policy-making. Critically, the decision to employ a combined governance/MLG approach was based on preliminary observations that 'governance' (rather than 'government') and MLG are vital and striking features of our chosen policy field: the greening of the European economy.

At this juncture, it is worth underscoring the point that seminal governance literature (Heritier and Rhodes 2011; Jordan and Schout 2006; Kohler-Koch and Eising 1999; Kohler-Koch and Rittberger 2006) invites us to consider the relationships between and the roles of three main sets of public policy actors: government, business and what might be labelled civil society.[7] The relationships and interactions between these actors combine to produce public policy. Empirically speaking, we observe EU level policy being determined or affected by international forums such as the United Nations Framework Convention on Climate Change (UNFCCC), the EU's own commission, parliament and other actors, national governments and subnational governmental bodies. We also witness private sector actors such as the 'big' energy producers endeavouring to influence policy in relation to this critical area. Additionally, civil society in the form of NGOs such as Greenpeace and Friends of the Earth (FoE) also play a role in helping to construct a European 'Green Economic' policy. In other words, the policy-making process has been and is characterised by 'governance' rather than 'government'. Then, given the peculiarities of the EU, we also invoke the idea of MLG (Bache and Flinders 2004; Conzelmann and Smith 2008; Fairbrass and Jordan 2004; Hooghe and Marks 2001, 2003; Jessop 2004; Jordan 2001; Knill and Tosun 2008; Kohler-Koch and Larat 2009; Marks 1993, 1996; Marks and Hooghe 2004; Peters and Pierre 2004; Piattoni 2009; Rosenau 2004), given that the EU exhibits a markedly multi-level or multi-centred character with actors from the international (above the EU), the regional (i.e. the EU's institutions), the national and the subnational all striving to set the 'green' policy agenda, shape that policy and then to varying degrees, implement the agreed policy.

The observations and reflections above then led to the common, underpinning research questions that have been used to shape this edited book. We now turn to those questions.

[7] The term 'civil society' is one of several alternatives in use that essentially points to the same type of organisation. Other labels include 'third sector organisations', 'interest group', 'lobby groups' and 'pressure groups'.

1.4.2 Central Research Questions

To further reinforce the collective effort of the contributors, in addition to highlighting the concepts above, the authors were also asked to address a set of common questions in each of their chapters. Whilst the contributors were given flexibility in terms of their research content about how to respond to the questions, each of the papers included in this volume has addressed one or more of the following questions:

- How is the term 'green economy' being defined in the context of your research?
- What role can businesses play in engendering a 'green economy'?
- What changes can/should businesses undertake with regard to the following in their endeavours to create or help build a 'green economy'?
- What incentives or opportunities do businesses require to encourage them to innovate to help develop a 'green economy'?
- What sort of funding structures/sources and types of capital would assist businesses to shift towards a 'green economy'?
- What types of political/economic environments are required to 'encourage' business organisations to assist in the construction of a 'green economy'?
- What forms of business organisation might be most effective in addressing the shift towards a 'green economy' (e.g. social enterprise, large multi-national, community based)?
- How might the form of business adopted affect or assist in creating 'green local communities'?
- How and to what extent might businesses help to eradicate poverty via their efforts with regard to the construction of a 'green economy' (locally, nationally, and internationally)?
- How do businesses, governmental and civil society organisations relate to one another in seeking to establish a vibrant 'green economy'?
- To what extent and how can 'green jobs' contribute to the construction of the wider 'green economy'?
- What lessons can be drawn for policy-making in this area?

In the concluding chapter of this volume, we summarise the responses to these questions and reflect on what the results reveal.

1.5 Structure and Contents

The seven chapters that form the core of this volume (excluding the Introduction and Chapter 9) were all selected because they highlight or spotlight particular issues relating to the 'greening' of the European economy. Chapter 2 is included because it sets out the terms of the debate about 'greening' an economy and highlights the practical policy issues and obstacles. Chapter 3 was selected because it adopts a more overtly theoretical stance and addresses key questions about the vital role(s) played by key governance actors such as governments in seeking to create a green economy. The first three chapters provide the context and tone for the chapters that follow.

Other contributions (Chapters 4–8) were chosen because they offer fresh empirical data and focus on particular national contexts in 'older' EU member states such as the UK and Germany (in the case of Chapter 6) or on 'newer' EU member states such as Romania (as is the case with Chapter 5). Additionally, the chapters proffered here were selected because they highlight the significant (potential or actual) role of the energy sector in helping (or hindering) the transition to low carbon or green European economy. In effect, evidence about the role played by the energy sector is one of the central themes or topics that lends coherence and commonality to the volume. Moreover, given that all of the chapters utilise certain shared underpinning frameworks and concepts (i.e. 'governance' and 'MLG'), all of the chapters grapple with the issue of the role played by a range of governance actors, at EU, national and subnational or local levels in the private, public and voluntary sectors in 'greening' the European economy. This again provides consistency and cohesion to the collection.

In further detail, Chapter 2 starts with a discussion of the definition of green economies and how this has changed over time. In particular, Benson, Fairbrass, Lorenzoni, O'Riordan and Russel discuss the origins of the term 'green economy', and how this concept re-emerged more than a decade ago in discussions across the globe amongst politicians, civil servants, business, NGOs, community interest groups, the media and academics. The authors argue that the notion of a green economy remains elusive and is deeply disputed, often poorly understood and unevenly applied. Their analysis traces the development of the concept, not only in Europe but beyond, in order to provide context for the deliberations in Europe. The chapter also outlines contemporary debates and identifies emerging themes in order to argue that the idea of a green economy, as currently practiced, requires urgent rethinking and application.

In Chapter 3, Rozema, Fairbrass and Vasilakos consider the ways in which policy actors may advance the notion of a 'green economy' by making it compatible with 'good governance'. As one way of shaping order in advanced industrialised societies, the idea of green economy translates into a discourse propagated by government and non-state actors where it is conceived as 'the right thing to do', thereby fitting current economic activity into governance arrangements which are also tailored to meet environmental objectives. The authors reflect on current theoretical debates about a 'green economy' in the EU as a conception of 'good governance', the latter being an umbrella concept encompassing principles of legitimate public policy-making such as accountability, transparency, public engagement or institutional reform. They conclude that a European green economy can be achieved as a product of 'good governance', whilst also simultaneously considered as 'the right thing to do'. This theoretical reflection reinvigorates interest in normative power and the will to govern as productive forces for governance, through its capacity to instil affinity with a particular rendition of economic ordering.

In Chapter 4, Hoerber, Agafonow and Akhabbar propose a change in the ownership structure of energy utilities through the introduction of social enterprises. This seems to be a pertinent approach, because in parallel to the EU 2020 strategy, the EU has introduced a Social Business Initiative (SBI). The authors of this chapter believe that the combination of both policies can change the ground rules of energy production and provision within the EU. To explain this, the authors use a theoretical model that draws on a MLG framework, which enables the analysis to consider the effects and interdependencies of governance on various actors of the energy sector, namely national governments and energy producers. Their analysis shows that although using social enterprises in the renewable energy sector will foster the emergence of greener communities, it is also more likely to benefit well-off estate owners than less affluent tenants. This effect could be reversed with the design of a regulatory framework that requires social enterprises to use a pricing policy that discriminates clients by their tenure status, charging more affordable prices to tenants only.

Davidescu in Chapter 5 discusses the experience of Romania in transitioning towards a green economy. As the author explains, until recently Romania had limited credentials with regard to ambitious environmental policy and a difficult transition to market economy and democracy. However, the country has surprisingly experienced the emergence of a green economy discourse separate from sustainable development and a range of green economy initiatives in niche sectors and across different levels of government, with a peak of activity in 2016–2017. The chapter links this to the agenda of a technocratic caretaker government, as well as the emergence of subnational actors from the environmental movement and local and regional level, who were able to successfully engage in green economy initiatives, bypassing the national government level. Using the example of the renewable energy sector, this chapter shows that significant growth in this area usually associated with the green economy, does not necessarily ensure either sustained or green practices.

Chapter 6 assesses the attempts of maritime port cities to use the green economy in a bid to overcome long-term structural disadvantages. Moulton, Osthorst, Deutz, Jonas and Wurzel argue that these cities perceive climate change not only as a threat but also as an opportunity for 'green' growth in the form of new technologies and industries (such as the renewable energy industry). However, the emerging literature on the green economy underlines the dangers of uneven chances to exploit economic opportunities, reinforced spatial competition, and the prevalence of technocratic, instead of transformative, strategies. The chapter uses as a case study Bremerhaven (Germany) and Hull (UK); two coastal cities that suffered major economic setbacks as a result of severe declines in local maritime industries (e.g. fisheries and shipbuilding). Albeit with differing strategies, both cities have turned to renewables, especially offshore wind, and the 'green' improvement of public housing as a source of jobs and growth. The analysis that is presented in this chapter shows how local green economies can develop, and what impact they may have on local economies. The cases also exhibit the challenges that cities can face in trying to maintain their role as centres for the green economy, including tough financial restrictions (a hallmark of the problems faced by structurally disadvantaged cities when conditions are exacerbated by austerity), regional competition and changing national policy contexts.

The changing role of energy companies in the context of European green economies is examined by Fernandez in Chapter 7. As the author explains, the traditional model of a European energy company has been characterised by big entities that usually play a relatively important role as national champions in terms of market share, assets value, vertical integration, political influence and employment volumes, among other factors. However, the last decade has seen these big firms losing market power to new entrants. This chapter uses the framework of green economy as the one that approaches macroeconomic issues through innovative ways, promoting green investments through the most adequate regulatory measures, and considering green energy as one of the sectors where these investments should be focused. The chapter goes on to point out the important role of energy companies in the transition of Europe into a green economy. The chapter also highlights the barriers that energy companies impose themselves through old fashioned strategies that do not take into consideration the wider demands from a much larger group of stakeholders in a changing society, and argues for the importance of embracing a business model that is proactive and in favour of change, rather than try to maintain the status quo.

In Chapter 8, Eadson and While examine how definitions of the green economy are shaped by and seek to shape norms and discourses of economic development. The authors draw on multi-level governance theories alongside literature from critical accounting to investigate ways that urban policy actors have sought to make the case for investment in the green economy. In doing so the chapter expands existing conceptualisations of the politics of calculation (in a multi-level governance context) to illuminate how calculations represent a range of assumptions about territory, the way people live and the nature of place and society in the present and the future. Empirically the chapter focuses on a series of 'Mini-Stern' reports commissioned by urban governments in England which took as inspiration Nicholas Stern's influential 2006 report on the economics of climate change. The authors analyse how these reports use various calculative devices relating to carbon reduction in order to justify, de-risk and legitimise what might be seen as experimental or risky policy options; and the implications for how cities are represented as a result.

Finally, in Chapter 9, the conclusions chapter, Vasilakos and Fairbrass provide a capstone commentary on the edited volume as a whole, returning to the underpinning research questions and conceptual frameworks, Governance and Multi-level Governance, summarising the findings of the eight case study chapters, and reflecting on the key results and what they reveal about the greening of the European economy, the limitations of the research conducted and presented, and outlining some ideas for further research.

References

Bache, I. and Flinders, M., eds. (2004). *Multi-level Governance*. Oxford: Oxford University Press.

Commission of the European Communities (2019) *Communication from the Commission to the European Parliament, the European Council, the Council, the European Economic and Social Committee and the Committee of the Regions*. The European Green Deal. COM (2019) 640 final. Brussels: European Commission.

Conzelmann, T. and Smith, R., eds. (2008). *Multi-level Governance in the European Union: Taking Stock and Looking Ahead*. Baden Baden: Nomos.

Fairbrass, J. and Jordan, A. (2004). Multi-level governance and environmental policy. In I. Bache and M. Flinders, eds., *Multi-level Governance*. Oxford: Oxford University Press, pp. 147–164.

Heritier, A. and Rhodes, M. (2011). *New Modes of Governance in Europe: Governing in the Shadow of Hierarchy*. Basingstoke: Palgrave Macmillan.

Hooghe, L. and Marks, G. (2001). *Multi-level Governance and European Integration*. Lanham, MD: Rowman & Littlefield.

Hooghe, L. and Marks, G. (2003). Unraveling the central state, but how? Types of multi-level governance. *American Political Science Review*, 97(2), 233–243.

Jessop, B. (2004). Multi-level governance and multi-level metagovernance. In I. Bache and M. Flinders, eds., *Multi-level Governance*. Oxford: Oxford University Press, pp. 49–74.

Jordan, A. (2001).The European Union: an evolving system of multi-level governance ... or government? *Policy and Politics*, 29(2), 193–208.

Jordan, A. and Schout, A. (2006). *The Coordination of the European Union: Exploring the Capacities of Networked Governance*. Oxford: Oxford University Press.

Knill, C. and Tosun, J. (2008). Emerging patterns of multi-level governance in EU Environmental Policy. In T. Conzelmann and R. Smith, eds., *Multi-level Governance in the European Union: Taking Stock and Looking Ahead*. Baden Baden: Nomos, pp. 145–162.

Kohler-Koch, B. and Eising, R., eds. (1999). *The Transformation of Governance in the European Union*. London: Routledge.

Kohler-Koch, B. and Larat, F., eds. (2009). *European Multi-level Governance: Contrasting Images in National Research*. Cheltenham: Edward Elgar.

Kohler-Koch, B. and Rittberger, B. (2006). Review Article: the 'governance turn'. *EU Studies, Journal of Common Market Studies*, 44, 27–49.

Marks, G. (1993). Structural policy and multi-level governance in the EC. In A. Cafruny and G. Rosenthal, eds., *The State of the European Community: The Maastricht Debate and Beyond*. Boulder, CO: Lynne Rienner, pp. 391–411.

Marks, G. (1996). An actor-centred approach to multi-level governance. *Regional and Federal Studies*, 6(2), 20–38.

Marks, G. and Hooghe, L. (2004). Contrasting visions of multi-level governance. In I. Bache and M. Flinders, eds., *Multi-level Governance*. Oxford: Oxford University Press, pp. 15–30.

Peters, B. and Pierre, J. (2004). Multi-level governance and democracy: a Faustian bargain? In I. Bache and M. Flinders, eds., *Multi-level Governance*. Oxford: Oxford University Press, pp. 75–89.

Piattoni, S. (2009). Multi-level governance: a historical and conceptual analysis. *Journal of European Public Policy*, 31(2), 163–180.

Rosenau, J. (2004). Contrasting visions of multi-level governance. In I. Bache and M. Flinders, eds., *Multi-level Governance*. Oxford: Oxford University Press, pp. 31–48.

2

The Green Economy

Changing Meanings in a Changing World

DAVID BENSON, JENNY M. FAIRBRASS, IRENE LORENZONI, TIM O'RIORDAN AND DUNCAN RUSSEL

2.1 Introduction

Chapter 1 established the research objectives and questions that provide coherence and common ground for the volume. Simultaneously, it provided the adopted theoretical approach of the work: namely, multi-level governance (MLG). This conceptual framework is employed as a lens for exploring the concept of greening the European economy. In keeping with the MLG approach, this chapter traces the development of the notion on a global scale, setting Europe in a wider international context, and then highlights current debates and emerging themes to offer a critique. The chapter outlines the conceptual setting that provides the backdrop to the remainder of the edited volume, in which European-focused case studies wrestle with the definitional issues and complex and testing practicalities of implementation.

The concept of the green economy has enjoyed a renaissance in recent years (Barbier and Markandya, 2013; Bailey and Caprotti, 2014; Russel and Benson, 2014; Loiseau et al., 2016; Gasparatos et al., 2017; New Economics Foundation, 2019), an idea that has its origins in earlier green economic thinking. The notion has enjoyed a renewed interest globally since 2008, when the near collapse of the global financial system and ensuing economic malaise that swept through countries in Europe, and beyond, in the wake of the so-called 'credit crunch' and banking crisis, led to the resuscitation of the concept as a potential remedy to the 'double crisis' of financial collapse and dangerous climate change (Bina and La Camera, 2011; Bina, 2013). Consequently, the green economy concept was advocated to national governments by the United Nations Environment Programme (UNEP) as part of its Global Green New Deal (GND) initiative (UNEP, 2009). Here, the creation of green jobs and environmentally light-touch industries were considered an obvious 'political fix' to these twin threats. Such arguments initially fell on fertile political ground in industrialised states where governments were quick to seize upon the notion of a green economy to inform sustainability-focused policymaking.

Building on this earlier thinking, in this chapter, we draw together different analyses to explore the changing concept of the green economy and its implementation on a global scale as a means of developing a more thorough and detailed examination of the European context. In so doing, we highlight three key arguments. First, economic instability and turmoil, and indeed the failure to provide decent living standards and offer consistent well-being for all within the existing social and ecological restraints, has significantly elevated the salience and importance of the green economy concept in academic and public policymaking discussions. Prior to the 2008 economic crisis, the idea of any green economy was rarely contemplated, even as a medium-term priority within established policy circles. Instead, the concept was largely confined to academic debates about sustainable development (for example, Pearce et al., 1989; Jacobs, 1992). Second, since 2008, there has been a divergence in interpretations of the green economy concept, with only limited implementation in practice. Third, while re-evaluation and review of the green economy concept provide an important opportunity for reorientating economic activity, ultimately the concept alone is not sufficient to enable and promote the transformations necessary to achieve desirable sustainability-focused economic and social outcomes. We contend that new conceptualisations, stressing the social fairness aspects of green economics, are required along with better prescriptions about how to implement the concept in practice.

This chapter adopts the following structure. It initially places the conceptualisation of the green economy in its social and historical context by tracing the evolution of the idea. It then maps the current conceptual, theoretical and empirical landscape within the green economy debate to show how it is being variably and opportunistically interpreted across multiple levels of governance in Europe and beyond, drawing upon overlapping and often competing concepts such as GNDs, green growth and the circular economy. Lastly, the chapter reflects on the potential for revising the green economy concept to account for current socio-economic and environmental conditions and emerging social mores.

2.2 A Social History of the Green Economy Concept

Earlier phases of green economic thinking can be traced via a philosophical focus on localism, new forms of environmental democracy, welfare economics, the *Limits to Growth* and sustainable development debates, notions of ecological modernisation and *Blueprints*, and the post-2008 green economy renaissance, arriving at its most recent political reincarnation in the form of the so-called GND (Commission of the European Communities (CEC), 2019). Given this eclectic history, the idea of a green economy is understood in a number of diverse and competing ways. We now explore a number of key interpretations in turn as they have developed over time.

2.2.1 The Enlightenment and Localism

Arguably, the green economy concept is rooted in eighteenth- and nineteenth-century philosophical traditions. The Enlightenment era had '... popularized ... [a] belief in progress, critical reasoning, natural rights, utilitarianism, laissez-faire economics, and environmental relativism'. (Andrews, 2006: 21) Nature was no longer viewed in 'divine' terms, but rather as a resource to be dominated and exploited by human endeavour. Unrestrained economic growth during the early Victorian period (in Britain, for example) brought both appalling social conditions for the burgeoning urban working classes (Engels, originally 1845, reprinted 1987) and rampant degradation of environmental stocks. As a reaction to the growing negative impacts of industrialisation, opinion formers from different traditions throughout Europe began to re-evaluate the relationship between economic growth and its social and environmental implications. At this time, radical thinkers such as Peter Kropotkin and Arthur Geddes (Meller, 1993) developed the beginnings of a deep 'green' economic agenda that eschewed exploitative capitalism and political centralisation in favour of local scale, cooperative self-sufficiency based on mutual exchanges (Kropotkin, originally 1902, reprinted 2006).

2.2.2 Environmental Limits

A subsequent wave of thinking grew out of developments in welfare economics in the mid twentieth century. Arthur C. Pigou (1952) helped to establish the notion of negative external effects, or externalities. These became manifest in rising levels of affluence across the Western world in the 1950s and 1960s, which were procured at a high cost in terms of acute environmental and social consequences (Connelly et al., 2012). Neo-classical economists such as Ezra J. Mishan (1967) drew on the Pigovian tradition to argue that without the appropriate level of protection of amenity rights, ever-increasing production could actually reduce overall societal welfare due to declining environmental quality. Mishan recognised that his solution, the introduction of pollution rights, raised significant issues over the quantification and hence the appropriate valuation of externalities (van der Straaten and Gordon, 1995). Nevertheless, his work helped to lay the foundations for the subsequent development of the green economy perspective.

Subsequently, the late 1960s witnessed the emergence of the concept of environmental limits. Kenneth Boulding (1966), via his metaphor of the 'spaceship economy', argued that contemporary economics tended to treat environmental resources as infinite. By the early 1970s, such ideas had gained traction with academics and policy actors. Along with the publication of the *Limits to Growth* by Meadows et al. (1972), influential thinkers such as Herman Daly (1977) and Walter Stahel and Geneviève Reday (1976) expanded the notion of scarcity and absolute limits, arguing that neo-classical economic theory downplayed the finite nature of environmental resources. These ideas were subsequently incorporated into current circular economy frameworks (see, for example, Geissdoerfer et al., 2017; Howard et al., 2018), discussed in Section 2.3 of this chapter.

2.2.3 Brundtland and Blueprints

Arguments about 'limits' were most famously addressed in the landmark United Nations-sponsored Brundtland Commission Report *Our Common Future* (World Commission on Environment and Development (WCED), 1987). The Commission sought to circumvent failings in traditional economic strategies through elaborating the concept of sustainable development that would meet '... needs of the present without compromising the ability of future generations to meet their own needs'. (WCED, 1987: 43)

Implicit within this definition is the view that sustainable development must not only enable prosperity that is more equitable but also offer the opportunity for all future citizens to be able to flourish in the changing circumstances bequeathed to them. This, in turn, places real constraints not only on natural resource depletion and the enhancement of the global commons, nature-support functions but also places a duty on technological development to ensure that the outcomes of any advances create equitable opportunities for all future generations, so that:

> In essence, sustainable development is a process of change in which the exploitation of resources, the direction of investment, the orientation of technological development, and institutional change are all in harmony and enhance both current and future potential to meet human needs and aspirations.
>
> *(WCED, 1987: 46)*

Various interpretations have since emerged from the Commission's conceptualisation of sustainable development. These can be summarised as sitting on a continuum that ranges from weak to strong (Baker, 2016).

One pivotal feature of the Commission's definition is the emphasis on the inter-generational maintenance of critical natural capital stocks. These characteristics proved to be hugely influential in the ground-breaking *Blueprint for a Green Economy* series (Pearce et al., 1989). For David Pearce and colleagues, sustainable development could be pursued as long as inter-generational equity is maintained through a 'constant capital' bequest comprising an aggregate of natural and human capital (Pearce et al., 1989: 48), providing a strong rationale for valuing environmental assets. Furthermore, the authors made the case for maintaining natural capital wherever possible due to the limited substitutability of many environmental resources. The *Blueprint* series also proved persuasive through its elaboration of valuing techniques such as cost-benefit analysis and market-based policy instruments for economic greening. Green economic thinking, as a whole, had by this point become divided over the substitutability of these natural stocks with other forms of capital (e.g. technological infrastructure or financial). Strong conceptions of sustainable development argue that substitution is non-permissible. Weaker interpretations suggest that development can be sustainable as long as the overall stock of different capitals is maintained (Gutés, 1996).

2.2.4 Ecological Modernisation

The arguments of the Brundtland Commission helped popularise important concepts focused around weaker but more widely politically acceptable notions of sustainable development. One such concept is ecological modernisation, which can be traced back to the early 1980s via the work of authors such as Joseph Huber and Martin Jänicke, and which found widespread favour in the post-Brundtland period (Mol and Spaargaren, 2000; Jänicke, 2008). In essence, ecological modernisation seeks to integrate environmental concerns into markets specifically, and the economy more broadly, through a variety of governance mechanisms such as regulation, market-based instruments and voluntary modes of steering (Mol et al., 2010). Problematically, these weaker market-led conceptions of the green economy continue to downplay environmental limits and make little reference to well-being and fairness themes. They rely on change enabled almost exclusively by technological innovation, underpinned by scientific developments and the decoupling of economic growth and environmental impacts. Ecological modernisation ideas initially found a receptive audience in the 'greener' European states such as Germany and Denmark but have subsequently been espoused, to varying degrees of success, in other national contexts (Mol et al., 2010). Notably, they have also underpinned the environmental policy of the European Union (EU) (Benson and Jordan, 2013).

2.2.5 Governance and Business

Political resistance to implementing sustainable development in the 2000s prompted another phase in the green economy discourse. This period placed greater emphasis on the putative role of business actors as key players in the delivery of sustainability, which relied on translating sustainability into corporate social responsibility (CSR) (see, for example, Carroll, 1979, 1991; Matten and Crane, 2005; Husted and Allen, 2006; Fairbrass and Zueva-Owens, 2012) at the level of the individual firm or industry. This line of thinking emerged partly because of the allegedly shifting roles of, and relationships between, public, private and third sectors as part of move away from government to governance. This, in turn, was thought to blur the lines of demarcation between these social actors (see, for example, Rhodes, 1997, 2000), although, arguably, the boundaries between such actors may have actually been fluid for some time previously but, perhaps not acknowledged.

Crucially, whilst in previous decades, society would most likely have turned to state actors to 'resolve' social, economic and environmental problems and crises, public sector bodies were finding themselves increasingly impotent in the face of globalisation and ever more interconnected global problems (Moon, 2004; Connelly et al., 2012). Consequently, governmental bodies began to solicit help from others such businesses and the third sector actors with regard to the delivery of sustainability goals (Albareda et al., 2008; Lozano et al., 2008; Fairbrass and Zueva-Owens, 2012). It was considered that powerful and better resourced private-sector corporations might have a greater capacity to realise sustainability goals. Some authors have even gone so far as to argue that corporations ought to shoulder these social, environmental responsibilities as well as economic ones to earn their 'licence to operate' (see, for example, Buhmann, 2016; Demuijnck and Fasterling, 2016).

To illustrate this new wave of thinking, it is worth particularly focusing on the reports that were prepared for the World Summit on Sustainable Development (WSSD) in Johannesburg in 2002, an event convened as a stocktake of the goals met since the Rio UN Conference on Sustainable Development in 1992, and which identified limited progress on implementing the ambitious Agenda 21 (Baker, 2016). As alluded to above, one of the main outputs of the WSSD was an agreement in the Johannesburg Plan of Implementation to strengthen operationalisation of sustainable development through Type II partnerships. Reflective of collaborative or relational governance, such partnerships were intended to enlist the engagement of multiple actors, including civil society and business in delivering specific projects. Such approaches then proliferated within a global partnership paradigm (Glasbergen et al., 2007). However, such pacts have proved to be highly controversial (see for example The Guardian, 2001). Some environmentalists were becoming increasingly doubtful about the willingness and ability of corporations to deliver sustainable development (see, for example, The Guardian, 2014). This broad failure, in part, has led to the continuing UN focus on global and universal sustainable development goals.

Similar patterns of thought and action have been replicated both at the EU level and in national arenas (such as the UK). During the 2000s, for example, the EU engaged in public consultations on CSR, produced a number of policy papers on the topic, and established stakeholder forums (that included public, private and voluntary sector actors) to debate the issue of sustainability and more particularly CSR (Commission of the European Communities (CEC) 2001, 2002, 2006). However, these events and policy papers were also viewed with some distrust and misgivings by many non-business actors given that in the European context one of the bones of contention centred on whether CSR should be mandated or voluntary (Fairbrass, 2011). Whilst CSR continued to be optional for corporations, this only underlined the fears and suspicions of other actors (the non-governmental actors, in particular) about the implausibility of the private sector as the guardian or promoter of CSR and sustainability (Fairbrass, 2011). More widely, others have highlighted the 'green-washing' practices of business organisations (see, for example, Bowen, 2014; Delmas and Burbano, 2011) in which firms appear to subscribe to and embrace sustainability goals and ambitions but simultaneously continue to operate a 'business as usual' approach, privileging profit over social benefits or environmental protection. Any residual faith that public policymakers and wider society may have had in the capacity of business to act in environmentally, socially and economically responsible ways may have been further eroded when the world entered a period of unprecedented financial and economic turmoil in the late 2000s, a development that some have attributed, in part, to business malpractice.

2.3 Mapping the Multi-level Green Economy Landscape: New Deals, Green Growth and Circularity

The green economy had already emerged as a profoundly disputed concept before 2008. This contestation had deep historical roots, as the idea was continually re-invented in order to reflect changing economic, social and environmental contexts. Current conceptions mirror this eclecticism: they are diffuse, confusing and bear the traces of the different elements of these earlier discursive waves. By scrutinising its multi-level political evolution since 2008, it is evident that several, often overlapping discursive themes, have now come to the fore that are centred on the notions of the GND, an extension of Keynesian demand management, green growth and the circular economy, the last of these being a concept that revives earlier closed-loop economy arguments.

2.3.1 Green New Deal and Green Growth

In past decades, faced with arguably the most serious global financial crisis since the 1930s, the United Nations Environment Programme (UNEP) sought to reinvigorate the green economy concept as a means of engaging business interests in the sustainability agenda. It sought to re-frame the green economy in the language of Keynesian macroeconomics. John Maynard Keynes had earlier theorised that ending the Great Depression of the 1930s was possible through government monetary policy (i.e. lowering interest rates) but also expansionary fiscal policy (i.e. increasing public expenditure) to create demand and hence stimulate job creation through a multiplier effect (Keynes, 1933). These ideas subsequently influenced Roosevelt's New Deal of 1933. Through its Global GND, the UNEP, therefore, recommended that national governments follow this interventionist thinking to use fiscal stimuli to support green industry, jobs and technological innovation, thereby re-inflating depressed economies (UNEP, 2009).

At this point, it is worth recalling the UN's definition of a green economy, which it characterises as:

> *...one that results in improved human well-being and social equity, while significantly reducing environmental risks and ecological scarcities.*
>
> *(UNEP, 2010: 5)*

Other global initiatives emerged in response to this agenda, particularly around the notion of green growth (Jänicke, 2012; Barbier, 2014). In 2009, all 30 members of the Organisation for Economic Co-operation and Development (OECD), many of whom are European states, signed the Green Growth Declaration in support of the UNEP recommendations. According to the Declaration, countries agreed to strengthen their:

> *...efforts to pursue green growth strategies as part of our response to the current crisis and beyond, acknowledging that "green" and "growth" can go hand-in-hand*
>
> *(OECD, 2009: 1).*

In this respect, governments recognised the importance of green investment and sustainable management of natural resources (OECD, 2009), with different policy instruments recommended in support. A Green Growth Strategy, designed to meet these aims, was published in 2011 (OECD, 2011). This Strategy, outlined in the OECD's report, *Towards Green Growth*, defines green growth as:

> *...fostering economic growth and development, while ensuring that natural assets continue to provide the resources and environmental services on which our well-being relies*
>
> *(OECD, 2011: 9).*

Green growth was subsequently endorsed by multilateral development institutions, including the Asian Development Bank and the World Bank. The latter published its strategy document *Inclusive Green Growth: The Pathway to Sustainable Development* in 2012 (World Bank, 2012), leading to the creation of the Green Growth Knowledge Platform with the OECD, UNEP and the Global Green Growth Institute (GGGI).

The EU had also reacted to these demands for action. In 2009, the European Commission had undertaken a review of its Sustainable Development Strategy (SDS), concluding that although the Union had taken a lead in mainstreaming sustainable development into policy in Europe, further action was required (CEC, 2009). In response, the European Commission and Council utilised the EU's overarching economic policy, the *Europe 2020 Strategy* (2010), to link economic prosperity to the achievement of environmental (mainly around greenhouse gas (GHG) emission reductions) and social (e.g. social exclusion and poverty reduction) goals. The main policy initiatives identified to pursue these aims were the European Fund for Strategic Investment (EFSI), adjustments to the Energy Union, enhancing existing climate change policy and promoting circular economy policies. As discussed below, the notion of the green economy was then subsumed by the circular economy agenda in EU policy circles after 2015 (Fitch-Roy *et al.*, 2019).

These international and supranational responses were, to an extent, converted into action at the national level reflecting the multi-level character of the policy issue. One of the most well-known national policies comes from South Korea, where the *Low-Carbon Green Growth* policy, which was originally adopted in 2008, was extended in response to the OECD and World Bank green growth agenda (Global Green Growth Institute, 2015). A Five-Year Plan was developed for the period 2009–2013 along with a *National Strategy for Green Growth (2009–2050),* based on the notion of low-carbon green growth in which climate emissions are reduced and green technologies, jobs and industries are stimulated. An ambitious national target to reduce GHG emissions by 30 per cent by 2020 was set to drive this policy forward. Other policy innovations included a Presidential Committee on Green Growth (PCGG) and the Korea Emissions Trading Scheme (K-ETS), which was established in 2015.

In other countries such as the UK, GND's thinking was also influential (Russel and Benson, 2014). Faced with an existential collapse of the banking system in 2008, the UK Labour Government had adopted an interventionist fiscal approach to support the economy, borrowing heavily to bail out ailing financial institutions. As explained by Russel and Benson (2014), the then newly formed 2010 Coalition (Conservative–Liberal Democrat) Government made strong rhetorical commitments to environmental investments through fiscal stimulus in what Prime Minister Cameron pledged would be the 'greenest government ever' (Cameron, 2010). Multiple pledges to environmental policy, particularly climate emissions reductions, were made as part of the Conservative's *Vote Blue, Go Green* modernisation agenda (Carter and Clements, 2015). This environmentally supportive position was also endorsed by their coalition partners, the Liberal Democrats, who were perceived as the most 'green' mainstream political party in the UK at the time.

In parallel, Barrack Obama had been swept to Presidential power in 2009 in the United States of America, pledging action on climate change as part of a wider federal fiscal stimulus for economic recovery (Russel and Benson, 2014). In common with the UK, the US economy had also been hit hard by the credit crunch financial crisis, culminating in the collapse of Lehman Brothers bank in 2008, which became synonymous with the systemic institutional financial mismanagement that had occurred under the Bush administration. One of the first policy acts by Obama was to agree to the $789 billion federal American Recovery and Reinvestment Act (ARRA) of 2009, which allocated $16.8 billion to the Department of Energy for energy efficiency and renewable energy provision in addition to significant funding for water-related projects (Congress.Gov, 2009). This approach reflected the New Deal rhetoric, in particular the ideas of influencers such as Van Jones (2008) who talked optimistically of the emergence of a green collar economy that would simultaneously address unemployment while also solving critical environmental problems.

2.3.2 *Circular Economy*

Another parallel discourse emerging alongside the GND and green growth is the circular economy. Although many definitions of the circular economy exist, essentially it equates to:

> *...an economic system that replaces the 'end-of-life' concept with reducing, alternatively reusing, recycling and recovering materials in production/distribution and consumption processes*
>
> *(Kirchherr* et al., *2017: 229).*

Its origins date back centuries (Ghisellini *et al.*, 2016) but modern interpretations relate to the closed-loop economy arguments of Walter Stahel and Genevieve Reday (Stahel and Mulvey-Reday, 1981; Stahel, 2016). Developed during the economic crisis of the 1970s, the notion of closed-loop production suggested that employment could be generated through greater recycling and reconditioning of waste products. Closed-loop economy arguments initially found favour with the European Commission in the 1970s, influencing elements of early European Economic Community (EEC) waste and resource use policy (Fitch-Roy *et al.*, 2019). They then evolved through more industry-specific concepts such as 'industrial ecology' (Jelinski *et al.*, 1992), to influence the *3R* (Reduce, Reuse, Recycle) policy agenda in Asia. In this respect, ASEAN has proved a significant 'transfer agent' (Stone, 2004) in translating these ideas into national industrial strategies. Japan has long prioritised the *3R* concept in national policy and could be considered both a pioneer and innovator of this policy approach. The Japanese *Basic*

Law for Establishing a Sound Material-Cycle Society 2000 and its associated plans form the basis of integrating the circular economy across society through comprehensive waste management and recycling measures.

Since 2012, the circular economy idea has rapidly evolved to become a favoured object of international policy worldwide, particularly in the EU, which first adopted its Circular Economy Package in 2015, updated in 2018. The diffusion of circular economy policy packages has occurred in parallel at the national level of governance. For example, in China, the *Circular Economy Promotion Law 2008* set the regulatory framework for the circular economy by compelling provinces to adopt plans for recycling and recovery (Su *et al.*, 2013). The Netherlands and its *Circular Economy Programme* (2016), Finland with its *Finnish Road Map to a Circular Economy 2016–2025* (SITRA, 2016), and Denmark's *National Strategy for the Circular Economy 2018* (The Danish Government, 2018) all provide other innovative examples. At the sub-national level of governance, provincial and state governments have also jumped on the circular economy bandwagon, with regions, provinces or states of the UK (i.e. Scotland), Belgium (i.e. Flanders), China (i.e. Hong Kong), Spain (i.e. Catalonia), Canada (i.e., Ontario) and Australia (i.e. New South Wales), amongst others, all introducing dedicated policies (Benson and Monciardini, 2018).

2.3.3 Green New Deal 2.0

A post-script to the initial wave of the GND was evident in 2019 (The Guardian, 2019a; The New York Times, 2019). In what we might term *GND 2.0*, Democrats in the USA revitalised this notion by introducing a Congressional Resolution (H.Res.109) in February 2019. This measure, promoted by Democrat Congresswoman Alexandria Ocasio-Cortez, called for a GND to be adopted by the federal government, aimed at job creation and reductions of GHG emissions to net zero over the next 10 years (The Washington Post, 2019). Despite pledges to promote renewable energy, clean manufacturing, upgrade infrastructure and create high-quality jobs, the Resolution met with predictable scepticism from Republicans. As a result, it failed to be adopted in Congress. However, inspired by these events in the US, UK grassroots activists in the opposition Labour Party then launched a campaign to make a GND official policy. The campaign sought to commit the Labour leadership to decarbonise the UK economy within 10 years, while guaranteeing green jobs, expanding public ownership of industry and increasing government spending on infrastructure (The Guardian, 2019a). Labour then announced plans for a green industrial revolution in tackling the climate emergency and generating green jobs, specifically by fitting solar panels to 1.75 million homes (The Guardian, 2019b). That said the current political preoccupation with Brexit (at the time of writing) might keep the green economy off the UK political agenda for some time to come.

2.4 Resolving the Double Crisis: A Critique of Contemporary Green Economy Approaches

As stated above, UNEP (2010) has defined the green economy as one that results in socio-economic improvements while significantly reducing environmental problems, but this begs the question: To what extent are current conceptions addressing the double crisis? Here, available evidence suggests that there is a significant gap between the green economy rhetoric and actual implementation at different levels of governance, reflecting tensions with counter-populist and neoliberal agendas in various political contexts.

When examining the contribution of current green economy initiatives to the improvement of human well-being and social equity, there are evident problems, particularly with its implementation at the national scale. Using the example of the UK, the political commitments of 2010 proved short-lived. This situation occurred as the consequence of an insidious shift in Government fiscal policy that moved away from GND thinking towards an overt austerity agenda as the economic crisis deepened and right-wing political antipathy strengthened towards environmental policy (Russel and Benson, 2014). Rather than being seen as a means of generating economic growth, environmental protection subsequently slipped down the government's list of priorities, to almost disappear as an issue by the time of the 2017 general election, with UK politics by this point dominated by Brexit concerns. Pursuit of an austerity-led economic approach, adopted at the expense of GND thinking since 2010, has failed to resolve critical sustainability issues, particularly growing social inequality. Indeed, the New Economics Foundation (NEF) (2019) refers to an economic system that is broken. Problematically for delivery of the green economy, this system, it argued:

> *. . .has delivered a decade of wage stagnation, left millions of people feeling squeezed and led to rising poverty and inequality*
>
> *(NEF, 2019: 3).*

The GND was also unsuccessful in securing a long-term foothold in US federal policy-making. Rather than becoming an interventionist attempt at Keynesian demand management, ARRA became a focus for a right-wing political backlash to Obama's policies in the form of the so-called *Tea Party*. This grassroots ultra-conservative movement, based upon libertarian values and a climate sceptic agenda, was instrumental in catalysing public support for the Republican Party in the 2010 midterm Congressional elections, helping it to increase the number of both Senate and House of Representative seats for the party. With his room for political manoeuvre circumscribed, Obama was gradually forced to row back on earlier commitments to fund social and environmental initiatives, also abandoning his flagship cap-and-trade climate policy (Russel and Benson, 2014). The Trump Presidential era, despite falling unemployment, has witnessed the attempted reversal of previous advances in US social-economic policy (such as *Obamacare*), in addition to introducing disproportionate tax cuts and threatening the funding of environmental policy implementation. Trump was typically scathing of the 2019 GND Resolution, suggesting that it proposed to 'permanently eliminate all Planes, Cars, Cows, Oil, Gas & the Military' (Trump 2019, quoted in The Washington Post).

A similar concern could be expressed when examining whether environmental risks, specifically climate risks and ecological scarcities have been addressed. On a global scale, green economy initiatives are doing little to abate a growing climate emergency. South Korea has struggled to meet its ambitious climate emissions reduction targets despite the *Low-Carbon Green Growth* policy, with the GGGI stating that:

> . . .*the [Republic of Korea] has not yet achieved substantial results in decoupling economic growth from GHG emissions*
>
> *(GGGI, 2015: 23).*

Significant opposition to the K-ETS was experienced from industry concerned about global competitiveness. Indeed, resistance from industry and the fossil fuel lobby had helped to thwart Obama's cap-and-trade policy in the USA (Russel and Benson, 2014), while a similar retrenchment by right-wing politicians in the UK Coalition government led to a watering down of decarbonisation targets in the National Energy Act in 2013. Subsequent policy support by the UK government for fracking of shale gas in a so-called dash for gas has so far been opposed by environmentalists (Bomberg, 2017), with little effect. However, this issue is now politically in limbo, reinforcing uncertainties as to how the UK will meet its long-term commitments for net-zero emissions under the Climate Change Act 2008.

The circular economy appears unlikely to address these failings in green economic implementation through reducing ecological resource use. Although a current buzzword among policymakers at international and national levels, with multiple circular economy policy packages emerging, it has been criticised for being less radical than supporters would argue. Critics highlight how current conceptions do not represent a transformative change to modern capitalism since they do not challenge its fundamental norms and values (Hobson and Lynch,

2016). For example, while the EU's Circular Economy Package contains specific measures in the form of directives to reduce plastic bag use and single-use plastic products in order to tackle land and marine pollution, it does not address the wider problem of a global economic system predicated on consuming oil-based plastics (Benson and Monciardini, 2018). Moreover, some have questioned whether it is possible to reorient entire economies away from linear modes of production and consumption towards greater circularity without attendant wholesale changes in both societal and political thinking, and economic governance (Benson and Monciardini, 2018).

Nevertheless, there are some signs that transformative change may be possible. One country that appears to be taking an alternative route is New Zealand. The Royal Society of New Zealand initially called for a shift towards a green economy in 2014. In its position paper, *Facing the future: towards a green economy for New Zealand*, the Royal Society stated that the country was ideally placed to pursue a greener development path (Royal Society of New Zealand, 2014). Under the leadership of Prime Minister Jacinta Ahern, a policy approach is being adopted that endorses this argument. New Zealand's Wellbeing Budget 2019 reflects a new way of thinking about the central government's role in economic policy. In contrast to the UK, where Her Majesty's Treasury has often blocked environmental policy (Russel and Benson, 2014), the New Zealand Treasury has instructed policymakers to move beyond the promotion of Gross Domestic Product (GDP) growth as the overriding objective of government, to integrating wider sustainability considerations into its decision-making. Although the academic idea of green national accounting is not new (e.g. Asheim, 2000), New Zealand along with Bhutan is one of the few countries to base its measurements of national development on non-GDP indicators. However, it still has a long way to travel to achieving a green economy. Figures from the OECD (2017) show that despite New Zealanders enjoying a high quality of life, their GHG emissions were actually increasing, up by 23 per cent on 1990 levels, even though 80 per cent of electricity was derived from hydropower. Agriculture, which accounted for 49 per cent of these emissions, has also generated other negative impacts through nitrification of soils, surface and ground waters (OECD, 2017). Even in New Zealand, touted as an exemplar of green economic practice, there is consequently a significant difference between the political rhetoric and action on the ground. While the New Zealand experiment seeks to incorporate specific well-being measures into its overall budget and to highlight the values of a society that places a greater weight on personal health and mental enrichment, it may well be that the costs of maintaining future dysfunctional societies will increase significantly if these objectives cannot be introduced more broadly.

2.5 Conclusions

In Europe, the green economy has emerged as a seemingly unifying political concept that proffers the possibility of resolving one of the most fundamental, complex and urgent global challenges: simultaneously addressing global society's need for economic, social and environmental well-being. While interpretations of the concept have varied from *Blueprints* to GNDs (see CEC, 2019), the underlying objective remains the same: to reconcile socio-economic advances with environmental protection through economic means. In this respect, the green economy is an important goal and theme for policymakers at multiple levels of governance in Europe and beyond. However, as our reflections above also highlight, there are fundamental difficulties in trying to translate ideas into political action. One evident problem is the current prevalent focus on moderating downstream demand through government steering of economic objectives without radically altering the upstream structures of supply, increasingly determined by the demands of global capital. These challenges are evident across the EU as this edited volume demonstrates in the chapters that follow.

We conclude that the green economy concept should be reformulated in order to account for a changing global context. The challenge of integrating environmental and social concerns into economic policy has assumed greater urgency due to growing pressures from climate change, overconsumption, social and economic inequality, and biodiversity loss. In addition, the dependability and trustworthiness of extant capitalist economic approaches have been subject to much more searching criticism, particularly in the light of the recently experienced high levels of unemployment and volatility in financial markets combined with continued erosion of disposable incomes (O'Riordan, 2014), and increasing inter- and intra-generational inequality (e.g. see the Resolution Foundation, 2018; New Economics Foundation, 2019). These suggest that classical market-based liberal economic models are inherently sub-optimal, requiring a paradigmatic shift (Kuhn, 2012) to restructure growth and job creation patterns within more ecologically sustainable and socially equitable parameters: in other words, the conversion to a 'true' green economy (for example, UNEP, 2011; New Economics Foundation, 2019). Currently, we appear to be at the tipping point of yet another shift in economic guidelines and incentives, which could, perhaps, lead towards greater human decency and fairness of treatment in the context of an age of fragmented civil rights. Such a transformation is most likely to be prompted by the pressing prospect of the potential extinction of the human species, as a cooperating and sustaining organism, living on a planet that is now gasping for breath.

References

Albareda, L., Lozano, J. M., Tencati, A., Midttun, A. and Perini, F. (2008). The changing role of governments in corporate social responsibility: drivers and responses. *Business Ethics: A European Review*, 17(4), 347–363.

Andrews, R. N. L. (2006). *Managing the Environment, Managing Ourselves*. New Haven, CT: Yale University Press.

Asheim, G. B. (2000). Green national accounting: why and how? *Environment and Development Economics*, 5(1), 25–48.

Bailey, I. and Caprotti, F. (2014). The green economy: functional domains and theoretical directions of enquiry. *Environment and Planning A*, 46(8), 1797–1813.

Baker, S. (2016). *Sustainable Development*. London: Routledge.

Barbier, A. B. and Markandya, A. (2013). *A New Blueprint for a Green Economy*, New York: Routledge.

Barbier, E. (2014). Is green growth relevant for poor economies? *Resource and Energy Economics*, 45, 178–191.

Benson, D. and Jordan, A. (2013). Environmental policy. In M. Cini and N. Pérez-Solórzano Borragán, eds., 4th ed., *European Union Politics*, Oxford: Oxford University Press.

Benson, D. and Monciardini, D. (2018). Governing the circular economy: multi-level comparative analysis. *Circular Economy Disruptions – Past, Present and Future*. 17–19 June, Exeter, UK.

Bina, O. (2013). The green economy and sustainable development: an uneasy balance between the imperatives of crisis management and persisting contradictions. *Environment and Planning C*, 31, 1023–1047.

Bina, O. and La Camera, F. (2011). Promise and shortcomings of a green turn in recent policy responses to the 'double crisis'. *Ecological Economics*, 70(12), 2308–2316.

Bomberg, E. (2017). Shale we drill? Discourse dynamics in UK fracking debates. *Journal of Environmental Policy & Planning*, 19(1), 72–88.

Boulding, K. (1966). The economics of the coming spaceship Earth. In H. Jarret, ed., *Environmental Quality in a Growing Economy*, Baltimore: Johns Hopkins University Press.

Bowen, F. (2014). *After Greenwashing: Symbolic Corporate Environmentalism and Society*. Cambridge: Cambridge University Press.

Buhmann, K. (2016). Public regulators and CSR: the 'social licence to operate' in recent United Nations instruments on business and human rights and the juridification of CSR. *Journal of Business Ethics*, 136(4), 699–714.

Cameron, D. (2010). Speech given by the Prime Minister at the Department of Energy and Climate Change on 14 May 2010. London: Cabinet Office.

Carroll, A. B. (1979). A three-dimensional conceptual model of corporate performance. *The Academy of Management Review*, 4(4), 497–505.

Carroll, A. B. (1991). The pyramid of corporate social responsibility: toward the moral management of organizational stakeholders. *Business Horizons*, 34(4), 39–48.

Carter, N. and Clements, B. (2015). From 'greenest government ever' to 'get rid of all the green crap': David Cameron, the conservatives and the environment. *British Politics*, 10(2), 204–225.

Commission of the European Communities (2001). Promoting a European framework for corporate social responsibility. COM (2001) 366 final. Brussels: European Commission.

Commission of the European Communities (2002). Communication from the Commission concerning corporate social responsibility: a business contribution to sustainable development. COM (2002) 347 final. Brussels: European Commission.

Commission of the European Communities (2006). *Implementing the partnership for growth and jobs: making Europe a pole of excellence on corporate social responsibility*. COM (2006)136 final. Brussels: European Commission.

Commission of the European Communities (2009). *Communication from the Commission to the European Parliament, the Council, the European Economic and Social Committee and the Committee of the Regions - Mainstreaming sustainable development into EU policies: 2009 Review of the European Union Strategy for Sustainable Development*. Brussels: European Commission.

Commission of the European Communities (2010) Europe 2020: a strategy for smart, sustainable and inclusive growth. Brussels: European Commission.

Commission of the European Communities (2019). *Communication from the Commission to the European Parliament, the European Council, the Council, the European Economic and Social Committee and the Committee of the Regions. The European Green Deal*. COM (2019) 640 final. Brussels: European Commission.

Congress.Gov (2009) *HRI – American Recovery and Reinvestment Act of 2009*. Washington DC: US Congress.

Connelly, J., Smith, G., Benson, D. and Saunders, C. (2012). *Politics and the Environment*, 3rd edn. London: Routledge.

Daly, H. (1977). *Steady-State Economics*. London: Earthscan.

Delmas, M. A. and V. C. Burbano (2011). The drivers of greenwashing. *California Management Review*, 54(1), 64–87.

Demuijnck, G. and Fasterling, B., 2016. The social license to operate. *Journal of Business Ethics*, 136(4), 675–685.

Engels, F. (1987). *The Condition of the Working Class in England*. London: Penguin.

Fairbrass, J. (2011). Exploring corporate social responsibility policy in the European Union: a discursive institutionalist analysis. *Journal of Common Market Studies,* 49 (5), 949–970.

Fairbrass, J. and Zueva-Owens, A. (2012). Conceptualising corporate social responsibility: 'relational governance' assessed, augmented, and adapted. *Journal of Business Ethics,* 105(3), 321–335.

Fitch-Roy, O., Benson, D. and Monciardini, D. (2019) Going around in circles? Conceptual recycling, patching and policy layering in the EU circular economy package. *Environmental Politics.* doi.org/10.1080/09644016.2019.1673996

Gasparatos, A., Doll, C.N., Esteban, M., Ahmed, A. and Olang, T.A. (2017). Renewable energy and biodiversity: implications for transitioning to a Green Economy. *Renewable and Sustainable Energy Reviews*, 70, 161–184.

Geissdoerfer, M., Savaget, P., Bocken, N.M. and Hultink, E.J. (2017). The circular economy–a new sustainability paradigm? *Journal of Cleaner Production*, 143, 757–768.

Ghisellini, P., Cialani, C. and Ulgiati, S. (2016). A review on circular economy: the expected transition to a balanced interplay of environmental and economic systems. *Journal of Cleaner Production,* 114, 11–32.

Glasbergen, P., Biermann, F. and Mol, A.P. J., eds. (2007). *Partnerships, Governance and Sustainable Development Reflections on Theory and Practice*. Cheltenham: Edward Elgar.

Global Green Growth Institute (2015). *Korea's Green Growth Experience: Process, Outcomes and Lessons Learned*. Seoul: GGGI.

Gutés, M. C. (1996). The concept of weak sustainability. *Ecological Economics*, 17(3): 147–156.
Hobson, K. and Lynch, N. (2016). Diversifying and de-growing the circular economy: radical social transformation in a resource-scarce world. *Futures*, 82, 15–25.
Howard, M., Hopkinson, P. and Miemczyk, J. (2018). The regenerative supply chain: a framework for developing circular economy indicators. *International Journal of Production Research*, 1–19.
Husted, B. and Allen, D. (2006). Corporate social responsibility in the multinational enterprise: strategic and institutional approaches. *Journal of International Business Studies,* 37(6), 838–849.
Jacobs, J. (1992). *Systems of Survival*, New York: Random House.
Jänicke, M. (2008). Ecological modernisation: new perspectives. *Journal of Cleaner Production, 16*, 557–565.
Jänicke, M. (2012). Green growth: from a growing eco-industry to economic sustainability. *Energy Policy*, 48, 13–21.
Jelinski, L.W., Graedel, T.E., Laudise, R.A., McCall, D.W. and Patel, C.K.N. (1992). Industrial ecology: concepts and approaches. *Proceedings of the National Academy of Sciences*, 89, 793–797.
Jones, V. (2008). *The Green Collar Economy*. New York: Harper Collins.
Keynes, J. M. (1933). *The Means to Prosperity*. London: Macmillan.
Kirchherr, J., Reike, D. and Hekkert, M. (2017). Conceptualizing the circular economy: an analysis of 114 definitions. *Resources, Conservation & Recycling*, 127, 221–232.
Kropotkin, P. (2006). *Mutual Aid: A Factor of Evolution*. Mineola NY: Dover Publications.
Kuhn, T. (2012, *The Structure of Scientific Revolutions: 50th Anniversary Edition*. Chicago: University of Chicago.
Loiseau, E., Saikku, L., Antikainen, R., Droste, N., Hansjürgen, B., Pitkänen, K., Leskinen, P., Kuikman, P. and Thomsen, M. (2016). Green economy and related concepts: an overview. *Journal of Cleaner Production*, 139, 361–371.
Lozano, J. M., Albareda, L., Ysa, T., Roscher, H. and Marcuccio, M. (2008). *Governments and corporate social responsibility*. Basingstoke: Palgrave
Matten, D. and Crane, A. (2005). Corporate citizenship: toward an extended theoretical conceptualization. *The Academy of Management Review*, 30(1), 166–179.
Meadows, D. H., Meadows, D. L., Randers, J. and Behrens, W. (1972). *The Limits to Growth*. London: Earth Island.
Meller, H. (1993). *Patrick Geddes: Social Evolutionist and City Planner*. London: Routledge.
Mishan, E. J. (1967). *The Costs of Economic Growth*. London: Staples Press.
Mol, A. P. J., Sonnenfeld, D. A. and Spaargaren, G., eds. (2010). *The Ecological Modernisation Reader*. London: Routledge.
Mol, A. and Spaargaren, G. (2000). Ecological modernisation. *Environmental Politics, 9* (1), 17–49.
Moon, J. (2004). Government as driver of corporate social responsibility. International Centre for Corporate Social Responsibility Research Paper Series, University of Nottingham, No. 20-2004.
New Economics Foundation (2019) *A Green New Deal in the UK*. London: New Economics Foundation.
O'Riordan, T. (2014). Sustainability beyond austerity: possibilities for a successful transition to a wellbeing society. *Analise Social*, 211, 497–520.
OECD (2009). *Declaration on Green Growth Adopted at the Meeting of the Council at Ministerial Level on 25 June 2009 [C/MIN(2009)5/ADD1/FINAL]*. Paris: OECD.

OECD (2011). *Towards Green Growth.* Paris: OECD Publishing. Available at http://www.oecd.org/greengrowth/towards-green-growth-9789264111318-en.htm

OECD (2017). *Environmental Performance Review of New Zealand.* Paris: OECD.

Pearce, D., Markandya, A. and Barbier, E. (1989). *Blueprint for a Green Economy.* London: Earthscan.

Pigou, A. C. (1952). *The Economics of Welfare,* London: Macmillan.

Resolution Foundation (2018). A new generational contract. The final report of the Intergenerational Commission. Accessed on-line on 30 November 2019 at https://www.resolutionfoundation.org/app/uploads/2018/05/A-New-Generational-Contract-Full-PDF.pdf

Rhodes, R. A. W. (1997). *Understanding governance.* Buckingham: Open University Press.

Rhodes, R. A. W. (2000). Governance and public administration. In J. Pierre, ed, *Debating governance. Authority, steering and democracy.* Oxford: Oxford University Press.

Royal Society of New Zealand (2014). *Facing the future: towards a green economy for New Zealand.* Accessed on-line on 30th November 2019 at https://sustainable.org.nz/sustainable-business-news/towards-a-green-economy-for-nz-where-to-now/

Russel, D. and Benson, D. (2014). Green budgeting in an age of austerity: a transatlantic comparative perspective. *Environmental Politics,* 23(2), 243–263.

SITRA Studies (2016). *Leading the cycle Finnish road map to a circular economy 2016–2025.* Accessed on-line on 30 November 2019 at https://www.oneplanetnetwork.org/sites/default/files/finnish_roadmap_to_a_circular_economy_2016-2025.pdf

Stahel, W. and Reday-Mulvey, G. (1981). *Jobs for Tomorrow, the Potential for Substituting Manpower for Energy.* New York: Vantage Press.

Stahel, W. (2016). The circular economy. *Nature,* 531, 435–437.

Stahel, W. R. and Reday, G. (1976). *Jobs for Tomorrow: The Potential for Substituting Manpower for Energy,* Report to the Commission of the European Communities. New York: Vantage Press.

Stone, D. (2004). Transfer agents and global networks in the 'transnationalization' of policy. *Journal of European Public Policy,* 11(3), 545–566.

Su, B., Heshmati, A., Geng, Y. and Yu, X. (2013). A review of the circular economy in China: moving from rhetoric to implementation. *Journal of Cleaner Production,* 42, 215–227.

The Danish Government (2018). *Strategy for circular economy.* Ministry of Environment and Food. Accessed on-line on 30 November 2019 at https://mfvm.dk/publikationer/publikation/pub/hent-fil/publication/strategy-for-circular-economy/

The Guardian (2001). *Sleeping with the enemy.* 4 September. Accessed on-line 25 September 2019 at https://www.monbiot.com/2001/09/04/sleeping-with-the-enemy/

The Guardian (2014). *Missed targets: when companies fail to keep their key sustainability promises.* 22 July 2014. Accessed on-line 25 September 2019 at https://www.theguardian.com/sustainable-business/blog/2014/jul/21/sustainability-goals-promise-broken-failure-target-walmart-disney

The Guardian (2019a). *What is the green new deal and how would it benefit society?* 11 February 2019. Accessed 25 September 2019 at: https://www.theguardian.com/us-news/2019/feb/11/green-new-deal-alexandria-ocasio-cortez-ed-markey

The Guardian (2019b). *Labour reveals plans to fit solar panels to 1.75m homes.* 15 May 2019. London: The Guardian.

The Netherlands (2016). *A circular economy in the Netherlands by 2050*, The Ministry of Infrastructure and the Environment and the Ministry of Economic Affairs, also on behalf of the Ministry of Foreign Affairs and the Ministry of the Interior and Kingdom Relations. Accessed on 29 November 2019 at www.government.nl/circular-economy.

The New York Times (2019). *What is the green new deal? A climate proposal, explained.* 21 February 2019. Accessed 25 September 2019 at https://www.nytimes.com/2019/02/21/climate/green-new-deal-questions-answers.html

The Washington Post (2019). *What's actually in the 'Green New Deal' from Democrats?* 10 February 2019.

UNEP (2009). *Rethinking the Economic Recovery: A Global Green New Deal.* Nairobi: UNEP.

UNEP (2010). *Green Economy. Developing Countries Success Stories.* Nairobi: UNEP.

UNEP (2011). *Introduction: Setting the Stage for a Green Economy Transition.* Nairobi: UNEP.

van der Straaten, J. and Gordon, M. (1995). Environmental problems from an economic perspective. In P. Glasbergen and A. Blowers, eds, *Environmental Policy in an International Context: Perspectives.* London: Arnold.

World Bank (2012). *Inclusive Green Growth: The Pathway to Sustainable Development.* Washington, DC: World Bank.

World Commission on Environment and Development (1987). *Our Common Future.* Oxford: Oxford University Press.

3

The Green Economy as Good Governance

The Right Thing to Do?

JAAP ROZEMA, JENNY M. FAIRBRASS AND NICHOLAS VASILAKOS

3.1 Introduction

Over the past few decades, policy actors in the public, private and third sectors across a range of tiers of governance, from the sub-national to the national and international, have wrestled with the idea of a green economy, often advocating it in the process. Such discussions have deliberated about whether and to what extent a green economy might prove to be an effective method with which to address and allay commonly expressed concerns about economic growth, where there are concerns that the latter is achieved at the expense of the environment. In a similar vein to the practitioner deliberations mentioned above, in parallel, scholars have also grappled with the notion of a green economy and how it might be linked to environmental objectives as part of a shift towards sustainability (see, for example, Arrow et al., 1995). The key question at this juncture is to ask: What do policy-makers and academics mean when they refer to a green economy?

One seminal conceptualisation of a 'green economy' is premised on a type of economics which:

> *...implies a rethink of the idea that we should design economic systems to meet the unconstrained desires of Homo economicus, whereby the economic person is assumed to weigh up the costs and benefits to himself or herself and to act so as to maximize the net benefits to the self*
>
> *(Pearce 1992: 3).*

Accordingly, in a green economy, economic agents could reasonably be expected to incorporate environmental considerations and targets into their planning and actions. Crucially, therefore, the concept embodies tensions about how to reconcile economic growth and environmental protection in the pursuit of sustainability goals.

Arguably, green economic thinking can be seen as being nested within a number of alternative worldviews (for example, Clapp and Dauvergne, 2011). For example, the United Nations (UN) states that:

> *...[t]he green economy approach seeks, in principle, to unite under a single banner the entire suite of economic policies and modes of economic analyses of relevance to sustainable development. In practice, this covers a rather broad range of literature and analysis, often with somewhat different starting points*
>
> *(cited in Brand, 2012: 28).*

Of course, whether such a goal is possible and how it could or should be achieved, is altogether another matter. The vexed question that faces green economy proponents is: In what ways can environmental and sustainability considerations be mainstreamed by economic actors who traditionally have been reticent on the subject, if not openly hostile to a reform of their conduct? Yet, despite these potential or actual barriers, as a concept, a green economy does have the potential to showcase ways in which a particular type of economic ordering can be advanced and attained.

In this chapter, we reflect on the idea of a green economy as a repository for norms about economic conduct in the European Union (EU), managed via supranational governance arrangements that include environmental objectives, and which are subsequently transposed into member states' legislation. Crucially, in this chapter, we contend that efforts to fashion a green economy in the EU constitute a process that creates an 'innocuous site' of policy-making, ostensibly in the interest of all (Swyngedouw, 2009). Such a process is one in which both state and non-state actors have increasingly deployed 'good governance' as a vehicle for legitimating conduct, led by public demands for taking 'appropriate action' at multiple levels of governance (Fairbrass and Jordan, 2004). Using the idea or slogan of 'good governance for sustainability', those actors who have a decisive role to play in bringing about green economic order thereby contribute to a narrative that claims that attaining a 'green economy' is essentially about 'doing the right thing'.

At this point, it is important to revisit a definition of the term 'governance'. According to one of the leading authors on the subject, governance:

> *...signifies a change in the meaning of government, referring to a new process of governing; or a changed condition of ordered rule; or the new method by which society is governed*
>
> *(Rhodes, 1996: 652–653).*

Governance, therefore, represents a set of mechanisms through which the 'will to govern' is expressed by 'conducting conduct' in such a way as to satisfy public demands. By extension, good governance is a system of hypothetically appropriate regulatory behaviour and actions, a system of representation in which policy procedures and decision outcomes are based on principles that may include:

> *...effectiveness and efficiency, the rule of law, participation, accountability, transparency, respect for human rights, the absence of corruption, toleration of difference, and gender equity*
>
> *(Meadowcroft, 2007: 300).*

Advocates of good governance values can promote the notion in or at various 'sites' of policy-making. These may include procedures, process manuals, (voluntary) agreements, guidance, terms of reference, user protocols and other rule-competent artefacts. Good governance supporters often present good governance ideals as 'normal', 'apolitical' and 'fair', and therefore beyond the need for any further discussion (Löwenheim, 2008; Swyngedouw, 2009).

Embedding the idea of good governance into conceptions of economic ordering is vital to understanding how policy, such as that represented by, in, and through a green economy, can be shaped and realised as a result of the demands by both public and private policy-making (Kemp *et al.*, 2005). For example, entrenching good governance into economic thinking could be regarded as being essential to the efforts to establish an enhanced public engagement with common-interest issues such as the low-carbon transition (United Nations Environment Program (UNEP), 2011). Accordingly, in this chapter, we argue that a green economy that has been acclaimed as a new *leitmotif* by diverse actor groupings, including government, businesses and civil society actors, which can be fleshed out by those supporters by the addition or inclusion of good governance in economic domains that until now exhibited much concern about the potentially adverse effects of economic growth on the environment.

Given the focus of this edited volume on Europe (and more particularly, the EU), the essential point to underscore at this point is that there have been significant efforts made over a number of years to mainstream green economic thinking into EU policy using the principles of openness, participation, accountability, effectiveness and coherence (Commission of the European Communities (CEC), 2001a). That said, the green economy idea is likely to be subject to supranational policy reform in order to make norms for 'proper' economic conduct compatible with other good governance domains (such as human rights, cultural diversity and improved labour conditions). The 'greening' of domestic economies, consequently, is a demand placed on EU member states given that this lower tier of governance is obliged to comply with EU policy targets that, amongst others, relate to carbon emissions, renewable energy supply and waste management (European Environment Agency, 2013, 2014).

In order to understand how the concept of a green economy has materialised in EU political debates in recent years, the chapter reflects on how current theoretical deliberations about green economic thinking have come to be conceived of as good governance amongst actors exhibiting a will to govern. Accordingly, the remainder of this chapter unfolds as follows. The next section further develops the notion of a green economy and outlines its discursive development throughout recent history (discussed in more detail in Chapter 2 of this volume). This chapter then proceeds by reflecting on a green economy as a real-world example of good governance, paying attention to the role played by various policy actors in managing ('conducting') conduct. The chapter demonstrates the link between governance and sustainability in the context of the EU, illuminating the ways in which the EU's green economy is operationalised through good governance at the European supranational level, taking into account the EU's role as a locus of normative power. The chapter closes with some concluding remarks.

3.2 The Green Economy as a Concept

The green economy, as a concept, is now an established topic for debate in academic literature (Pearce *et al.*, 1989; Pearce, 1992; Lafferty and Hovden, 2003; Hamdouch and Depret, 2010; Barbier, 2011, 2012; Borel-Saladin and Turok, 2013; Cashmore *et al.*, 2014; Ehresman and Okereke, 2015), as well as being widely debated amongst policy-makers and practitioner communities who are focused on the issues of sustainability and its challenges and measurement. That said, and as shown in Chapter 2 of this volume, the idea is still evolving, shaped by wider economic and societal developments and crises. The recognition of the substantial and extensive environmental degradation resulting from widespread industrialisation has provoked counter-movements, some of which advocate subsistence and self-sufficiency, pointing to the exploitative character of capitalism (Robbins *et al.*, 2011). With the publication of an influential report by the Club of Rome, *Limits to Growth* (Meadows *et al.*, 1972), economic growth was regarded as being a function of, and contingent on, the Earth's carrying capacity. That report presented a vision in which economic growth would have to be held in check if 'nature' were to be preserved. Measuring the impact of human populations on the environment, via the idea of an ecological footprint, stems from this vision. The report *Our Common Future* (World Commission on Environment and Development, 1987), better known as the Brundtland Report, similarly proved to be a watershed in the conceptual development of the idea of reconciling 'economy' with 'ecology'. It considered equality both across and within generations, in terms of access to natural capital stocks, as the key indicator of what since then has become known as sustainable development.

Given the thinking emerging in past debates, arguably, government intervention would seem to be a key component in any attempt to steer societies and economies towards more sustainable structures of production and consumption (Barbier, 2011, 2012; Droste *et al.*, 2016). However, government involvement is by no means the only source of influence in rethinking or reshaping economic conduct. To fully appreciate the development of a green economy, it is vital to understand that some free-market advocates conceive of a green economy as 'capitalism reinvented'. As Bailey and Caprotti (2014) argue, the social forces of capital may well benefit from a process of economic reordering that is on a par with capital accumulation and profit maximisation (see Bina, 2013). This means that a green economy could, potentially, at least in part, be shaped by actors pursuing (economic) self-interest. Moreover, some particularly powerful actors may be able to propagate a particular interpretation of sustainability through their economic conduct (Goodman and Salleh, 2013; Wanner, 2015; Cavanagh and Benjaminsen, 2017). As Büscher *et al.* (2014) have indicated, market instruments such as derivatives, carbon trading and ecotourism are increasingly deployed to advance 'green capitalism'. Yet conversely, it has been argued that the making of a green economy lacks top–down coordination. In such a vision, change of conduct could emanate from what Bailey and Caprotti (2014) have labelled the 'green cultural economy', which represents an assemblage of knowledge, resources, (counter-) discourses and networks in which alternative views to that of the mainstream economic model nest.

Some versions of a green economy closely resemble the concept of 'ecological modernisation', an idea that may provide a template for greening existing economic structures (Mol, 2002). Arguably, most ecological modernists aspire to combine multiple objectives into a programmatic approach, aimed simultaneously towards environmental protection and economic growth. Ecological modernisation may be seen as being intrinsically 'optimistic' (Bailey *et al.*, 2011), in so far as it conceives of economy and ecology as being not only mutually inclusive but also reinforcing. Such a perspective offers business models that could have recourse to sustainability in order to improve products, penetrate new consumer groups or, in the longer term, reduce costs. Such a harmonious view of economy and ecology takes issue with the 'negative' and 'adversarial' limits-to-growth perspective of earlier decades (Meadows *et al.*, 1972). Themes of harmony, mutual inclusiveness and joint incentives are evident in the thinking. Accordingly, the pronouncements of some mainstream policy circles argue that:

> *...the greening of economies need not be a drag on growth*
> *(United Nations Environment Program, 2011: 16).*

A green economy may require some adjustment in economic conduct in order to internalise sustainability. Embedding sustainability into core economic domains and public spending areas is one possible method for modifying behaviour and thinking. Consider, for instance, the greening of fiscal cycles (Russel and Benson, 2014). Another strategy is to entrench sustainability into a technocratic agenda, where sustainability solutions are explicitly sought through science and best-available-technologies (Swyngedouw, 2009; Bailey and Caprotti, 2014). The utilisation of such instruments would suggest that major steps could be taken towards creating a green economy, yet this leaves unquestioned the underlying rationalities of existing economic structures as entrenched in extant institutions. Furthermore, a technology-driven approach adopted and operated by businesses, enlisted for sustainability purposes, may ignore broader questions about social equity and global resource redistribution (McAfee, 1999; Brown *et al.*, 2014).

Critically, the notion of a green economy, at its very core, could be a repository for particular understandings of sustainable development and the relationship between economy and ecology. Yet, some of the actors who could bring about a genuine 'green economy' have also been associated with preserving vested economic interests (Lorek and Spangenberg, 2014). To some extent, any private sector involvement in a green economy might be considered to be self-serving given the business mandate to maximise private gain, thus, effectively treating sustainable development as a marketable good (Büscher *et al.*, 2014). Sustainability governance must, therefore, be critically evaluated for its ability to trigger real change in economic attitudes and conduct.

3.3 The Green Economy as Good Governance?

We begin this section by posing a number of contentious and difficult questions. First, how has the idea of a green economy come to be equated with the notion of good governance according to some conceptualisations? Second, and conversely, in what way has good governance come to be seen as the means for legitimating sustainable development? Third, who decides on the appropriateness and rightfulness of economic growth in terms of its sensitivity to the environment? Fourth, and finally, when can we conclude that a right balance has been struck between economic growth and the environment?

By way of a response, we would argue that decision-making *power* is a key attribute for the making of economic policy within the operating space of good governance, via which route a green economy could establish as the 'right thing to do'. However, power is not evenly distributed within society but held selectively by certain actors (Castree, 2010; Sullivan, 2013; Büscher *et al.*, 2014; Wanner, 2015). This tends to result in a green economy being operationalised according to the economic rationalities of certain public as well as private actors (i.e. those who hold power) exhibiting rule-competence and agenda-setting powers, ultimately substantiating policy change.

Before addressing the question of legitimacy, it is helpful to provide some insights into the relationship between governance and sustainability. Given that both concepts have come to popularity more or less at the same time (late 1980s, early 1990s), certain parallels can be drawn. Kemp *et al.* (2005: 13) contend that both governance and sustainability *'are children of similar history and parentage'*. Arguably, in recent years, specific governance arrangements for sustainability have been tailored to fit the particular task of mainstreaming sustainability into economic policy and other decision arenas.

Given that sustainability, as a public policy narrative, has matured in recent years, so too has governance-encompassing efforts to balance economy and ecology. The concept of sustainable development (World Commission on Environment and Development (WCED), 1987), in particular, has expedited rule-competence and institutional guidance in light of developments that highlight and focus on the environmental consequences, both negative and positive, of economic activities. This is not to say that economic activities and transactions have become substantively 'greener'. Rather, as regards economic conduct it has become increasingly more difficult, if not impossible, to gloss over or ignore sustainability or to remain reticent about it.

Furthermore, it is noteworthy that in some versions of a green economy, the social pillar seems to be embedded in the definitions that key actors apply to the concept. For example, the United Nations Environment Program (2011: 16) states that

> *. . .in its simplest expression, a green economy is low-carbon, resource efficient, and* ***socially inclusive***
>
> *(emphasis added).*

The definition above displays sensitivity to the cross-linkages between ecology and a public demand for being involved in environmental decision-making. In this way, public participation can be considered to be part of a green economy. However, it does not mean that green economy decision-making is necessarily more open to the public. It may well be a case of certain key actors simply paying 'lip service' to those operating beyond the democratic mandate.

Additionally, seeing a green economy as a 'win-win' scenario is only one possible perspective. Some may regard economic and environmental interests as being aligned and compatible and discuss the ways in which these interests could (or should) be internalised into decision-making, including the rules and legislation that govern economic conduct. Such a symbiotic relationship between sustainable development and good governance is possible. As Kemp *et al.* (2005) have argued, sustainable development and good governance reflect a shared vision that 'going green' is the new 'normal'. Both may be seen as normative ideas about how to improve policy conduct (van Zeijl-Rozema *et al.*, 2008). However, good governance itself is by no means a set of fixed, ahistorical values that are, or should be, innate to governing systems across the globe. Rather, good governance also follows the logic of its time. It can take the form that society wants it to take, premised on dominant values of good conduct. Crucially, over the period of time that the idea of good governance has been used, it has steadily been transformed into a discourse associated with globalisation (Doornbos, 2003).

By regulating the conduct of governmental bodies, powerful actors may be able to provide templates for 'good' public policy according to the interests they seek to defend. Arguably, good governance is mediated by the predominant rationality that prevails at any given point in time. Potentially, for example, this could mean that environmental advocacy groups would campaign for market-based interventions such as carbon offsetting. Therefore, it shows they may choose to legitimise carbon-intensive practices. It could also mean today's environmental advocacy groups may combine with private sector actors to create ‘strange-bedfellow coalitions' (see Fairbrass, 2013; Fitch Roy *et al.*, 2019), creating discursive constructs that emphasise the use of technology to ‘fix’ environmental problems, 'cleantech' being a noteworthy example (Caprotti, 2012). Carbon offsetting and technological solutions, in these cases, are often promoted as a form of ‘good' conduct, in so far as the results can be evaluated and are vetted by relevant stakeholders (Mol, 2002).

The key challenge when attempting to analyse power is, therefore, to detect how incumbent actors install their economic visions via a good governance discourse. A green economy, from this standpoint, might provide a repository of norms about how economies could be made 'twenty-first century proof' and, therefore, relate to public expenditure, democracy and social inclusion, amongst other issues. Some powerful actors display a will to govern by appealing to these norms. Some incumbent actors assert that it is in the interest of sustainability to construct a green economy according to capitalist rationalities, with uncritical support for market solutions as a way to police misconduct (Büscher *et al.*, 2014). In this vein, those subjected to such rationalities may act as agents who spread capitalist behaviour in the guise of sustainable development. Through ‘governing from a distance’ (Rutherford, 2007), powerful actors can instil interests in ‘subordinates’ as if these were their own. This suggests that the freedom to favour one form of economic conduct over another is ‘regulated’, and therefore necessarily limited. Crucially, private sector involvement in the creation of a green economy can take place in the sub-politics of sustainability. This is a process that does not amount to representative democracy, although accountability may be achieved via mechanisms such as annual reviews or third-party certification and labelling (Chan and Pattberg, 2008). For example, for Janković and Bowman (2014), the framing of climate change as corporate strategy hints at the ‘ontological dislocation’ of what was previously a science-intensive policy arena. Instead, it has become a field through which business self-interest can be advanced whilst appearing to serve goals of sustainability.

In parallel, as a scholarly domain, political ecology has become heavily infused with debates about, and thus necessarily critiques of, the idea of a green economy (Cavanagh and Benjaminsen, 2017). Efforts to design economies, which, could harness both economic growth and sustainability, may only serve particular ends and may indicate a particular disposition towards the pertinence of ecology in relation to business conduct. For example, notions of environmental 'market-isation', 'privatisation' and 'commodification' (Castree, 2010) as well as the 'financialisation' (Sullivan, 2013) or 'neoliberalisation' of nature (Wanner, 2015) have emerged to signal the appropriation of ecology within certain types of a green economy (Büscher and Fletcher, 2015). To this list can arguably be added the potential co-optation of environmental advocacy groups in neoliberal models of a green economy (Adams, 2017; Fitch-Roy *et al.*, 2019), often to ensure funding.

3.4 The European Union: Good Governance for Sustainability

Overall, we have now reached a point where a sizeable body of academic literature reflects on the ways in which a green economy may contribute to achieving sustainability objectives. In this respect, some authors refer a twenty-first century paradigm shift (Bina, 2013; Bowen and Frankhauser, 2011). Yet beyond the field of environmental economics, little scholarly attention has been paid to the means to enact such changes. Consequently, here, we argue there has been only limited attention to the forces that may thwart or expedite actual, substantive, real-world change. We would, therefore, argue that most theoretical reflections fail to properly address the economic rationalities underpinning a green economy. The 'fixing' rather than 'shifting' (Bina, 2013) of economic systems dominates. This is a major challenge for accomplishing change in economic conduct (Barbier, 2011) and is particularly pertinent in the context of a multi-level (good) governance polity such as the EU.

Against this background, Bailey *et al.* (2011) have characterised the EU's metamorphosis in recent years being one from a 'controller' to an 'enabler' in the pursuit of environmental objectives, such as carbon emission reduction. Arguably, the EU has legitimised this shift away from traditional command-and-control policies through its focus on effectiveness and efficiency, further reinforced by its ambition to boost the global competitiveness of European businesses (Bailey *et al.*, 2011). Earlier, the EU's desire for economic integration (attained via an internal market) had already necessitated a gradual shift towards efficiency through creating a level-playing field for member states. This is mirrored in the evolution of the EU's Environmental Action Programmes (EAPs), where from the early 1980s onwards:

...issue linkage between the internal market and environmental policies became a key driver for programming and activities. Environmental emission standards needed to be harmonized to avoid distortions to industry competitiveness

(European Environmental Bureau, 2006: 19).

The European Environmental Bureau, which is a membership organisation comprising civil society actors across all EU member states, noted that a green economy had become formal EU policy during the 1990s. Following the publication of the Brundtland Report (1987), the EU espoused the idea that economy and ecology are mutually supportable through sustainable development:

'Sustainable development' gradually became a normative reference for environmental policy in the EU from the beginning of the 1990s onwards. The incorporation of the environmental dimension and the systematic search for "no regret strategies" were promoted. In other words, win-win situations were identified where both environmental and economic objectives could benefit

(European Environmental Bureau, 2006: 21).

Given the contentious nature of command-and-control policies, the EU began to favour the depoliticisation of environmental action within its boundaries. In parallel, the EU advanced norms for good governance as a solution with which to overcome the deadlock between public demands for environmental action and private interests in maintaining the *status quo*. In commenting on EU environmental policy in the early 2000s, the European Environmental Bureau (2006: 27) observed that:

The political strategy (...) is to postpone potentially contentious and controversial political decisions to later phases or to avoid them altogether by relying on cooperative approaches to environmental policy making. Cooperative approaches with industry, such as integrated product policies, the wider use of standardisation for environmental policies, voluntary agreements, cooperation with Member States' expert fora, or both (e.g. chemicals policy reform) rank high on the political agenda in order to manage complex risks (...). It is evident that those new governance approaches relieve the legislator and strengthen the role of private and public professionals with specific technical skills.

Acting as an 'enabler' or 'facilitator', the EU attempted to avoid prescribing precisely in what ways supranational environmental policy should be transposed into member states' legislation. From the late 1980s and early 1990s onwards, having recourse to fiscal incentives or voluntary agreements became an official EU environmental policy (European Environmental Bureau, 2006). This policy direction gained traction particularly as the result of a fear that new measures designed to combat climate change could be introduced. The EU has subsequently adopted a target-led policy approach to cutting down carbon emissions, so as minimise the disturbance to the domestic industries of member states. Accordingly, for example, member states are given some license to devise national schemes for implementing the Emission Trading System (ETS), a critical facet of the EU's environmental policy package. Instead of 'commanding' or 'controlling', the EU guides national efforts through policy reform, further institutionalising emission trading as a form of public–private governance (Bailey *et al.*, 2011).

The role of the EU as 'enabler' has eventually culminated in the construction of a so-called 'enabling framework', first introduced in the seventh Environment Action Programme (EAP) that guides environmental action towards 2020. Such a strategy permits flexibility in bringing about change. It is considered vital to facilitating a green economy. The seventh EAP, agreed by the European Parliament and the Council of the European Union, states that:

> *...[t]he Union should also further intensify its contribution to initiatives that facilitate the transition towards an inclusive and green economy at international level, such as the promotion of appropriate enabling conditions, the development of market-based instruments and indicators beyond GDP, consistent with its internal policies*
> *(European Parliament and Council of the European Union, 2013: 198).*

Recall that the EU's earlier *White Paper on European Governance* (CEC, 2001a) had already identified certain principles for good governance, which could give rise to more flexible working arrangements between the EU and its member states, thereby attaching value to the involvement of a range of stakeholders outside government in co-decision-making, co-operation and co-regulation. Through its 'open method of coordination', the EU deploys soft-binding instruments such as guidelines, statistics or manuals to work with member states in the transposition of supranational policy into national legislation. Arguably, by bringing national governments on board, this process aims to resolve the so-called EU 'democratic deficit' arising from the ineffectiveness of the EU's institutions (European Commission, European Council and European Parliament) and to address interdependencies between, and within, supranational policy-making (Jordan and Schout, 2006). The 2001 White Paper proposed a number of action points designed to create a more decentralised, flexible and integrative working relationship between the EU and its partners in policy-making. It considers environmental policy a potential pilot area for showcasing such institutional reform.

Within the EU, good governance is seen as a means of tackling the challenges associated with cross-sectoral, multi-stakeholder and multi-level interdependencies, thereby aiming to rebuild confidence in the supranational project as a vehicle of common interest. It could offer opportunities for actors operating outside the EU institutions to access a wide number of policy areas, sustainable development being a prominent one. According to the 2001 White Paper, EU policies should be generated via principles such as openness, stakeholder participation, accountability and the effectiveness and coherence of supranational policy. These tenets of good governance could help shape a common vision on the future of the EU, which has been described as follows:

Refocusing policies means that the Union should identify more clearly its long-term objectives. These may, with the overall objective of sustainable development, include improving human capital, knowledge and skills; strengthening both social cohesion and competitiveness; meeting the environmental challenge; supporting territorial diversity; and contributing to regional peace and stability

(CEC, 2001a: 28).

One notable example of EU good governance, explicitly related to environmental policy-making, is the enforcement of sustainable development as well as protecting and improving environmental quality as common provisions in the Treaty of the EU, first adopted in Maastricht in 1992 and subsequently consolidated. Analogous to the Brundtland Report, in its treaty, the EU advocates achieving the ambition of sustainable development in Europe, which is:

...based on balanced economic growth and price stability, a highly competitive social market economy, aiming at full employment and social progress...

(EU, 2012, Article 3).

This ambition is listed amongst other objectives associated with human rights, cultural diversity and public participation. The EU's sustainable development strategy (CEC, 2001b) and the *2020 Strategy* (CEC, 2010), the latter preceded by the *Lisbon Strategy*, have subsequently framed the ambition in terms of objectives for good governance, such as exhibited in the strategy on sustainable development:

...achieving the vision offered by sustainable development requires urgent action; committed and far-sighted political leadership; a new approach to policymaking; widespread participation; and international responsibility

(CEC, 2001b: 4).

Governance for sustainability in the EU is manifested in several ways, both supranationally and within national policy domains. Setting standards for professional conduct is an important field for exerting influence on economic conduct. For example, in the past decade, the EU has adopted a regulation (European Parliament and Council of the European Union, 2010) that prevents illegally harvested timber and timber products from being placed on the European market. Another example is found in one of the EU's member states: namely, the Code for Sustainable Homes in the United Kingdom (UK) (Department for Communities and Local Government, 2008), which addresses sustainability in the housing sector. The code proposes new professional standards that are intended to improve energy efficiency, water usage and the ecological footprint of materials used for new homes. The UK government describes the code as a 'mark of quality', but also as a 'signal to the future'. Instruments such as these are increasingly deployed to maintain a minimum standard of ecological sensitivity in sectors known to have an adverse impact on the environment (see Gibbs and O' Neill, 2015).

Good governance for fostering a 'green economy' in the EU sphere of influence is a question of *procedure* as much as it is one of *substance*. Often these two dimensions go hand-in-hand, with formal initiatives driving the evolution of mainstream governance attributes such as accountability, transparency and public scrutiny in EU policy and conduct. The EU's *Better Regulation Agenda*, which is designed to make supranational decisions more timely and sound, marries environmental considerations into a longer list of good governance attributes, thus obfuscating the roles of means and ends in supranational policy-making. It states that:

> *Applying the principles of better regulation will ensure that measures are evidence-based, well designed and deliver tangible and sustainable benefits for citizens, business and society as a whole [...] This legislation is essential for sustainable development, for the single market that drives our economy and for unlocking the investments needed to support jobs and growth. It underpins the European social model and gives meaning to the rights and freedoms that citizens cherish, including their security and right to justice. It also helps us respond to common challenges such as energy security and protecting the environment and the climate*
>
> *(CEC, 2015: 3).*

The *Better Regulation Agenda* serves as an example of mainstreaming an idea through policy coherence, ideally having a substantive impact on the quality of the environmental policy. It coincides with the role the EU has attributed to the environment in its current Cohesion Policy, which indicates the EU's priorities in terms of investment to be achieved through the good governance of supranational funding (CEC, 2014). Improving the environment is enumerated amongst other objectives such as creating jobs and growth, investing in people, supporting enterprises, strengthening research and innovation and modernising transport. The EU further mainstreams environmental policy by incorporating its cohesion objectives into rules for proper engagement between its corpus and member states. This includes a stronger focus on results, a simplification of the rules for conduct, strengthening the urban dimension and fighting for social inclusion and the need for economic reform in member states who benefit from funds.

Some of the examples mentioned above represent interventions in economic conduct by changing the 'rules of the game' through formal institutions. Nevertheless, formal institutions are subject to 'refocusing' in EU parlance (CEC, 2001a). Kemp *et al.* (2005) in their appraisal of the aforementioned White Paper, contend that:

> *...[t]he intent of the White Paper on European Governance [...] is to make formal institutions – which are increasing in size and number – more accessible, accountable, and relevant to the general populace and to retain a higher degree of relevancy, credibility, and legitimacy in the average person's mind*
>
> (*Kemp* et al., *2005: 18-19).*

Kemp *et al.* (2005) also note that EU policy-makers have focused on redesigning formal institutions with the aim of facilitating the development of 'governance for sustainability' and with the goals of reducing hierarchy and bureaucracy. This could also be seen as a normative disposition towards environmental policy-making, marking a shift away from command-and-control and towards market-based instruments (Jordan *et al.*, 2003; Meadowcroft, 2009).

Congruent with the idea of ecological modernisation (as discussed in section 2 of this chapter and in Chapter 2), market-based instruments seem to offer a promising range of options for instilling desired conduct, and as such, have been 'rediscovered' by governments in making public policy (Lascoumes and Le Gales, 2007). Market-based instruments are intended to stimulate sustainable behaviour, not merely to legally restrict behaviour that is considered unsustainable. Examples of such instruments are ecolabels or voluntary agreements, which attest to optimism about the possibility of substantiating environmental progress without coercion. These fit into the EU's supranational agenda of conducting environmental policy-making through 'soft' instruments. Market involvement is one dimension of the EU's role as an 'enabler' or 'facilitator' of collective action, consistent with its approach to good governance as discussed above. The failure or success of the green economy is, therefore, potentially at the mercy of the voluntary contributions of state and non-state actors.

Formal institutions, arguably, can furnish an antidote to the 'incoherent', 'fragmented' and *'ad hoc'* character of sustainability governance (Gupta and Sanchez, 2012). The transposition of sustainability principles into legislation is a key requirement for the real-world realisation of a 'green economy'. Yet, partly due to the problematic nature of political authority in the international sphere of action (Abbott and Bernstein, 2015), governance for sustainability is intrinsically driven by voluntary commitment of states. Furthermore, corporate social responsibility is often conducted on the basis of voluntary private sector involvement, particularly in the EU (see Fairbrass, 2011), notwithstanding corporate actors' efforts to build legitimacy for the decisions they take (Schouten and Glasbergen, 2011). Yet, voluntary agreements are important for the 'governancing' of sustainability, as they are flexible in bringing diverse actor groupings together in thinking about ways to improve public policy.

By focusing on attempts to redefine the institutional environment in which governance for sustainability is nested, the question arises as to what extent the EU remains a normative power (Manners, 2002), and by extension a 'green power' (van der Heijden, 2010) in the field of environmental sustainability. Normative power relates to the ability to have an ideational impact: that is, *'to think of the ideational impact of the EU's international identity/role as representing normative power'* (Manners, 2002: 238). If a green economy is to strike a balance between uninhibited economic growth and strong environmental protection, then good governance offers a challenge in terms of setting hard-binding targets. The erosion of hard-binding supranational regulation by good governance mechanisms, for reasons of political feasibility, say, or renewed democratic and civil legitimacy could affect (adversely) the normative power potential of supranationalism.

3.5 Conclusions

In this chapter, we have reflected in what ways policy actors can advance the notion of a green economy by making it compatible with or equivalent to good governance, taking the multi-level governance structure of the EU as a test case. Further reflecting on the multi-level nature of EU (good) governance and the greening of the European economy, we find that actors in the public, private and third sectors at international, EU, national and sub-national levels of governance may be capable of (and willing to) designing and implementing such an economy. In reaching these conclusions, we draw on Rhodes (1996) and his conception of governance and combine that with an understanding of good governance that implies the strengthening of the conduct of decision-making by focusing on principles such as effectiveness and efficiency, accountability, transparency, the rule of law, institutional reform and/or public engagement. All of these characteristics may be considered 'good', 'just' and 'fair': the 'right thing to do'. We conclude that a European green economy can be achieved via good governance and may, simultaneously be considered the 'right thing to do'.

During our deliberations, we have also observed that the idea of sustainable development as generally understood, and the EU's sustainability policy, in particular, seems to be a 'critical enabler' for the creation of a green European economy. Crucially, some would claim that sustainable development is inherently 'optimistic' and portrays a symbiotic relationship between economy and ecology, thus dispensing with the 'adversarial' view that trade-offs between economic growth and environmental sustainability (re)present a zero-sum game. However, for critics of the idea of a green economy, given the ways in which the notion is conceived in existing policy discourses (essentially as a solution to the adverse effects of capitalism), it may prove difficult to break through the vernacular of good governance. The optimistic message of 'ecology meets economy' obfuscates tensions between sustainability and market capitalism. Furthermore, it may also be challenging to convince the public that good governance (i.e. the 'right thing to do') genuinely marks a deep-seated change in thinking, especially as it is played out in the innocuous and hum-drum 'sites' of policy-making such as process manuals, guidance or user protocols, which are largely unnoticed or unread by the public. Consequently, a green economy, in good governance terms could be seen as a form of:

> *...a neoliberal governmentality that has replaced debate, disagreement and dissensus with a series of technologies of governing that fuse around consensus, agreement, accountancy metrics and technocratic environmental management*
>
> *(Swyngedouw, 2009: 604).*

Based on our observations and deliberations, we also conclude that the 'conduct of conduct' is a critical lever in the framing of a green economy as a type of good governance. Moreover, policy actors in positions of power who exercise a 'will to govern' can advance particular ends according to their own economic rationality. They may attempt to shape the sustainability agenda according to rationality of 'green growth' and 'profit maximisation', allegedly all taking place within environmental limits. As a consequence, in effect, we find that the idea of a green economy can become a depoliticised construct (Swyngedouw, 2009): that is, one that is designed to solve problems rather than to question its conceptual foundations. In this way, where the 'will to govern' is directed towards environmental management, a range of measures to shape a green economy can be reduced to a template for appropriate action. Arguably, technology could become the force driving managerial approaches to sustainability. In this way, a technocratic rendition of sustainability could bring about convergence between good governance and 'green growth'. That is, ultimately, by conceiving a green economy as mainly as a technical or technocratic exercise, it may render it devoid of politics and that may be an unfortunate or unhelpful outcome.

References

Abbott, K. W. and Bernstein, S. (2015). The high-level political forum on sustainable development: orchestration by default and design. *Global Policy*, 6(3), 222–233.

Adams, W. (2017). Sleeping with the enemy? Biodiversity conservation, corporations and the green economy. *Journal of Political Ecology*, 24(1), 243–257.

Arrow, A., Bolin, B., Constanza, Dasgupta, P., Folkee, C., Holling, C. S., Jansson, B-O., Levin, S., Mäler, K-G., Perrings C. and Pimentel, D. (1995). Economic growth, carrying capacity, and the environment. *Ecological Economics*, 15(2), 91–95.

Bailey, I. and Caprotti, F. (2014). The green economy: functional domains and theoretical directions of enquiry. *Environment and Planning A*, 46(8), 1797–1813.

Bailey, I, Gouldson, A. and Newell, P. (2011). Ecological modernisation and the governance of carbon: a critical analysis. *Antipode*, 43(3), 682–703.

Barbier, E. (2011). The policy challenges for green economy and sustainable economic development. *Natural Resources Forum*, 35(3), 233–245.
Barbier, E. B. (2012). The green economy post Rio+20. *Science*, 338(6109), 887–888.
Bina, O. (2013). The green economy and sustainable development: an uneasy balance? *Environment and Planning C*, 31(6), 1023–1047.
Borel-Saladin, J. M. and Turok, I. N. (2013). The green economy: incremental change or transformation? *Environmental Policy and Governance*, 23(4), 209–220.
Bowen, A. and Frankhauser, S. (2011). The green growth narrative: paradigm shift or just spin? *Global Environmental Change*, 21(4), 1157–1159.
Brand, U. (2012). Green economy – the next oxymoron. *GAIA – Ecological Perspectives for Science and Society*, 21(1), 28–32.
Brown, E., Cloke, J., Gent, D., Johnson, Ph. H. and Hill, C. (2014). Green growth or ecological commodification: debating the green economy in the global south. *Geografiska Annaler B*, 96(3), 245–259.
Büscher, B. and Fletcher, R. (2015). Accumulation by conservation. *New Political Economy*, 20(2), 273–298.
Büscher, B., Dressler, W. and Fletcher, R. (2014) *Nature Inc.: Environmental Conservation in a Neoliberal Age*. Tucson: University of Arizona Press.
Caprotti, F. (2012). The cultural economy of cleantech: environmental discourse and the emergence of a new technology sector. *Transactions of the Institute of British Geographers*, 37(3), 370–385.
Cashmore, M., Richardson, T. and Axelsson, A. (2014). Seeing power in international development cooperation: environmental policy integration and the World Bank. *Transactions of the Institute of British Geographers*, 39(1), 155–168.
Castree, N. (2010). Neoliberalism and the biophysical environment 1: what 'neoliberalism' is, and what difference nature makes to it. *Geography Compass*, 4(12), 1725–1733.
Cavanagh, C. J. and Benjaminsen, T. A. (2017). Political ecology, variegated green economies, and the foreclosure of alternative sustainabilities. *Journal of Political Ecology*, 24(1), 200–216.
CEC. (2001a). *European Governance: A White Paper*. Brussels: Commission of the European Communities.
CEC. (2001b). *A Sustainable Europe for a Better World: A European Union Strategy for Sustainable Development*. Brussels: Commission of the European Communities.
CEC. (2010). *Europe 2020: A Strategy for Smart, Sustainable and Inclusive Growth*. Brussels: European Commission.
CEC. (2014). *An Introduction to EU Cohesion Policy 2014–2020*. Luxembourg: Publications Office of the European Union.
CEC. (2015). *Better Regulation for Better Results – An EU Agenda. Communication from the Commission to the European Parliament, the Council, the European Economic and Social Committee and the Committee of the Regions*. Strasbourg: European Commission.
Chan, S. and Pattberg, P. (2008). Private rule-making and the politics of accountability: analyzing global forest governance. *Global Environmental Change*, 8(3), 103–121.
Clapp, J. and Dauvergne, P. (2011) *Paths to a Green World: The Political Economy of the Global Environment*. Cambridge, MIT Press.
Department for Communities and Local Government. (2008). The code for sustainable homes: setting the standard in sustainability for new homes, London: Communities and Local Government Publications.
Doornbos, M. (2003). "Good governance": the metamorphosis of a policy metaphor. *Journal of International Affairs*, 57(1), 3–17.

Droste, N., Hansjürgens, B., Kuikman, P., Otter, N., Antikainen, R., Leskinen, P., Pitkänen, K., Saikku, L., Loiseau, E. and Thomsen, M. (2016). Steering innovations towards a green economy: understanding government intervention. *Journal of Cleaner Production*, 135(1), 426–434.

Ehresman, T. G. and Okereke, C. (2015). Environmental justice and conceptions of the green economy. *International Environmental Agreements: Politics, Law and Economics*, 15(1), 13–27.

European Environment Agency (2013). *Towards a Green Economy in Europe. EU Environmental Policy Targets and Objectives 2010–2050*. Copenhagen: European Environment Agency.

European Environment Agency (2014). *Resource-efficient Green Economy and EU Policies*. Copenhagen: European Environment Agency.

European Environmental Bureau (2006). *EU Environmental Policy Handbook: A Critical Analysis of EU Environmental Legislation*. Brussels: European Environmental Bureau.

European Parliament and Council of the European Union (2010). *Regulation No. 995/2010 of the European Parliament and of the Council of 20 October 2010 laying down the Obligations of Operators Who place Timber and Timber Products on the Market*. Official Journal of the European Union, L295, 23-34.

European Parliament and Council of the European Union (2013). *Decision No 1386/2013/ EU of the European Parliament and of the Council of 20 November 2013 on a General Union Environment Action Programme to 2020 "Living well, within the limits of our planet"*, Official Journal of the European Union, L354, 171–200.

European Union (2012). *Consolidated Version of the Treaty on European Union*, Official Journal of the European Union, C326, 13–45.

Fairbrass, J. (2011). Exploring corporate social responsibility policy in the European Union: a discursive institutionalist analysis. *Journal of Common Market Studies*, 49 (5), 949–970.

Fairbrass, J. (2013). Natural allies or strange bedfellows? The emerging relations between business, civil society, and government in response to the challenge of climate change. In: Monaghan, E., Wurzel, R., Jonas, A. E. G., Gibbs, D., Connelly, J. and Eden, S., eds, *New Climate Alliances*. York: Centre for Low Carbon Futures, 19–22.

Fairbrass, J. and Jordan, A. (2004). Multi-level governance and environmental policy. In: Bache, I. and Flinders, M., eds, *Multi-level Governance*. Oxford: Oxford University Press, 147–164.

Fitch-Roy, O., Fairbrass, J. and Benson, D. (2019). Ideas, coalitions and compromise: reinterpreting EU-ETS lobbying through discursive institutionalism. *Journal of European Public Policy*, http://doi.org/10.1080/13501763.2019.1567573

Gibbs, D. and O'Neill, K. (2015). Building a green economy? Sustainability transitions in the UK building sector. *Geoforum*, 59, 133–141.

Goodman, J. and Salleh, A. (2013). The "green economy": class hegemony and counter-hegemony. *Globalizations*, 10(3), 411–424.

Gupta, J. and Sanchez, N. (2012). Global green governance: embedding the green economy in a global green and equitable rule of law polity. *RECIEL*, 21(1), 12–22.

Hamdouch, A. and Depret, M-H. (2010). Policy integration strategy and the development of the "green economy": foundations and implementation patterns. *Journal of Environmental Planning and Management*, 53(4), 473–490.

Janković, V. and Bowman, A. (2014). After the green gold rush: the construction of climate change as a market transition. *Economy and Society*, 43(2), 233–259.

Jordan, A. and Schout, A. (2006). The Coordination of the European Union: Exploring the Capacities of Networked Governance. Oxford: Oxford University Press.

Jordan, A., Wurzel, R., Zito, A. R. and Brückner, L. (2003). European governance and the transfer of "new" environmental policy instruments (NEPIs) in the European Union. *Public Administration*, 81(3), 555–574.

Kemp, R., Parto, S. and Gibson, R.B. (2005). Governance for sustainable development: moving from theory to practice. *Internatio*nal Journal of Sustainable Development, 8 (1–2), 12-30.

Lafferty, W. and Hovden, E. (2003). Environmental policy integration: towards an analytical framework. *Environmental Politics*, 12(3), 1–22.

Lascoumes, P. and Le Gales, P. (2007). Introduction: understanding public policy through its instruments – from the nature of instruments to the sociology of public policy instrumentation. *Governance*, 20(1), 1–21.

Lorek, S. and Spangenberg, J. H. (2014). Sustainable consumption within a sustainable economy – beyond green growth and green economies. *Journal of Cleaner Production*, 63, 33–44.

Löwenheim, O. (2008). Examining the state: a foucauldian perspective on international "governance indicators". *Third World Quarterly*, 29(2), 255–274.

Manners, I. (2002). Normative power Europe: a contradiction in terms? *Journal of Common Market Studies*, 40(2), 235–258.

McAfee, K. (1999). Selling nature to save it? Biodiversity and green developmentalism. *Environment and Planning D*, 17(2), 133–154.

Meadowcroft, J. (2007). Who is in charge here? Governance for sustainable development in a complex world. *Journal of Environmental Policy & Planning*, 9(3–4), 299–314.

Meadowcroft, J. (2009). What about the politics? Sustainable development, transition management, and long term energy transitions. *Policy Sciences*, 42(4), 323–340.

Meadows, D. H., Meadows, D. L., Randers, J. and Behrens, W. W. (1972). *The Limits to Growth: A Report for the Club of Rome's Project on the Predicament of Mankind.* London: Earth Island.

Mol, A. P. J. (2002). Ecological modernization and the global economy. *Global Environmental Politics*, 2(2), 92–115.

Pearce, D. (1992). Green economics. *Environmental Values*, 1(1), 3–13.

Pearce, D., Markandya, A. and Barbier, E. (1989). *Blueprint for a Green Economy.* London: Earthscan.

Rhodes, R. A. W. (1996). The new governance: governing without government, *Political Studies*, 44(4), 652–667.

Robbins, P., Hintz, J. and Moore, S.A. (2011). *Environment and Society: A Critical Introduction.* Chichester: Wiley-Blackwell.

Russel, D. and Benson, D. (2014). Green budgeting in an age of austerity: a transatlantic comparative perspective. *Environmental Politics*, 23(2), 243–262.

Rutherford, S. (2007). Green governmentality: insights and opportunities in the study of nature's rule. *Progress in Human Geography*, 31(3), 291–307.

Schouten, G. and Glasbergen, P. (2011). Creating legitimacy in global private governance: the case of the roundtable on sustainable palm oil. *Ecological Economics*, 70(11), 1891–1899.

Sullivan, S. (2013). "Banking nature?" The spectacular financialisation of environmental conservation. *Antipode*, 45(1), 198–217.

Swyngedouw, E. (2009). The antinomies of the postpolitical city: in search of a democratic politics of environmental production. *International Journal of Urban Regional Research*, 33(3), 601–620.

United Nations Environment Program. (2011). *Towards a Green Economy: Pathways to Sustainable Development and Poverty Eradication*. Nairobi: United Nations Environment Program.

van der Heijden, H-A. (2010). *Social Movements, Public Spheres and the European Politics of the Environment: Green Power Europe?* Basingstoke: Palgrave.

van Zeijl-Rozema, A., Cörvers, R., Kemp, R. and Martens, P. (2008). Governance for sustainable development: a framework. *Sustainable Development*, 16(6), 410–421.

Wanner, T. (2015). The new "passive revolution" of the green economy and growth discourse: maintaining the "sustainable development" of neoliberal capitalism. *New Political Economy*, 20(1), 21–41.

World Commission on Environment and Development (1987). *Our Common Future*. Oxford: Oxford University Press.

4

On the Verge of a Second Revolution in the European Union's Utilities Market for Energy Production?

The Role of Social Enterprises

THOMAS HOERBER, ALEJANDRO AGAFONOW AND AMANAR AKHABBAR

4.1 Introduction

This chapter explores the possibility of a second revolution in the sector of energy utilities. The term *utilities* covers the production of electric power, natural gas, water, sewerage and, more recently, the Internet, although this chapter is limited to the production of energy. The first revolution in the production of energy occurred at the turn of the twentieth century, when it became possible to open up the use of the utility infrastructure to multiple providers. For the first time, competition in the production of energy was possible, thus preventing the monopolistic practices that a single provider was likely to adopt in the presence of well-known barriers to the entry of competitors.

The second revolution concerns a new kind of provider, i.e. social enterprises. The emergence of this kind of enterprise has involved a change in the ownership structure of the utilities market, which is likely to increase either the quantity supplied or the quality of the product, or a combination of both. In other words, the quantity/quality mix of a good or service can be increased or improved if one moves away from the principle of full-dividend distribution to shareholders, thus reinvesting profits in the enterprise beyond what is profitable for a residual claimant. Hence, we see for the first time big energy producers turning to renewable energy production, but also small and medium enterprises breaking into the green energy market, often on the basis of a social business model.

In line with the issues and problems set out in Chapter 1 of the edited collection, this chapter now explores a possible change in the ownership structure of energy utilities through the introduction of social enterprises. This seems to be a pertinent focal point because, in parallel to the European Union (EU) 2020 strategy (Commission of the European Communities (CEC), 2009, 2010), the EU has launched a Social Business Initiative (SBI) (CEC, 2011). The combination of both the EU 2020 strategy and the SBI may change the ground rules of energy production and provision within the EU, which is why we have chosen to refer to it, probably somewhat grandiloquently, as the second revolution in the production of energy. Hence, we delve into the normative objective function of social enterprises and how it fits in with the inclusive growth strategy of EU 2020 (CEC, 2009, 2010).

The EU 2020 framework demands a 20 per cent increase in renewable energy by 2020 (CEC, 2009). Achieving that target has proved difficult for national and sub-national actors involved in the energy sector. In addition, the SBI is promoting the creation of social enterprises or social businesses (CEC, 2011)—terms which the EU uses interchangeably. A social business is defined by the European Commission as 'an operator in the social economy whose main objective is to exert a social impact rather than make a profit for owners or shareholders. It operates by providing goods and services for the market in an entrepreneurial and innovative fashion and uses its profits primarily to achieve social objectives' (CEC, 2011: 2).

The EU may have prompted a change in the ownership structure of the utilities market after laying the foundations for the creation of social enterprises. A greater number of social enterprises competing side by side with for-profit enterprises is likely to lead to a change in ownership structure, because, despite both kinds of enterprises producing for the market and striving to be financially sustainable, a deviation from profit maximization and full-dividend distribution in social enterprises is deemed to affect property rights (Steinberg, 2006). Social enterprises have no owners to claim the appropriation of profits from the operation of utilities. Although social enterprises are privately owned, the party or parties who control the enterprise do not profit financially when net revenues are ploughed back into the business, instead of being credited to owners or distributed to shareholders (Agafonow, 2015, 2019).

That calculated deviation from profit maximisation, which in social enterprises is meant to benefit disadvantaged customers, has been interpreted in the case of UK-based social enterprises as a way to tackle fuel poverty, facilitating capacity building within disadvantaged communities by fostering an *enabling environment* (van der Horst, 2008). In the case of social enterprises in the renewable energy sector of Belgium, Huybrechts and Mertens (2014) have interpreted the logic of these initiatives as constituting a solution to the problem of excessive market power, which, as will be noted next, was historically the reason why governments nationalised utility companies, that is, to prevent the profiteering that stems from a dominant position in the utilities sector.

However appealing the social business solution may appear, and notwithstanding differences in the policy environment that drive community-based initiatives for energy production (Bauwens, Gotchev, and Holstenkamp, 2016; Bauwens, 2016), we believe that the creation of social enterprises will be constrained by the same forces which in the twentieth century prevented the creation of consumer-cooperative utilities in most of Europe, with the exception of Denmark, that is, Europe's predominantly urban structure combined with the transiency of urban dwellers that reduced the ability of utility firms to accumulate capital (Hansmann, 1996).

To fathom the institutions of the energy sector, this chapter takes into account the relationships between government, business and civil society, thus partially building on the multi-level governance (MLG) theoretical perspective. Since the liberalisation of the European internal electricity market (European Union, 1997), the EU has become a major actor in the energy sector. New small and medium energy producers are breaking into the European energy market. This multitude of actors justifies the choice of the MLG approach (Bache and Flinders, 2004; Conzelmann and Smith, 2008; Fairbrass and Jordan, 2004; Hooghe and Marks, 2001, 2003; Jessop, 2004; Jordan, 2001; Jordan and Schout, 2006; Knill and Tosun, 2008; Kohler-Koch Larat, 2009; Kohler-Koch and Eising, 1999; Kohler-Koch and Rittberger, 2006; Marks, 1993, 1996; Marks and Hooghe, 2004; Peters and Pierre, 2004; Piattoni, 2009; Rosenau, 2004; Windhoff-Heritier and Rhodes, 2011). Together, these actors produce public policy. For the EU more specifically, MLG accounts for the reality that international (i.e. above the EU), regional (i.e. EU institutions), national and sub-national actors, all influence the European energy policy.

In a nutshell, this chapter reaches the conclusion that the higher the proportion of real-estate owners as compared to tenants in the population, and the lower the fixed costs to be financed, the more favourable the structural conditions will be for social enterprises to break into the utilities market. This hypothesis brings us to a counterintuitive observation, namely that, while social enterprises are by their very nature supposed to cater for a disadvantaged clientele, those who are most likely to benefit from social enterprises will in fact be the better-off, because they are most likely to own property and thus to benefit from the production of affordable energy services by social enterprises.

4.2 Research Questions

We provide tentative answers to two of the research questions that motivate this book: (1) How and to what extent might businesses help eradicate poverty through their efforts with regard to the construction of a *green economy*? and (2) How might the form of business adopted affect or assist in creating *green local communities*? In striving to offer answers, the chapter sheds light upon the relation between the underlying interests of the population affected by the utilities sector and the form of business adopted by social enterprises, which has an effect on the interests of European citizens both in decreasing energy prices and in fulfilling EU environmental objectives.

4.3 The First Revolution in the Energy Sector: The Economics of Natural Monopoly and Imperfect Competition

Energy is at the heart of the EU's sustainability policy. The 2020 EU strategy regarding sustainability has two pillars: (1) mitigation of greenhouse gas (GHG) emissions and (2) energy policy (CEC, 2009, 2010). Both are dealt with through market-based tools, namely the EU Emission Trading Scheme, on the one hand, and the liberalisation of the electricity and gas market, on the other. The liberalisation of the industry is meant to make possible the emergence of both a decentralised energy sector and decentralised energy producers using small green devices, such as photovoltaic installations on façades and roofs (solar panels). These decentralised structures in a competitive market are referred to in this chapter as *bottom-up economic structures*. In this section, we first consider the twentieth century, early *top-down economic structure* of the European energy sector, and then we turn to the decentralisation of the industry, or its bottom-up organisation.

Until the late twentieth century, the energy sector was a top-down organised sector. In 1992, it was observed that '[t]he commercial and technological structure of energy markets is inherently anti-competitive' (Padgett, 1992: 53). Since the energy sector is characterised by fixed costs in energy generation (notably the electricity power plants) and in networks, it is a typical case of natural monopoly. The particular features of energy technologies and markets, that is, very high fixed costs and natural monopolies, account for the top-down structure. In Europe, until recently, the 'greater part [of energy suppliers and networks] was in the hands of state or regional monopolies' (Padgett, 1992: 53).

There were good reasons why the energy sector was organised as top-down structure. As Chick and Nelles (2007) put it, '[t]he potential for liberalizing markets in energy... in turn begs the question of why such industries were organized in monopoly form' (278). Like rail networks, energy networks (mainly electricity grids and gas pipelines) operate on the basis of very high fixed costs and very low operating costs and hence near-zero marginal cost. Importantly enough, and seldom pointed out in the literature, the use of networks displays one additional feature: they are non-rival goods, and, as such, they can be considered non-rival excludable goods, or *club goods*. Since Buchanan's 1965 paper 'An Economic Theory of Clubs', it has been acknowledged that the production of such club goods raises coordination problems for users to cover production costs according to their consumption preferences (Buchanan, 1965).

Because of high fixed costs and the club-good nature of energy networks, they remained natural monopolies for a long time, and they were subject to a familiar policy dilemma. The latter involves either (1) practising marginal cost (MC) pricing, which entails losses for the network owner but is actually a social welfare optimum, or (2) employing average cost pricing (or Ramsey-Boiteux pricing; see Boiteux, 1971) at the risk of not reaching the social welfare optimum but at least securing a break-even point for the enterprise (Henry, Matheu and Jeunemaitre, 2001). The latter solution is a second best, because average cost pricing maximises social surplus under a zero-profit, zero-loss constraint. This issue has been studied since the very dawn of the marginalist revolution, with John Stuart Mill advancing a theoretical analysis of natural monopolies, which included gas supply as a case in point (Mosca, 2008). Later, Léon Walras developed an early marginalist approach to the analysis of natural monopolies, stating the following:

> *Laying a second system of water or gas pipes in a city where there is already one that could satisfy all the needs, building a second network of roads in a country where there is already one that is enough for all the communications, would be an absurd way of chasing after economies.*
>
> *(quoted in Mosca, 2008: 333)*

It was Harold Hotelling who put together the various marginalist treatments of the issue. In his 1938 article 'The General Welfare in Relation to Problems of Taxation and of Railway and Utility Rates', Hotelling dealt with optimal pricing in fixed cost industries, like 'electric power plants, waterworks, railroads and other industries in which the fixed costs are large' (1938: 242). The first best solution is to apply marginal pricing, covering losses due to fixed costs through flat-rate taxes (the only taxes that do not introduce price distortion in the economy). It follows that energy networks were not suitable for a decentralised organisation and should remain organised in a top-down fashion.

While it makes no economic sense to have several competing energy grids, energy generation may in principle be organised in numerous competing power plants. Although this wisdom is at the core of privatisation and liberalisation policies in Europe, one cannot ignore that not only energy grids, but also energy-generating machinery, like a dam, a wind mill and solar and nuclear power plants, are production units whose main costs are fixed and whose actual operating costs are low. Thus, energy generators face the same pricing dilemma as energy grids. However, they need not be managed as a unified, single entity, which for an electricity grid would not make sense. Electricity produced by *multiple* power plants is distributed by *one* grid. Hence, while networks are club goods because of their non-rival characteristics, power plants are rival goods. Whether power plants are run by one monopolistic company or several competing companies matters, because in the former case the price of electricity is driven up, above a socially optimum price, by monopoly power, while in the latter the price is driven too low by competition to cover the fixed costs of operation.

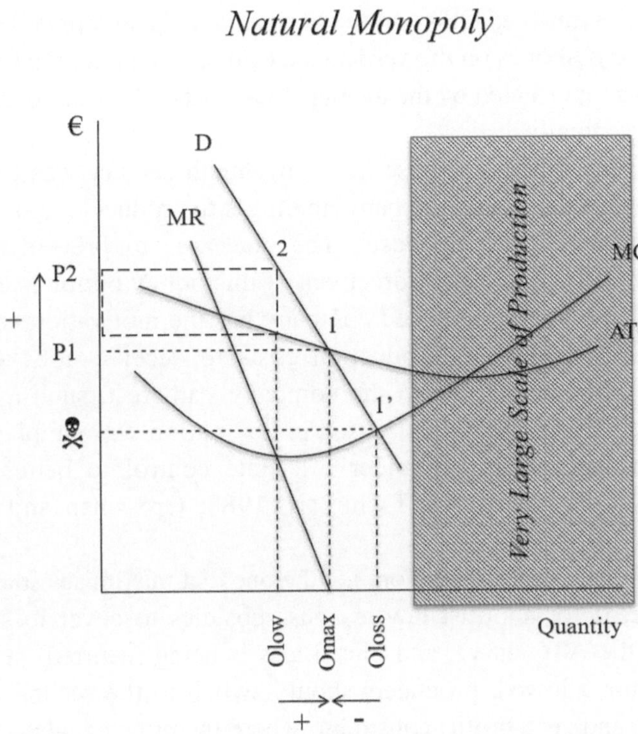

Figure 4.1. *Natural monopoly* (authors' own). When the costs that have already been incurred and cannot vary as a result of management decisions (i.e. sunk costs) are very large, as in utilities, it is not possible to follow the standard of efficiency that requires setting a price equal to marginal costs. If, under these circumstances, the standard of efficiency is followed, the supply would be as much as Oloss on the horizontal axis, at a price level indicated with a skull and crossbones on the vertical axis. The latter means that at this price, the firm would not cover its production costs. Thus proprietary utility providers have a vested interest in producing a quantity Olow on the horizontal axis at a price of P2 on the vertical axis, which is too high a price and too low a quantity. Consequently, the public would be underserved. The stretched MC and ATC curves illustrate large sunk costs that move the intersection of the two curves at a distant future in the shaded area *Very Large Scale of Production*. This may also be illustrated with L-shaped curves that never intersect, but that would erroneously suggest that the firm's growth is limitless.

That is illustrated in Figure 4.1, which shows that for-profit utility providers have an interest in producing a quantity Olow on the horizontal axis, at a price P2 on the vertical axis. Because this is too high a price and too low a quantity, the public would be underserved in respect of a good (i.e. electricity in the present case) considered of key importance for economic growth and development. The standard of efficiency requires that the company sets a price equal to marginal costs, supplying as much as Oloss on the horizontal axis, at a price level indicated with a skull and crossbones on the vertical axis. At such a price, the firm would not be covering costs represented by the average total cost (ATC) curve, hence running out of money eventually.

The conventional policy response in the twentieth century was to regulate the pricing behaviour of the utility company, forcing it to produce as much as Omax at a price of P1, hence covering costs. The goal was to prevent overcharging customers at P2. However, the enforcement of this policy option is expensive for a government, because the regulated company has the motivation and the means to conceal information about production costs to deceive policy-makers into setting a price more favourable to the company's interest, such as somewhere between P1 and P2. Another widely used policy option was simply to take over the utility company, placing it under full state control to better enforce the desired pricing at P1 (Berg and Tschirhart, 1988; Grossman and Cole, 2003; McNabb, 2005; Moss, 2005).

MC pricing is the first best solution, i.e. the one that maximises social welfare at Oloss. However, if for antitrust law reasons subsidies to cover losses (note that Oloss is below the ATC curve, and thus a loss is being incurred) at this scale of production are not allowed, producers should switch to the second-best solution under zero-loss (and zero-profit) constraint, where the price equals ATC at Omax. Hence, if by adopting MC pricing generators incur a loss, why would new generators enter the electricity wholesale market? This scenario discourages potential entrants, because competition would only lower prices, thus bringing losses or leading to the emergence of a monopoly. In other words, the energy-generation market does not display the right characteristics for bottom-up structures to flourish.

The current situation in the EU electricity market confirms this view. As stated in the Capgemini Consulting report on the European energy market: 'The chaotic situation on the electricity wholesale markets has continued with larger time intervals of negative prices' (Lewiner, 2014: 5), accompanied by disinvestment and decommissioning. Where competition and MC pricing are possible, the profitability allowed by high fixed costs power plants decreases dramatically. That occurred during the US and British liberalisation experiences, and it has raised issues for nuclear power plant management, because, with increasingly competitive markets, marginal pricing has led to wholesale market prices below average cost for nuclear power plants.

The existence of fixed costs in energy generation raises the question of why it would make sense to organise the energy sector as a competitive market. Although liberalisation policies in the energy sector can be viewed as a genuine revolution, we have found that the economic arguments in its favour falter in some respects.[1] The EU energy policy, however, actively promotes such an option, following the principle of *unbundling* (European Union, 1997). Viewing energy networks as natural monopolies, the EC encouraged the vertical disintegration of former national energy champions, separating network ownership from generation. However, generation technologies still involve significant fixed costs.

For technological reasons, renewable technologies fit well with decentralised organisations. Wind farms and solar installations can be grouped in cooperatives or operated by consumer-owned companies. Furthermore, a differentiated product can be offered, like green energy. Although one unit of electricity (say, 1 kW/h) looks like any other unit in the eye of the consumer, *green energy* does not look the same as nuclear energy or fossil-fuel energy. Hence, owing to differentiated energy products, competition offers a backdrop for the EU to promote another business model in the European energy sector, namely social businesses or social enterprises.

4.4 Social Business in European Sustainability Discourse

In the EU, the concept of sustainable development became an integral component of the legal and constitutional framework of the Single European Act, which came into force in 1987. It became more deeply entrenched with each revision of the Treaty and was enhanced and re-affirmed in the Lisbon Treaty of 2009 (European Union, 2012). Since 1987, however, there has been a great deal of debate as to its real meaning. Much about sustainable development can be criticised, such as the prolonged absence of common energy policy in the EU, only partly remedied by the creation of the common internal energy market in 1996 (European Union, 2003). Despite the firm opposition the EC has faced from the vested interests nursed by traditional energy producers, the EU now promotes another business model, namely social businesses or enterprises, for the EU energy sector (CEC, 2014).

Further evidence of environmental degradation and resource depletion continued to emerge throughout the 1970s and 1980s. The search for a new model of development advocated in 1972 in the Stockholm Declaration, a model that would take economic and environmental objectives into account, did not bear fruit until the publication of the Brundtland Report (World Commission on Environment and Development, 1987). That report identified three pillars of sustainable development, ecological, economic, and social, which marked the shift

[1] See the discussion in Kwoka (2006), according to which, 'While often suspected of inferior cost performance, the evidence here shows that publicly owned utilities achieve costs comparable to those under competition' (146).

from sustainability to the new model of sustainable development. Furthermore, inter-generational equity and public participation in decision-making were called for. The challenge was to achieve a balance between all pillars in a model of sustainable development to be adopted globally (CEC, 2014). Since 1987, the sustainable development discourse has become accepted as a new model to achieve sustainability. Sustainable development has become the hegemonic political discourse on sustainability, in contrast with other discourses, including the call for *de-growth* inspired by Georgescu-Roegen (1979) (see also Slim, 2013). Sustainable development provides the context in which decisions are made about how to resolve the tension between economic growth, environmental protection and social justice.

After 2007, the discourse on developing *a low-carbon green economy*, focusing on job creation, has become a nodal point in the European political discourse. Based on the writings of Jeremy Rifkin (2011) and with support from the European Parliament, this notion was adopted by other European institutions, led by the European Commission (2014), and the governments of some EU member states, notably Germany and the UK. To achieve a low-carbon or green economy, three requirements need to be met: (1) protecting the environment; (2) creating jobs; and (3) securing the energy supply (EC, 2014). These concerns accompany the argument of ecological modernisation (Barnes and Hoerber, 2013), which looms large in the European discourse. Jeremy Rifkin is one of its leading advocates, positing that, '[t]he entire industrial infrastructure built on the back of fossil fuels is ageing and in disrepair' (2011: 1). Rifkin argues that locating the environment at the centre of the economy would help to achieve the sustainable use of natural resources. As a result, environmental protection, energy security, and economic benefits would accrue from the transition to a green economy. A more precise and concise conceptualisation of the sustainability discourse is illustrated in Figure 4.2.

This argument suggests a narrowing down of the sustainability discourse as a general tendency over time, although the chronology can only be tentative, not least because the discourse has been developing continuously, but it gives an indication of the major changes of terms and contents used in the various periods. The extremes, much mooted at the outset, such as zero growth and radical green movements, are today no longer viable elements of the sustainability discourse and certainly fall outside the mainstream of the current discourse.

The suggested narrowing of the discourse over time could also be interpreted as a trend towards a progressive closure of the European discourse. This would mean that, in Europe, common norms and values are developing around the several aspects of sustainability, including the notion of social business, which, on the one hand, can be seen as uniting the industrialist discourse, through its business aspects, with the environmental discourse, and, on the other, through aspects of the

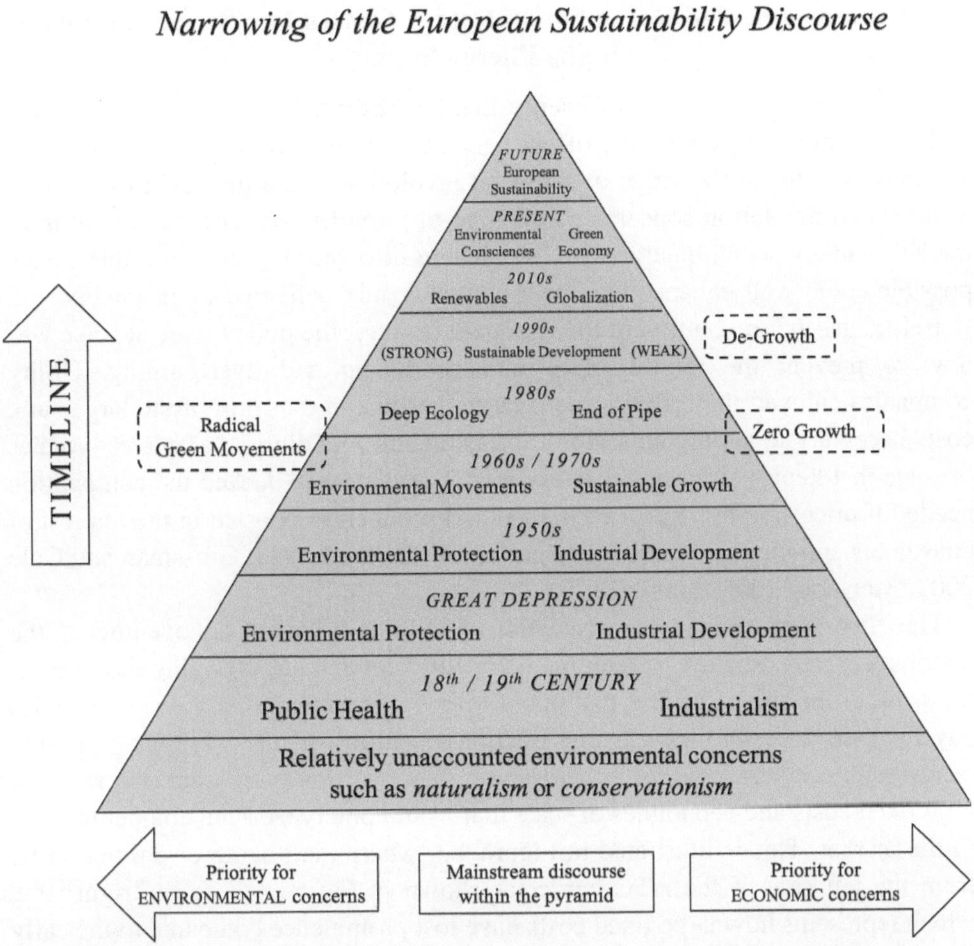

Figure 4.2. *Narrowing of the European Sustainability Discourse* (Barnes and Hoerber, 2016: 245). The different terms used in the sustainability discourse in Europe show that the concept of sustainability has become more precisely defined through integration. The notion of Social Business is one element in this process of a clearer definition, in this case, of sustainable development, and thus of the narrowing of the European sustainability discourse. This process may lead to 'sustainability' becoming an element in the creation of a European identity.

green economy. The EU as a governance institution plays a particularly important role in this process because it has built up expertise and competence in the field of sustainability; hence the EU can cater for social, economic and environmentally sustainable development issues better than any member state on its own (Hoerber, 2013). However, it is also very clear that national and sub-national actors and even civil society play a major role in the implementation and the updation of the sustainability discourse (CEC, 2014).

4.5 Towards a Second Revolution in Energy Generation: Social Enterprises in the Energy Sector

In the EU, the liberalisation of energy markets, especially the electricity market and renewable energy sources, offers new opportunities to social entrepreneurs. We may be thus on the verge of a second revolution in the provision of utilities. This second revolution concerns a new kind of provider breaking into the utilities market, namely social enterprises. The change in ownership structure they make possible could well enhance the quantity/quality mix delivered to customers.

Before the first revolution of the twentieth century, the policy issue at stake was how to prevent the utilities from underproducing and overcharging. Utility companies enjoyed the protection of market barriers in the form of the large sunk costs necessary to set up the sector's infrastructure, building on ample economies of scale that kept their costs relatively low. These markets lacked the competition needed if prices are to be kept restrained and production boosted in the interest of consumers and the public at large (Berg and Tschirhart, 1988; Grossman and Cole 2003; McNabb, 2005; Moss, 2005).

The first revolution in the provision of utilities involved an opening of the distribution infrastructure to multiple competing companies, changing the rules of the game from one of natural monopoly to one of competition, where companies pay for their access to the existing distribution infrastructure while skipping the heavy sunk costs of building it themselves, thus overriding the market barriers of high fixed costs and economies of scale that would otherwise keep competitors out of the market. This is illustrated in Figure 4.3, where the pricing of utilities shifts from the left side of the ATC curve (as shown in Figure 4.1) to the right side, which represents how large fixed costs have lost prominence compared to the early twentieth-century scenario when the sector's infrastructure was still being built. The full range of pricing strategies starting at point 2, passing through 1' and until 1 along the demand (D), shows the possibility of *managerial discretion* that contravenes profit maximisation in a governance structure with separation of ownership and control. The utility company would turn the largest profit at point 2, below which the marginal revenue (MR) intersects the MC.

Although point 2 on D is beneficial for owners or shareholders, because the company is widening the gap between costs and revenues that makes possible the generation of handsome dividends, it lays a burden upon vulnerable customers who cannot afford price P2. The second revolution we referred to concerns a deliberate deviation from profit maximisation for customers' sake, involving a change in the ownership structure of the utilities market with the potential to increase the quantity/quality mix of utilities. This result may be achieved if full dividend distribution to shareholders can be prevented and profits reinvested

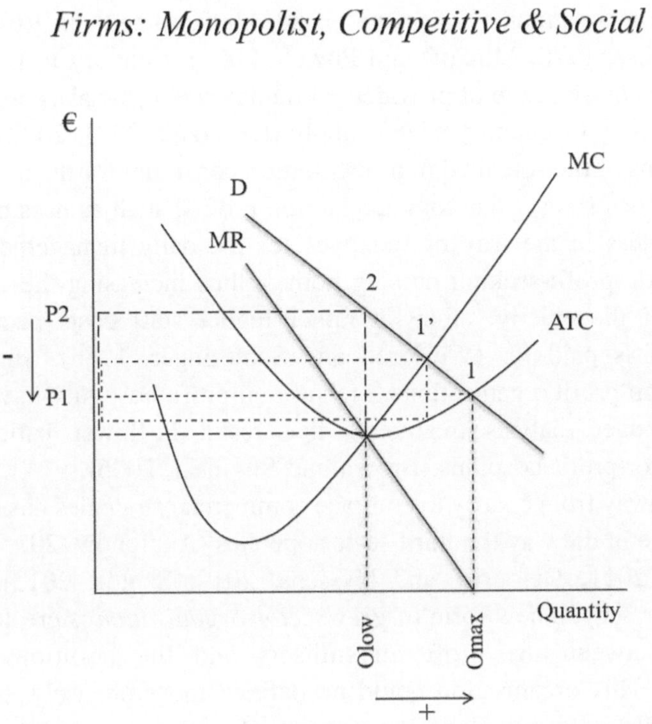

Figure 4.3. *Utility market open to competition* (authors' own). In a utility market open to competition, because sunk costs are reduced by making the existing infrastructure available to new providers, the pricing of utilities shifts from the left side of the ATC curve (as in Figure 4.1) to the right side of the ATC curve as illustrated here. The largest profit a firm could turn would be at point 2, below which the marginal revenue (MR) intersects the marginal cost (MC). Although point 2 on D is beneficial for owners or shareholders because the company is increasing the difference between costs and revenues that makes possible the appropriation of handsome dividends, it puts a burden upon vulnerable customers who cannot afford price P2. The second revolution in utility provision concerns a calculated deviation from P2 for the customers' sake. Achieving the latter is possible if we can prevent full dividend distribution to shareholders, reinvesting profits into the enterprise beyond what is profitable for a residual claimant, pricing utilities at point 1 along D to produce as much as Omax.

in the enterprise beyond what is profitable for a residual claimant (Agafonow, 2015, 2019).

Such a pricing strategy has long been known in the production of human services by commercial non-profit organisations, namely non-profit agencies that *sell* rather than donate their production. Instead of resorting to traditional charitable practices, these organisations charge a fee to customers without seeking to maximise profits. Because they are 'non-profit', they are legally banned in many countries from distributing dividends to shareholders, which is known as a non-distribution constraint (Hansmann, 1980, 2000; James and Rose-Ackerman, 2013; Newhouse, 1970; Minkoff and Powell, 2006). Contrary to the proposition that the ownership structure of providers of human services makes no difference as regards the quality or quantity of the supply (Le Grand, 2003, 2007), research on the implications of the so-called non-distribution constraint for the quantity/quality mix of output has shown that commercial non-profits, such as nursing homes, for instance, use less in the way of sedatives for the daily management of elderly patients than do profit-seeking nursing homes, thus increasing the quality of the experience for the elderly, albeit at rather higher staff costs because a more qualified staff is paid for (Weisbrod and Schlesinger, 1986). Similarly, other commercial non-profit organizations, such as non-profit hospitals, have been found to provide longer dialysis treatments that result in lower patient mortality compared to for-profit hospitals (Brown and Slivinski, 2006).

The move away from charity to embrace commercial strategies has been deemed a major change in the way the third sector operates (Agafonow, 2015, 2019; Bacq and Janssen, 2011; Defourny and Nyssens, 2010; Santos, 2012). Through a commercial strategy, a new form of *grey-sector organisation* is created, operating somewhere between the profit maximisers and the traditional non-profit organisations. This organisation could be defined more precisely as a non-loss, non-divided firm committed to the pursuit of a social goal (Agafonow and Donaldson, 2015; Yunus and Weber, 2007, 2010).

4.6 Are Social Enterprises Likely to Spearhead This Second Revolution?

Bottom-up solutions for the provision of utilities were not, however, unknown in the twentieth century. Examples of this form of organisation were found in consumer cooperatives in rural areas of the United States, while the predominant model of such provision in Europe was state-owned monopolies, with the exception of Denmark, where consumer-cooperative utilities were common (Hansmann, 1996). The reason for this ownership-structure pattern lies in the urban/rural divide found on both sides of the Atlantic.

First, consumer-cooperative utilities were rare in Europe, because its predominant urban structure made it difficult to meet the utility firms' needs of capital on account of the higher transiency among urban dwellers. Expecting to change residence, dwellers were reluctant to tie up their resources in fixed capital. Second, there was the all too familiar clash of interests between real-estate owners and tenants, with consumer-cooperative utilities contributing to capitalising the value of real-estate to the advantage of owners. Consumer-cooperative utilities were more common in the United States and Denmark, countries with relatively larger rural areas because farms were generally able to meet the utility firms' capital needs, and the interests among farm owners were more homogeneous.

Thus, utilities helped to enhance the capital value of farms (Hansmann, 1996).

In this context, regulated monopolies are in sharp contrast with small energy providers. First, regulated monopolies were, for the most part, either state monopolies or private monopolies regulated by the state. In contrast, social enterprises are usually based in smaller communities and provide services, including energy, for those communities. Secondly, the ownership structure is different. In regulated monopolies the owner was either the state or private investors—a mix existed in many different national contexts. Ownership in social enterprises resides neither with the state nor with a person aiming at capturing profits for private purposes. Finally, this leads us to the major ideological struggles between nationalised energy providers and free marketers.

The arguments ran from the immorality of profiting from merit goods, such as energy, on the left-wing of the political spectrum, to the accusation that nationalisation concentrated too much power in the hands of too few people (Hoerber, 2014). This leads to Elinor Ostrom's thesis that there are other solutions than state control and free markets in the economy. In her seminal work 'Beyond Markets and States: Polycentric Governance of Complex Economic Systems' (2010), she proved that under certain conditions small communities can handle their business better than nationalised companies and investor-owned companies. The social business model for small energy providers, which the authors of this chapter propose as a viable solution for the European energy sector, may be based on similar principles, although that line of enquiry has not been fully explored here.

The technological change fostered by the implementation of the principle of unbundling (European Union, 1997), thus reversing the vertical integration of former national energy champions, has also helped to tackle one of the barriers that, in the twentieth century, prevented the emergence of bottom-up solutions, or consumer-cooperative utilities, in most of Europe, that is, the need for large amounts of capital to fund the building of the infrastructure in the first place. Since the existing infrastructure has been, in a sense, democratised by making it available to providers who can now rely on the investment of a smaller amount of capital (i.e. costs are already sunk in the existing infrastructure now made available to new providers), bottom-up solutions seem to be more feasible in the twenty-first century.

Feasibility will be tested, however, by the remaining second barrier that in the last century accounted for the absence of bottom-up solutions in most of Europe, that is, the divergence of interests between real-estate owners and tenants, since a steady supply of high-quality utilities enables owners to capitalise on the value to their assets. The success of bottom-up solutions will depend on two foreseeable factors. First, the distribution of the population by tenure status, illustrated in Chart 4.1, and, second, the relative lower volume of fixed costs involved in power generation technologies.

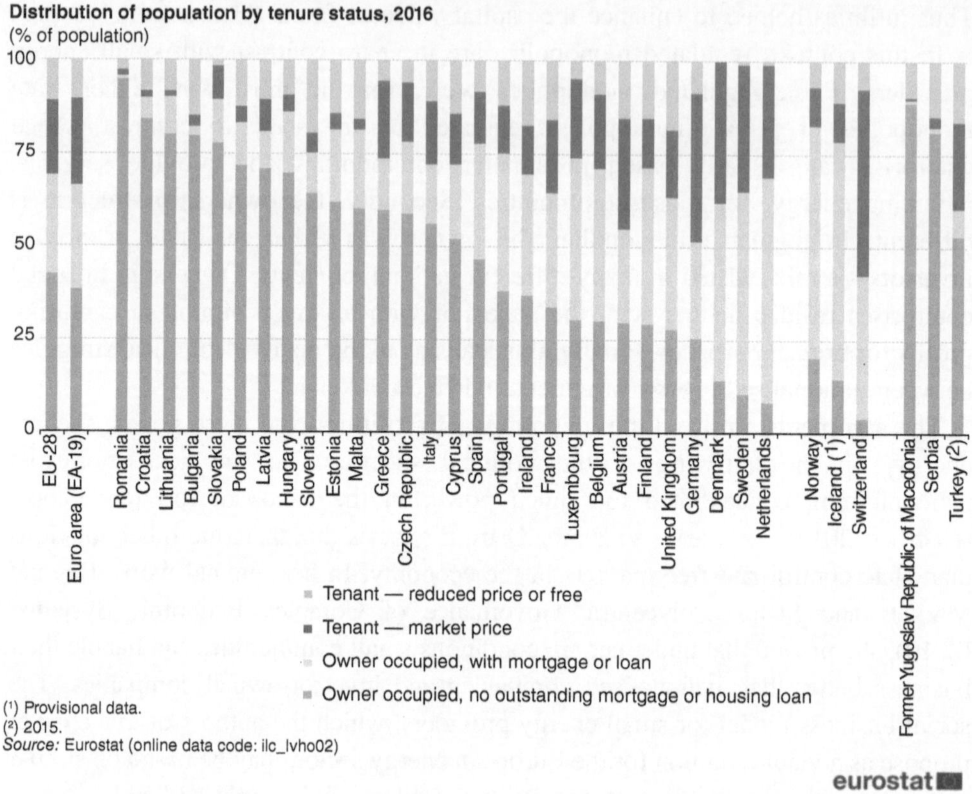

Chart 4.1. Distribution of population by tenure status, 2016 (per cent of population), Eurostat.

Thus, we argue that the higher the proportion of real-estate owners as opposed to tenants in the population and the lower the volume of fixed costs to be financed, the more favourable the structural conditions are for bottom-up solutions in the provision of utilities. This hypothesis leads to a surprising implication, namely that, although social enterprises are supposed to cater for disadvantaged customers, those who are most likely to patronise utility social enterprises are not the disadvantaged but the well-off, because they are more likely to be real-estate owners and therefore to benefit from the existence of utility social enterprises.

4.7 Conclusions

It is time to return to the first research question that motivated this chapter: How and to what extent might businesses help eradicate poverty through their efforts with regard to the construction of a green economy? The analysis indicates that, despite received wisdom on social enterprises as a means of poverty reduction, their impact on poverty is likely to be marginal in the specific sector of renewable energy. Well-off real-estate owners will benefit the most, insofar as social enterprises are able to charge a customer-friendly price for the energy supplied (P1 in Figure 4.3), thus contributing to capitalising on the value of owners' real estate.

However, it is important to observe that a reversal of this possibility may ensue as a consequence of a social-enterprise pricing policy that discriminates clients by their tenure status, charging more affordable prices to tenants only. This kind of policy, however, depends on regulatory policies the examination of which falls outside the scope of this chapter.

The second question was: How might the form of business adopted affect or assist in creating green local communities? The analysis does point to greener local communities. Irrespective of who benefits the most from customer-friendly prices, whether real-estate owners or tenants, a reduction in the price charged for renewable energy will increase the demand for it, as might be expected.

The rationale of this whole chapter finally draws on two prominent phenomena in the EU. First, we can discern today the acceptance of sustainable development as the dominant discourse, replacing both extreme ecological and industrialist discourses. Second, we can see that the EU is becoming interested in alternative organisational models that, without abandoning the growth model, are certainly moderating it towards a more sustainable economic activity in favour of environmental and social concerns.

Lastly, the real possibility of social enterprises venturing into green energy production might depend on a not-negligible degree on their unintended contribution to the capitalization of the value of the real state. Bottom-up initiatives for energy production flourished in the twentieth century wherever there was a convergence of interests between producers and consumers, such as in rural areas of the United States and Denmark, where consumer-cooperative utilities emerged to help capitalise the value of farms. Similarly, today's green energy production by social enterprises may be most feasible wherever the proportion of real-estate owners is higher than that of tenants in the population (see Chart 4.1), and the fixed costs to be financed are low. The implications of this conjecture are somewhat paradoxical, that is, even though social enterprises are expected to serve a disadvantaged clientele, those who are most likely to benefit from utility social enterprises may be property-owning, well-off people.

References

Agafonow, A. (2015). Value creation, value capture, and value devolution: where do social enterprises stand? *Administration & Society*, 47 (8), 1038–1060.

Agafonow, A. (2019). From hybrid organizations to social-purpose hierarchies: toward a transaction cost economics of social enterprises. *Journal of Interdisciplinary Economics*, published ahead of print: 1–20. doi: 10.1177/0260107919846791.

Agafonow, A. and Donaldson, C. (2015). The economic rationale behind the social business model: a research agenda. *Social Business*, 5 (1), 5–16.

Bache, I. and Flinders, M., eds. (2004). *Multi-level Governance*. Oxford: Oxford University Press.

Bacq, S. and Janssen, F. (2011). The multiple faces of social entrepreneurship: a review of definitional issues based on geographical and thematic criteria. *Entrepreneurship & Regional Development*, 23 (5–6), 373–403.

Barnes, P., Hoerber, T., eds. (2013) *Sustainability Discourse in the European Union - Reconciliation of Energy and Environmental Policies*. London: Routledge.

Bauwens, T. (2016). Explaining the diversity of motivations behind community renewable energy. *Energy Policy*, 93 (June), 278–290.

Bauwens, T., Gotchev, B. and Holstenkamp, L. (2016). What drives the development of community energy in Europe? The case of wind power cooperatives. *Energy Research & Social Science*, 13 (March), 136–147.

Berg, S. V. and Tschirhart, J. (1988). *Natural Monopoly Regulation. Principles and Practice*. Cambridge: Cambridge University Press.

Boiteux, M. (1971). On the management of public monopolies subject to budgetary constraints. *Journal of Economic Theory*, 3 (3), 219–240.

Brown, E. and Slivinski, A. (2006). Nonprofit organizations and the market. In W. W. Powell and R. Steinberg, eds., *The Nonprofit Sector. A Research Handbook*, 2nd edn. New Haven and London: Yale University Press, pp. 140–158.

Buchanan, J. (1965). An economic theory of clubs. *Economica*, 32 (125), 1–14.

CEC (2006). Services of general economic interest. Opinion prepared by the state aid group of EAGCP. Brussels.

CEC (2009). Directive 2009/28/EC of the European Parliament and of the Council of 23 April 2009 on the promotion of the use of energy from renewable sources and amending and subsequently repealing Directives 2001/77/EC and 2003/30/EC

CEC (2010). Communication from the Commission: Europe 2020, a strategy for smart, sustainable and inclusive growth. Brussels.

CEC (2011). Communication from the Commission to the European Parliament, the Council, the European Economic and Social Committee and the Committee of the Regions. Social Business Initiative: Creating a favourable climate for social enterprises, key stakeholders in the social economy and innovation. Brussels.

CEC (2013). *Social Economy and Social Entrepreneurship. Social Europe Guide Volume 4*. Luxembourg: Publications Office of the European Union.

CEC (2014). A map of social enterprises and their ecosystems in Europe. Brussels.

Conzelmann, T. and Smith, R., eds. (2008). *Multi-Level Governance in the European Union: Taking Stock and Looking Ahead*. Baden-Baden: Nomos.

Defourny, J. and Nyssens, M. (2010). Conceptions of social enterprise and social entrepreneurship in Europe and the United States: convergences and divergences. *Journal of Social Entrepreneurship*, 1 (1), 32–53.

European Commission (2014). A Map of Social Enterprises and Their Ecosystems in Europe. Brussels.

European Union (1997). Directive 96/92/EC of the European Parliament and of the Council of 19 December 1996 Concerning Common Rules for the Internal Market in Electricity. *Official Journal of the European Communities,* 40 (January): 20–29.

European Union (2003). Directive 2003/54/EC of the European Parliament and of the Council of 26 June 2003 Concerning Common Rules for the Internal Market in Electricity and Repealing Directive 96/92/EC. *Official Journal of the European Communities*, 46 (July): 37–55.

European Union (2012). Consolidated version of the treaty on the functioning of the European Union. *Official Journal of the European Communities*, 55 (October): 1–407.

Fairbrass, J. and Jordan, A. (2004). Multi-level governance and environmental policy. In I. Bache and M. Flinders, eds., *Multi-level Governance*. Oxford: Oxford University Press, pp. 147–164.

Georgescu-Roegen, N. (1979) *La décroissance - Entropie – Écologie - Économie*. Paris: Editions Sang de la terre.

Grossman, P. Z. and Cole, D. H., eds. (2003). *The End Natural Monopoly: Deregulation and Competition in the electric power industry*. Oxford: Elsevier Science.

Hansmann, H.B. (1980). The role of nonprofit enterprise. *The Yale Law Journal*, 89 (5), 835–901.

Hansmann, H.B. (1996). *The Ownership of Enterprise*. Cambridge and London: The Belknap Press of Harvard University Press.

Hansmann, H.B (2000). Nonprofit firms. In *The Ownership of Enterprise*, 227–245. Cambridge and London: The Belknap Press of Harvard University Press.

Henry, C., Matheu, M. and Jeunmaitre, A., eds. (2001). *Regulation of Network Utilities: The European Experience*. Oxford: Oxford University Press.

Hoerber, T. C. (2013). *The Origins of Energy and Environmental Policy in Europe: The Beginnings of a European Environmental Conscience*. London and New York: Routledge.

Hoerber, T. C. (2014). *A Converging Post-War European Discourse - War Experience, Changing Security Concepts, and Research and Education*. Lanham: Lexington.

Hooghe, L. and Marks, G., eds. (2001). *Multi-level Governance and European Integration*. Oxford: Rowman & Littlefield Publishers.

Hooghe, L. and Marks, G. (2003). Unraveling the central state, but how? Types of multi-level governance. *American Political Science Review*, 97 (2), 233–243.

Hotelling, H. (1938). The general welfare in relation to problems of taxation and of railway and utility rates. *Econometrica*, 6 (3), 242–269.

Huybrechts, B. and Mertens, S. (2014). The relevance of the cooperative model in the field of renewable energy. *Annals of Public and Cooperative Economics*, 85 (2), 193–212.

James, E. and Rose-Ackerman, S. (2013). *The Nonprofit Enterprise in Market Economics*. London and New York: Harwood Academic Publishers and Routledge.

Jessop, B. (2004). Multi-level governance and multi-level metagovernance. In I. Bache and M. Flinders, eds, *Multi-level Governance*. Oxford: Oxford University Press, pp. 49–74.

Jordan, A. (2001). The European Union: an evolving system of multi-level governance . . . or government? *Policy and Politics*, 29(2), 193–208.

Jordan, A. and Schout, A., eds. (2006). *The Coordination of the European Union: Exploring the Capacities of Networked Governance*. Oxford: Oxford University Press.

Knill, C. and Tosun, J. (2008). Emerging patterns of multi-level governance in EU Environmental Policy. In T. Conzelmann and R. Smith, eds., *Multi-level Governance in the European Union: Taking Stock and Looking Ahead*. Baden Baden: Nomos, pp. 145–162.

Kohler-Koch, B. and Eising, R., eds. (1999). *The transformation of governance in the European Union*. London: Routledge.

Kohler-Koch, B. and Larat, F., eds. (2009). *European multi-level governance: contrasting images in national research*. Cheltenham: Edward Elgar.

Kohler-Koch, B. and Rittberger, B. (2006). The 'governance turn' in EU studies. *Journal of Common Market Studies*, 44 (Special Issue), pp. 27–49.

Kwoka, J. E. (2006). The role of competition in natural monopoly: costs, public ownership, and regulation. *Review of Industrial Organization*, 29 (1–2), 127–147.
Le Grand, J. (2003). Motivation, Agency, and Public Policy: Of Knights and Knaves, Pawns and Queens. Oxford: Oxford University Press.
Le Grand, J. (2007). The Other Invisible Hand: Delivering Public Services Through Choice and Competition. Princeton: Princeton University Press.
Lewiner, C. (2014). European Energy Markets Observatory. Paris.
Marks, G. (1993). Structural policy and multi-level governance in the EC. In A. Cafruny and G. Rosenthal, eds., *The State of the European Community: The Maastricht Debate and Beyond*. Boulder, CO: Lynne Rienner, pp. 391–411.
Marks, G. (1996). An actor-centred approach to multi-level governance. *Regional and Federal Studies*, 6 (2): 20–38.
Marks, G. and Hooghe, L. (2004). Contrasting visions of multi-level governance. In I. Bache and M. Flinders, eds., *Multi-level Governance*. Oxford: Oxford University Press, pp. 15–30.
Martin, C. and Nelles, H. V. (2007). Nationalisation and privatisation: ownership, markets and the scope for introducing competition into the electricity supply industry. *Revue Economique*, 58 (1), 277–293.
McNabb, D. E. (2005). *Public Utilities. Management Challenges for the 21st Century*. Cheltenham and Northampton: Edward Elgar Publishing.
Minkoff, D. C. and Powell, W. W. (2006). Nonprofit mission: constancy, responsiveness, or deflection? In W. W. Powell and R. Steinberg, eds., *The Nonprofit Sector. A Research Handbook*, 2nd edn. New Haven & London: Yale University Press, pp. 591–611.
Mosca, M. (2008). On the origins of the concept of natural monopoly: economies of scale and competition. *The European Journal of the History of Economic Thought*, 15 (2), 317–353.
Moss, D. L., ed. (2005). *Network Access, Regulation and Antitrust*. London and New York: Routledge.
Newhouse, J. P. (1970). Toward a theory of nonprofit institutions: an economic model of a hospital. *The American Economic Review*, 60 (1), 64–74.
Ostrom, E. (2010). Beyond markets and states: polycentric governance of complex economic systems, *The American Economic Review*, 100 (3), 641–672.
Padgett, S. (1992). The single European energy market: the politics of realization. *JCMS: Journal of Common Market Studies*, 30 (1), 53–76.
Peters, B. and Pierre, J. (2004). Multi-level governance and democracy: a Faustian bargain? In I. Bache and M. Flinders, eds., *Multi-level Governance*. Oxford: Oxford University Press, pp. 75–89.
Piattoni, S. (2009). Multi-level governance: a historical and conceptual analysis. *Journal of European Public Policy*, 31 (2), 163–180.
Rifkin, J. (2011). *The Third Industrial Revolution: How Lateral Power Is Transforming Energy, the Economy, and the World*. Palgrave Macmillan. New York.
Rosenau, J. (2004). Contrasting visions of multi-level governance. In I. Bache and M. Flinders, eds., *Multi-level Governance*. Oxford: Oxford University Press, pp. 31–48.
Santos, F. M. (2012). A positive theory of social entrepreneurship. *Journal of Business Ethics*, 111(3), 335–351.
Slim, A. (2013). The Impact of De-Growth (La Décroissance) on the Discourse of Sustainability. In P. Barnes and T.C. Hoerber, eds., *Sustainable Development and Governance in Europe: The Evolution of the Discourse on Sustainability*. Oxford and New York: Routledge, pp. 48–60.

Steinberg, R. (2006). Economic theories of nonprofit organizations. In W.W. Powell and R. Steinberg, eds., *The Nonprofit Sector. A Research Handbook*. New Haven and London: Yale University Press, pp. 117–139.

van der Horst, D. (2008). social enterprise and renewable energy: emerging initiatives and communities of practice. *Social Enterprise Journal*, 4 (3), 171–185.

Weisbrod, B. A. and Schlesinger, M. (1986). Public, private, nonprofit ownership and the response to asymmetric information: the case of nursing homes. In S. Ros-Ackermann, eds., *The Economics of Nonprofit Institutions. Studies in Structure and Policy*. New York and Oxford: Oxford University Press, pp. 133–151.

World Commission on Environment and Development (1987). *Our Common Future*. Oxford and New York: Oxford University Press.

Windhoff-Héritier, A. and Rhodes, M., eds. (2011). *New Modes of Governance in Europe: Governing in the Shadow of Hierarchy*. Basingstoke: Palgrave Macmillan.

Yunus, M. and Weber, K. (2007). *Creating A World without Poverty. Social Business and the Future of Capitalism*. New York: Public Affairs.

Yunus, M. and Weber, K. (2010). *Building Social Business. The New Kind of Capitalism That Serves Humanity's Most Pressing Needs*. New York: Public Affairs.

5

'Great Expectations'

The Green Economy Discourse and Practice in Romania

SIMONA DAVIDESCU

5.1 Introduction

The concept of green economy (GE) has experienced a revival in the wake of the global financial crisis of 2008, which makes it particularly relevant for understanding developments in contexts where environmental and social crises have been persistent, such as transition economies. While the concept has moved into mainstream policy discourse in both developed countries and at the level of international organisations, transition economies and developing countries are lagging behind (Moyo, 2014). This chapter looks at the extent to which the GE agenda is nothing more than 'business as usual' focused on green growth, or a truly transformational discourse (Ferguson, 2015). Furthermore, research on the GE discourse in the global South has differentiated between four main contrasting discourses, reflecting 'a fundamental disagreement over the politics of the green economy': ('green resilience', 'green growth', 'green transformation' and 'green revolution') (Death, 2015: 2207). Looking at the links between the evolution of the discourse and policy agendas, another classification focuses on interpretations of the agenda in the global South, along 'incrementalist', 'reformist' and 'transformative' lines (Faccer et al., 2014).

This chapter is part of an edited volume that not only proposes to chart the rise of the GE discourse in a European Union (EU) facing crisis and transformation (Dinan et al., 2017) but also committing to tackle climate change, in terms of reform of energy production and consumption, as well as backing international action, under the Paris Climate Agreement. The focus is on an unlikely case of green state, Romania, with a reputation for being a 'laggard' with regard to environmental policy, having had a difficult transition to a market economy and democracy, and being seen as a country with the second-highest rate of people in poverty and social exclusion in the EU (37.4% in 2015) (Eurostat, 2017). This adds to the edited volume a case study on a new member state illustrative of the tensions between economic development and environmental protection, under conditions of economic crisis.[1] The expectation is that attention to the GE discourse would be limited from the part of the government, as economic development would be a priority under conditions of crisis and the main drivers for the adoption of a more ambitious discourse would be businesses, in the absence of pressure from below for environmental protection.

Despite these expectations, businesses have struggled to use the GE discourse to halt the dismantling of the incentives system in the renewable energy sector in 2013–2015, after an unexpected period of success in reaching the 2020 targets (Davidescu, 2018). Furthermore, a year later, the government was driving the adoption of a more ambitious GE discourse in 2016–2017, under a technocratic caretaker government, linked to the emergence of a policy entrepreneur at the head of the Environment ministry. The range of GE initiatives and programmes had increased substantially during this period, when Romania was keeping pace with international developments, and these diffused from the national to the local level, with the support of a range of local actors, including the voluntary sector.

The main research questions addressed in this chapter are inter-related. We start by asking how was the GE being defined in Romania and looking at the types of initiatives linked to the GE to assess how do businesses, governmental and civil society organisations relate to one another, cutting across governance levels, in seeking to establish a vibrant green economy. The chapter turns next to the renewable energy sector as a case study, to explore what are the green credentials of this sector, what types of political/economic environments are required and what incentives or opportunities do businesses need to encourage them to innovate to help develop a green economy.

The chapter uses semi-structured interviews (2013–2016) with non-governmental organisations (NGOs) and officials from Environment and Economy Ministries, documentary analysis and legislative process tracing of policy documents of the European Commission and the Romanian Government, public statements in press reports, policy reports, energy statistics and media coverage in Romania and at the EU level.

Multi-level governance (MLG) provides a particularly useful model for grasping the interplay between domestic and EU-level politics, as well as an alternative to traditional state-centred government, exploring how the EU works in practice and the linkages that connect multiple levels of governance (Stephenson, 2013). MLG provides a toolkit for understanding how governance arrangements come into existence and how lobbying and negotiations are conducted across levels or

[1] Only 6% of Romanians consider the environment, climate and energy as important issues facing their country (Eurobarometer, 2017: 11).

bypassing the domestic level (Hooghe and Marks, 2001). We are interested in observing this process of 'continuous negotiation among nested governments at several territorial tiers' (Marks, 1993: 392). While MLG has been a part of Western European states transformation, as a result of the European integration process (Tortola, 2017), it is less clear how useful this model would be to explain policy-making in the Eastern European Member states, with a legacy of strong states, top-down policy-making and implementation and weaker civil societies, such as Romania (Buzogany, 2015). In this chapter, we argue that the adoption of global environmental norms such as the GE in Romania has entailed the building of transnational links and actors and has empowered the subnational level, consistent with MLG's 'multiscalar configurations of authority' (Tortola, 2017: 245).

The structure of the chapter follows the emergence of the GE discourse in Romania alongside that of sustainable development (SD) and traces its evolution at both national and local levels. While at the national level the central impetus was provided centrally by the Ministry of Environment, at the local level it was NGOs and local mayors that led the way, with the support of foreign funding and technology. Some changes in niche sub-sectors had the potential to survive the change in government, and small municipalities were leading by example. Post 2018, the focus had shifted towards one of these niche sub-sectors, the circular economy, this time driven from the bottom-up by NGOs and developed at the level of the regions. A much wider transformation and arguably with greater chances to promote the GE agenda was the renewable energy support scheme. The next section of the chapter looks at how an extensive incentive system was set up in Romania in 2008, it generated a significant level of investment and growth of the renewables sector beyond expectations, only to result in systematic gradual dismantling until 2017, as a result of perceived costs and resistance by veto players (Davidescu et al., 2018).

5.2 Theoretical Framework

Using MLG (Marks, Hooghe and Blank, 1996; Stephenson, 2013) to uncover the interplay of a range of actors at multiple levels is particularly suitable for this case study. Governance on the environment in 'weak states', such as Romania, relies on 'cooperation and joint resource mobilization of stakeholders affected by those policies' (Agrawal and Lemos, 2007, cited in Buzogany, 2015: 903). MLG has been useful to explain the 'true nature of policy-making in unitary and centralised states' (Cairney, 2012: 155), as policy-making in the new EU member states tends to be reactive to top-down adjustment pressures emanating from the EU (Sedelmeier, 2011). There has been only recent emphasis on how these states have engaged with new modes of governance in the environmental sector, looking at how non-state actors are involved in the policy process (Buzogany, 2015; Parau, 2015). This literature emphasises the relative weakness of both administrative and societal actors in Romania and the fact that governments give priority to the 'creation of a strong and stable governmental structure with clear division of responsibilities' (Buzogany, 2015: 914). This suggests that type one of MLG would be more suitable to explain developments in this policy area, as it refers to a relatively clear separation of powers by territory (local, regional, national, supranational), while type two (Hooghe and Marks, 2001) is associated with changes that empower sub-state and non-state actors and overlapping jurisdictional levels (Bevir, 2009: 134–136). Furthermore, with regards to our case study on renewable energy, the use of MLG could help better understand the policy backlash and dismantling in this area. The complexity of MLG has had an impact on public accountability, on transparency and clarity of responsibilities (Bevir, 2009: 136–137) and it could shed light on the increasing unpopularity of RES policies, once costs to a range of consumers became apparent (Davidescu et al., 2018).

In the case of environmental policy-making more generally, the literature has looked at how multi-level interactions in this area are less formalised, but still evident, with some member states providing 'hard cases' when centralised authority is concerned, and states act as gatekeepers. The proliferation of actors that might have competing agendas, can often lead to unintended consequences (Fairbrass and Jordan, 2004). We find in the case of Romania a similar process in which the national executive initially had difficulties in predicting and controlling the course of policy-making (ibid.), and the only way of taking back control was through policy dismantling, instead of a change in policy instruments (Davidescu, 2018).

Given the increased interest in the GE agenda in recent years in Romania, this chapter will go beyond tracing the emergence of the discourse and its links to 'sustainable development', to assess the economic and social impact of renewable energy sources (RES) and policies have made in practice, in order to link them to a GE (Moyo, 2014: 40) and illustrate potential conflicts between underlying assumptions and practice, focusing on trade-offs, set-backs and missed opportunities. Faccer et al., (2014) distinguish between three different types of GE discourse: 'incrementalist', 'reformist' and 'transformative' discourses, each characterised according to the degree of change they demand of the prevailing global economic paradigm. Romania adopted an 'incrementalist' discourse (Faccer et al., 2014), consistent with its initial understanding of SD (Davidescu, 2013). This was a pro-growth stance, based on the prevailing economic paradigm, focused on cost avoidance, including environmental costs, offering no alternative to the use of a gross domestic product as a measure of progress, limited debate on environmental limits and a focus on job creation (Faccer et al., 2014: 645–647).

5.3 The Emergence of a Green Economy Discourse in Romania

This chapter looks at the emergence of the GE discourse closely linked to SD in the 2008–2015 period, followed by a significant change towards establishing GE as a distinctive discourse after 2015. The strategic documents adopted by Romanian authorities before 2015 explicitly linked the GE discourse with SD and climate change (CC) (Anghel et al., 2013: 14). There were several types of documents that were considered by the Romanian Government as having relevance for the transition to a green economy: broad strategies (The National Strategy for Sustainable Development Orizonturi 2013–2020–2030 and the draft National Strategy for Climate Change 2013–2020), and sectoral policies. The latter followed EU legislation in thirteen areas considered vulnerable in terms of climate change: industry, agriculture and fisheries, tourism, public health, constructions and infrastructure, transport, water resources, forestry, energy, biodiversity, education, insurance and recreational activities (Anghel et al., 2013: 13). Unlike the discourse on sustainable development, where the development of a strategy had involved a reflection on its meaning and a policy network involving experts from a wide range of organisations (Davidescu, 2013), there had been no consistent use of the term, and no emerging GE policy network at the national level. Overall engagement with the GE was superficial in this period, and the term used interchangeably with sustainable development.

The emergence of a GE discourse, distinctive from SD, was linked to the restructuring of the Romanian Ministry of Environment, Waters and Forests (MEWF) under the leadership of Minister Cristiana Pașca Palmer, in November 2015. The new minister wanted to 'stimulate a change of paradigm' (Romanian Government, 2016) and made it a personal mission to adopt an unprecedented programme of measures on the GE (Agerpres, 2016). Her prior work as head of unit and respectively analyst on CC in Directorate General (DG) DEVCO and DG CLIMA, had focused explicitly on the GE agenda. The minister actively engaged in setting a policy agenda designed to bridge the gap between domestic and international level discourse and governance. The package of measures adopted in a very short time was unprecedented in scope and range of stakeholders, trying to link the private, voluntary and public sectors, as well as national and local levels of government, in an attempt to stimulate green business, green consumer behaviour and green education. This intended to replace the reputation of environmental protection as a 'barrier for economic development' by linking it with a 'competitive advantage of the transition to a GE with low carbon emissions and a circular economy' (MEWF, 2017: 81). The discourse employed in this period was consistent with a 'green growth' discourse, with an emphasis on jobs and innovation and where environmental changes and programmes were seen as an economic opportunity (Death, 2015).

However, the programmes were limited to niche areas of the GE (ecotourism, ecoagriculture, ecobusiness, circular economy, green buildings, eco-mobility and conserving biodiversity) (MEWF, 2017: 82), while key areas such as recycling and renewables were either lagging way behind EU standards (Commission of the European Communities (CEC), 2017) or support schemes were being dismantled as soon as targets had been achieved (Davidescu, 2018). The programmes run by MEWF were going to be funded from the Environment Fund, set up in 2005 as an economic-financial instrument collecting taxes on the basis of the 'polluter pays principle'. Despite the popularity of some programmes for which funding was supplemented (Programme 'green house' and 'green house plus', programme 'Rabla' for replacing old cars and 'Rabla plus' for electric cars), given the short mandate, not all were operational by the time the government changed in January 2017. These were 'left ready for implementation' after a process of public consultation, with Ministerial Orders already in place (MEWF, 2017: 81–90).

The MEWF facilitated the creation for the first time of a group of experts working closely with the minister on the GE agenda, and a new unit within the structure of the Ministry: the Department of green economy, climate change and sustainable development (DGECCSD). The remit of DGECCSD included work on a new strategy and ensured coordination with other ministries (Interview 1, 20 July 2016). A new economic strategy was drafted, with substantial sections on the green economy: 'Competitive Romania: A Project for sustainable economic growth' (Romanian Government, 2016), for which the Ministry of Economy took the lead. There was hope that this unprecedented level of inter-ministerial 'partnership' and involvement of stakeholders in consultations (businesses, NGOs and local authorities), together with a preliminary legal basis, will be sufficient to put pressure on the next government to continue the programmes and allocate further funding (Interview 2, 20 July 2016). There was a further project to develop a 'White paper on the green economy', that proposed an 'alternative model of green growth', rather than the classic development model in the 'Competitive Romania' strategy, based on partnerships with the private sector and examples of best practice at local level and funded through the Environment Fund (Interview 1, 20 July 2016). Instead, the Ministry published a 'Manifesto for a Green Romania' that acted as a summary of policy initiatives at the end of the mandate: emphasising the short time in office of this technocratic government (400 days) and the extraordinary range and speed of decision-making (300 decisions promoted, 'one every 36 hours') (MEWF, 2017: 2).

However, with the change of government in January 2017, a deep political crisis linked to corruption ensued, raising concerns about democratic backsliding (Gotev, 2017), coupled with a change of overall government priorities and populist policies, such as increased salaries and pensions, as well as tax cuts. This made it unlikely that the GE drive would continue beyond the usual 'lip service'. There were some positive developments in terms of institutional continuity, as the DGECCSD survived within the Ministry of Environment with slightly reduced personnel. Furthermore, marking ten years of EU membership, the Minister Grațiela Leocadia Gavrilescu, proposed a joint statement on common values and priorities, including sustainable development, 'The Environment Declaration', signed by thirteen former ministers of environment (Agerpres, 2017).

The position of the Government showed how important its role can be in fostering green economies 'either by providing contexts favourable to green industries development or by engaging directly in the promotion of environmentally friendly industries' (Daugbjerg & Halpin, 2010, p. 142). The evolution of the GE discourse in Romania showed the central importance of the Ministry of Environment as the key top-down initiator of policy initiatives, and the dominance of type one MLG arrangements in which the separation of powers by territory is clear and the funding for programmes at regional and local level is disbursed from the top.

However, alongside central level initiatives, parallel developments had taken place at a local level, following initiatives from environmental NGOs, local mayors and business entrepreneurs, bypassing the national level administration. These type two multilevel governance arrangements empowered sub-state actors and relied almost exclusively on foreign funding, for example from Swiss and Norwegian governments and businesses.

The 'Green Cities – Green Regions' programme (2015–2017) was developed and implemented by environmental NGOs in direct partnership with twenty local authorities (TERRA Mileniul III and R20- Regions for Climate Action Switzerland and the Association of Romanian Municipalities), to train local experts, develop action plans and encourage local projects for cutting greenhouse gas emissions (TERRA Mileniul III, 2015). This was coupled with other projects from TERRA, showing that GE and SD agendas were intertwined, as NGOs followed closely developments in the EU policy agenda and international funding bodies agendas, pre-dating the changes in discourse at the level of the central government (Interview 4, 25 July 2013). Examples of other programmes from TERRA Mileniul III involved a wide range of stakeholders from voluntary, private and public sector and local and regional level. 'Sustainable development of local communities through effective selective waste collection' (2015–2016), was run in partnership with the Association of Habitat Land Owners and the Institute for Public Policy, and the 'Eco-innovative solutions for sustainable rural development' programme (2015–2016), promoted biofuels in collaboration with the private sector, using Norwegian government funding.

A further pioneering project developed in the north-western part of the country was reminiscent of the 'green resilience' discourse of defensive reaction to crisis

(Death, 2015: 2212), as a way to empower local communities. This had drawn on foreign know-how and funding (in this case Chinese investment) and the support of a local entrepreneur, Mayor Arnold Klingeis. The project in the small town of Avrig in Western Romania was to transform it into an energy-independent 'smart city'. The plans of local authorities over a nine-year period were to start using exclusively alternative RES powered systems from a variety of RES technologies sourced/developed locally (primarily solar, hydro, biomass and biogas) for transport and heating and their own electricity distribution grid (Miron, 2014). This would be consistent with the discourse on 'green resilience', rather than 'green growth' (Death, 2015) promoted by the Romanian government, as it went beyond emphasising job creation and emission reductions, in order to invest in new technology and include green stimulus policies at the local level.

While there had been no overlap between the GE policy networks for the type one and two of MLG, the supportive framework of policies at the national level has given new lease of life to local level actors that were already engaged in small projects spearheaded by NGOs who were able to secure external funding. While there was no clear evidence of learning across levels, there was some continuity of discourse and practices at the local and regional level, despite a new government in place since 2017 that has shown little interest to engage with a broader environmental policy agenda and with the GE discourse in particular. A more recent development showed this trend continues. From 2018, the focus had shifted towards a sub-sector of the GE agenda, the 'circular economy'. In Romania, the initiative on developing a new 'Strategy for Romania's Transition to a Circular Economy 2020–2030' was initiated from the bottom-up and has empowered the regions, while the Ministry of Environment has taken a supportive back seat. Following a joint initiative from the European Economic and Social Committee and the European Commission, 24 organisations from across the EU were selected in a competitive process to be part of the coordinating network for the 'European Circular Economy Stakeholder Platform'. Romania was represented in this forum by the 'Circular Economy and Environment Institute 'Ernest Lupan' from Iasi (IRCEM), a regional research institute and think tank with an NGO status, thus empowering for the first time an organisation from one of the less developed regions in Romania (IRCEM, 2019). IRCEM was tasked with the drafting of a new national circular economy strategy, funded by the EU that would focus mainly on building networks of partners (businesses, policy-makers, academics and NGOs) across the seven regions of Romania on different sectors: textiles, water management, smart cities, waste management, packaging, energy efficiency. Although the strategy will be drafted in collaboration with the Ministry of Environment, the process was driven by IRCEM as the main recipient of EU funding for this project and a member of the coordinating group for this platform

(IRCEM, 2019). This governance arrangement is an example of type two MLG, with an expectation that this level of engagement and ownership from sub-national actors, members in European networks, cutting across levels, has the potential to ensure that this latest national strategy would be implemented in practice and have effects in all the regions, unlike previous SD strategies (Davidescu, 2013).

5.4 Renewable Energy and the Green Economy

The previous section of the chapter has shown the extent to which in Romania the GE discourse was put into practice in a range of niche and relatively small size policy programmes at both national and local levels. The next section tries to uncover why a policy area such as renewable energy, which is associated in the literature with the GE discourse (Toke, 2011), has not been incorporated in the GE discourse as an example of success when this was high on the agenda (2016–2017). There were significant barriers and unintended consequences that have prevented this sector from capitalising on the GEdiscourse. This was the result of the interplay of a number of factors, from high levels of legislative uncertainty, to grid capacity problems, increased costs for consumers (Davidescu et al., 2018), followed by retroactive measures of highly visible, active policy dismantling (Davidescu, 2018).

In the early 2000s, Romania's Environmental Performance Review (United Nations, 2001) noted that the renewable energy sector in Romania was negligible in terms of energy production, due to 'no incentive for private investment in this field' (United Nations 2001: 185). By 2013, Romania was considered one of the most attractive countries for investors in renewable energy, with one of the most generous support schemes in the EU (Gellner, 2013) and investments in excess of 8 billion Euros. Explaining how this spectacular increase was possible is relevant for the GE discourse, as the main rationale for adopting a renewable energy support scheme in 2008 (Law 220/2008) was to stimulate foreign direct investment in a green sector and create jobs.

The scheme became appealing to investors because of its wide range of support measures. It offered a guaranteed connection to the grid and created a market in green certificates (GCs) (equivalent to 1MWh of electrical energy from RES) differentiated on the type of technology (one for hydropower, two for wind, three for biomass and four for solar energy). To ensure the smooth functioning of the market, minimal and maximal values of the GCs were set by an independent national regulator ANRE and tax exemptions were applied.[2] Setting mandatory annual quotas of green energy meant distributors were obliged to acquire GCs and

[2] This involved, 'a guarantee of maximum 50% of the value of the medium or long term loans or tax and fee exemptions or discounts for reinvested profit, for three years from the commissioning of the investment' (The Diplomat, 2013; Law 220/2008).

then passed on the costs to final consumers (Davidescu et al., 2018). As investment soared, Romania was able to reach its 2020 target of 24 per cent renewable electricity in the energy mix as soon as 2014.

An additional effect of the supporting legislation was the creation of multi-level, cross-cutting networks of supportive actors. Sub-sector umbrella organisations, specialised in lobbying and consultancy, such as the Romanian Wind Energy Association (RWEA), started promoting 'unity of action' amongst networks of actors, bringing together energy producers, turbine manufacturers, firms delivering associated services in constructions, transportation, insurance, accountancy, environmental consultancy, law firms and even banks, cutting across levels, as some were transnational firms and others were locally based (RWEA, 2013). Similar associations proliferated since then for all types of renewables, working with domestic NGOs and lobbying national and local level institutions, as well as the European Commission directly and through their membership in similar European-wide organisations (Davidescu, 2017).

As policy-makers were surprised by the success of the support scheme, the initial decision by the government, the regulator ANRE and the grid operator Transelectrica was to stall connections and amend legislation repeatedly[3] (Davidescu, 2018). This was done by controlling the number of GCs on the market, granting exemptions and reducing the set annual quota, creating a climate of uncertainty for businesses, in the hope that this will slow down new investments and alleviate costs to final consumers (Davidescu et al., 2018).

The networks of actors cutting across different levels, such as the RWEA, started to lobby the European Commission directly, expressing concern about the dismantling of the support scheme and asking for support (Interview 5, 20 July 2013 and Interview 6, 15 July 2016), but this came at a time when other countries in the EU were equally engaging in policy dismantling (Burns et al., 2018), and the level of ambition for the EU's 2030 targets was lower than expected (Burgin, 2015).

The issue of costs has been central to the backlash on RES and trumped the 'green' credentials of the scheme. There were significant distortions to the GCs market and unintended consequences resulting from the government and the regulator's attempts to cuts costs for consumers. The measures used were gradual exemptions to large industrial consumers and frequent amendments by emergency legislation (Davidescu, 2018). These had a range of unintended consequences, resulting in large fluctuations in the value of GCs, market distortion that encouraged corrupt practises in concluding 'preferential' contracts for some RES big producers, while others (usually small second generation of domestic

[3] From 2013 to 2016 a number of nineteen amendments to Law 220/2008.

investors) could not sell their GCs and were going bust (Davidescu et al., 2018).

The Romanian case emphasises what most conservative critics were bemoaning, the emphasis on 'growth' at the expense of 'green', while progressive voices were concerned that the concept of GE represented business as usual rather than a fundamental shift in the prevailing macroeconomic paradigm (Faccer et al., 2014: 643). Similar to the findings by Moyo (2014), there seemed to be a limited socio-economic impact of RES policies in terms of the empowerment of local communities and local, small-scale businesses.

The main drive of the incentive system was to attract large foreign and medium-size domestic investors. When the costs associated with RES became apparent, the government preferred to dismantle the support scheme through legislative amendments, rather than change the incentive system. Domestic small and medium-size producers were arguing that a change to feed-in-tariffs would encourage more sustainable small scale and individual investment, but this was not considered a viable option by the government (Interviews 6, 15 July 2016 and 3, 6 July 2016). This was consistent with the critique in the literature that GE can be used instrumentally and is marred with contradictions within the discourse and practice, as it can reinforce a 'commodification of nature through the bio-economy' (Death, 2014: 3).

Furthermore, the 'green' credentials of RES were undermined by frequent reports in the media and from environmental NGOs of unsustainable and corrupt practices related to permits for RES projects in nature protected areas and small hydro plants running rivers dry, especially at the local level and often with the approval of the Environment Guard, institution tasked with permitting and implementation (Terra Mileniul III, 2011: 30). Research on the GE discourse encourages a deeper reflection on 'whether transitions to a GE might produce new power relations of inequality and injustice' (Death, 2014: 3).

Moreover, the 'success' of RES was not necessarily translated in a surge in 'green jobs', beyond the building phase (usually low skilled jobs), as technology and know-how were imported (Interview 3, 6 July 2016; Dobre, 2013). A working document from the European Commission accounts for how the RES support scheme had contributed to the GE in Romania (CEC, 2015). The entire energy sector in Romania had a much higher percentage in terms of employment than the rest of the member states (in particular in the coal sector), with a share of 1.4 per cent. However, for the renewable sub-sector, in 2013, the employment was of 0.22 per cent, below the EU average of 0.53 per cent (CEC, 2015).

The significant increase in RES did not address issues such as phasing out polluting energy sectors. The intermittent nature of RES and lack of technological innovation and investment in smart grids and interconnectors produced imbalances and questions of long term sustainability (Davidescu et al., 2018). Overproduction in summer could not be stored or exported and a surge in demand in winter saw a return to coal power plants as the default option (Interview 3, 6 July 2016). These earlier opportunities to promote the GE on a wider scale were squandered. This chapter argued that this did not amount to an energy transition or significant job creation, but instead was linked to socially and politically unacceptable costs and scepticism over the future of renewable energy over the following decades.

5.5 Conclusions

This chapter's contribution to advancing research using MLG as a theory of public policy (Tortola, 2017: 245) was to uncover how international norms such as the GE made it into the national level discourse. In doing so, the emphasis was on how political alliances can be formed 'across territorial levels, sectoral boundaries and the divide between public and private' (Christiansen 1997: 66) and how subnational level actors can be empowered.

Despite a recent surge in interest in the GE discourse in Romania and significant investment and capacity in 'green' sectors such as renewable energy, it is difficult to identify a homogenous and consistent position on the issue, as different actors have often competing agendas and priorities. This chapter has shown that the emerging GE in Romania was limited to initiatives in small niche sectors and under threat of policy reversal with every change of government, as this was not entrenched in the way of doing things and dominant development narrative. Even in 'success' sectors such as renewable energy', 'green' credentials were limited because of unsustainable practices and unpopularity linked to higher costs for consumers. The RES support scheme ended in 2016, exactly at the time when MEWF was starting a GE offensive in other niche areas. Overall, initiatives related to the GE seem highly dependent on the availability of funding and support from key government actors, highlighting the limited extent to which the GE discourse had a transformative effect on the development agenda at the national level. There was some potential for more initiatives from the sub-national level, but this amounted to a patchy range of initiatives and networks.

The chapter uncovered evidence that type one MLG dominates and has led to the development of more coherent networks of actors and policies, but there were issues related to sustaining these practices and implementing strategies from one government to another. Type two MLG has the potential to survive changes in government, as actors within these networks rely on funding from external sources, but this dependency on foreign funding means continuity beyond the timeframe of the programme would be difficult.

Different articulations of the GE discourse coexisted in the period from 2008 to 2015 in Romania, dominated by 'green growth' at the national level, which sees the environment as an economic opportunity at a time of crisis (Death, 2015: 2213) and some occasional examples of 'green resilience' through development programmes empowering communities at local and regional level (Death, 2015: 2212). After 2015, for the first time, albeit briefly, the discourse moved towards a more ambitious 'green transformation', with green stimulus packages in niche areas, realigning the domestic and international level discourse (Death, 2015: 2215), followed by a limited engagement with both the discourse and the implementation in practice of previous policies. However, this move of the discourse on the ambition scale showed limited learning and socialisation of actors within the new GE discourse.

List of interviews

Interview 1 – Government Expert on green economy, MEWF, 20 July 2016, Bucharest.

Interview 2 - Government Expert on governance and administration, MEWF, 20 July 2016, Bucharest.

Interview 3 – Expert, Ministry of Energy, 6 July 2016, Bucharest.

Interview 4 – NGO president, 25 July 2013, Bucharest.

Interview 5 – Lobbyist, Romanian Wind Energy Association (RWEA), 20 July 2013, Bucharest.

Interview 6 – RES small investor, Biomass, 15 July 2016, Bucharest.

References

Agerpres (2016). Ministrul Mediului: Pentru Romania, economia verde este o oportunitate de dezvoltare si stimulare a competitivitatii in noi sectoare de crestere economica, 9 June 2016, H : 10 :30, Bucharest. https://www.agerpres.ro/economie/2016/06/09/ministrul-mediului-pentru-romania-economia-verde-este-o-oportunitate-de-dezvoltare-si-stimulare-a-competitivitatii-in-noi-sectoare-de-crestere-economica-10-30-06 [Accessed on 10 August 2017].

Agerpres (2017). Prima 'Declaratie privind protectia mediului in Romania', semnata miercuri la Bucuresti. *Romanian National Press Agency*, 07/07/2017, h: 11:45, Bucharest. www.agerpres.ro/mediu/2017/06/07/prima-declaratie-privind-protectia-mediului-in-romania-semnata-miercuri-la-bucuresti-11-45-46 [Accessed on 10 August 2017].

Agrawal, A. and Lemos, M.C. (2007). A Greener revolution in the making? : environmental governance in the 21st century' *Environment: Science and Policy for Sustainable Development*, 49, 36–45.

Anghel, L., Vanghele, J.C. and Vieru, R. (2013). *Green Jobs. Studiu la nivel national cu privire la situatia actuala in cee ace priveste locurile de munca verzi in Romania*, Project co-financed by the European Social Fund, AMPOSDRU, Development of Human

Resources 2007–2013, Invest in People! http://proiect.locuridemuncaverzi.ro/upload/pdf/studiu-national_A4_final_LA+Anexe_preview.pdf [Accessed on 11 July 2015].
Bevir, M. (2009). *Key Concepts in Governance*. London: Sage.
Bürgin, A. (2015). National binding renewable energy targets for 2020, but not for 2030 anymore: why the European Commission developed from a supporter to a brakeman, *Journal of European Public Policy*, 22(5), 690–707.
Burns, C., Tobin, P. and Sewerin, S. eds. (2018). *The Impact of the Economic Crisis on European Environmental Policy*. Oxford: Oxford University Press.
Buzogany, A. (2015). Building governance on fragile grounds: lessons from Romania. *Environment and Planning C*, 33, 901–918.
Cairney, P. (2012). *Understanding Public Policy: Theories and Issues*. London: Palgrave Macmillan.
CEC (2015). Commission Staff Working Document, Country Factsheet Romania, State of the Energy Union', Brussels, 18 November 2015.
CEC (2017). Waste: Commission refers Romania to Court of Justice for failing to adopt national measures on waste management and waste prevention. Brussels, 27 April 2017. http://europa.eu/rapid/press-release_IP-17-1047_en.htm [Accessed on 10 July 2017].
Christiansen, T. (1997). Reconstructing territorial space: from territorial politics to multi-level governance. In K.E. Jørgensen, ed., *Reflective approaches to European governance*. Basingstoke: Palgrave Macmillan.
Daugbjerg, C. and Halpin, D. (2010). Generating policy capacity in emerging green industries: the development of organic farming in Denmark and Australia. *Journal of Environmental Policy & Planning*, 12(2), 141–157.
Davidescu, S. (2013). The Sustainable Development Discourse in post-Communist Central and Eastern Europe: the case of Romania. In P. Barnes and T. C. Hoerber, eds., *Sustainable Development and Governance in Europe. The evolution of the discourse on sustainability*. London: Routledge, pp. 163–176.
Davidescu, S. (2017). The Europeanization of renewable energy policy in Romania. In I. Solorio and H. Jorgens, eds., *A Guide to EU Renewable Energy Policy: Comparing Europeanization and Domestic Policy Change in EU Member States*. Cheltenham: Edward Elgar, pp. 204–223.
Davidescu, S. (2018). Environmental policy in times of crisis: Romania's troubled transition'. In C. Burns, P. Tobin and S. Sewerin, eds., *The Impact of the Economic Crisis on European Environmental Policy*. Oxford: Oxford University Press, pp. 133–151.
Davidescu, S., Hiteva, R. and Maltby, T. (2018). Two steps forward, on step back: renewable energy transitions in Bulgaria and Romania. *Public Administration*, 96(6), 11–25.
Death, C. (2014). The green economy in South Africa: global discourses and local politics. *South African Journal of Political Studies*, 41(1), 1–22.
Death, C. (2015). Four discourses of the Green Economy in the Global South. *Third World Quarterly*, 36(12), 2207–2224.
Dinan, D., Nugent, N., and Paterson, W., eds. (2017) *The European Union in Crisis*. London: Palgrave.
Diplomat, The (2013). Romanian Renewable Energy Overview, on-line edition, Bucharest, available at www.energyguide.ro [Accessed on 15 March 2014].
Dobre, M. (2013). Energia verde cauta specialist, dar nu (prea) ofera locuri de munca. *Carrers Online*. http://www.cariereonline.ro/energia-verde-cauta-specialisti-da-nu-prea-ofera-locuri-de-munca?page=0,0 [Accessed on 17 October 2016].
Eurostat (2017). Europe 2020 indicators – poverty and social exclusion. June 2017. http://ec.europa.eu/eurostat/statistics-explained/index.php/Europe_2020_indicators_-_poverty_and_social_exclusion [Accessed on 10 August 2017].

Faccer, K., Nahman, A. and Audouin, M. (2014). Interpreting the green economy: emerging discourses and their considerations for the Global South. *Development Southern Africa*, 31(5), 642–657.

Fairbrass, J. and Jordan, A. (2004). Multi-level Governance and Environmental Policy. In I. Bache and M. Flinders, eds., *Multi-level Governance*. Oxford: Oxford University Press.

Ferguson, P. (2015). The green economy agenda: business as usual or transformational discourse? *Environmental Politics*, 24(1), 17–37.

Gellner, A. (2013). A confrontation between lobbyists, round two. The Diplomat 'Romanian Renewable Energy Overview', on-line edition, Bucharest, available at www.energyguide.ro [Accessed on 15 March 2014].

Gotev, G. (2017). Junker, Timmermans issue stern warning against Romania's "backtracking". *Euractiv*, 1 February 2017, Brussels. https://www.euractiv.com/section/elections/news/juncker-timmermans-issue-stern-warning-against-romanias-backtracking/ [Accessed on 10 May 2017].

Hooghe, L. and Marks, G. (2001). *Multilevel Governance and European Integration*. Lanham, MD: Rowman &Littlefield.

IRCEM (2019). Romania's strategy for the transition to a circular economy ROCES, 2020–2030', Iasi. https://www.ircem.ro/roadmap-for-developing-a-strategy-on-the-circular-economy-in-romania/ [Accessed on 10 June 2019].

Marks, G. (1993). Structural policy and multi-level governance in the EC. In A. Cafruny and G. Rosenthal, eds., *The State of the European Community: The Maastricht Debate and Beyond*. Boulder, CO: Lynne Rienner, pp. 391–411.

Marks, G., Hooghe, L. and Blank, K. (1996). European integration from the 1980s: state-centric vs. multi-level governance. *Journal of Common Market Studies*, 34(3), 341–378.

Ministry of Environment, Waters and Forestry (MEWF) (2017). Manifest pentru Romania Verde: 400 de zile de guvernare tehnocrata de mediu. Ministru Cristiana Pașca Palmer. November 2015–January 2017. http://www.mmediu.ro/articol/manifest-pentru-romania-verde/2090 [Accessed on 10 October 2017].

Miron, R. (2014). The socioeconomic impacts of local energy programmes: a case study of Avrig, Romania. *Management of Environmental Quality: An International Journal*, 25(3), 352–360.

Moyo, T. (2014). Green economy/growth policies and their implementation in the context of the renewable energy sector: The case of Mozambique, South Africa and Zimbabwe. *International Journal of African Renaissance Studies - Multi-, Inter- and Transdisciplinarity*, 9(2), 39–60.

Parau, C.E. (2015). Environmental Network Governance in Romania: Transnational Norm Entrepreneurs in the Shadow of the EU. In L. Stan, ed., *Post-Communist Romania at 25: Linking Past, Present and Future*. Boulder CO: Rowman & Littlefield.

Romanian Government (2016). Romania Competitiva: Un proiect pentru o crestere economica sustenabila. Strategy, Ministry of Economy. http://www.economie.gov.ro/romania-competitiva [Accessed on 10 October 2017].

RWEA (2013). Despre RWEA. http://rwea.ro/despre-noi/despre-rwea/ [Accessed on 15 May 2014].

Sedelmeier, U. (2011). Europeanisation in new member and candidate states. *Living Reviews in European Governance*, 6(1).

Stephenson, P. (2013). Twenty years of multi-level governance: 'Where Does It Come From? What Is It? Where Is It Going? *Journal of European Public Policy*, 20(6), 817–837.

TERRA Mileniul III (2011). Analiza factorilor de divergenta dintre actorii relevanti in sectorul energiei din surse regenerabile. CNCSIS funded project, Bucharest. http://terramileniultrei.ro/wp-content/uploads/2013/04/Studiu-final.pdf [Accessed on 10 October 2014].

TERRA Mileniul III (2015). Orase Verzi – Regiuni Verzi [2015–2017]. 2 April 2015, Project website. http://terramileniultrei.ro/portfolio/orase-verzi-regiuni-verzi-2015-2017/ [Accessed on 10 August 2017].

Toke, D. (2011). Ecological modernisation, social movements and renewable energy. *Environmental Politics*, 20(1), 60–77.

Tortola, P.D. (2017). Clarifying multilevel governance. *European Journal of Political Research*, 56, 234–250.

United Nations (2001). *Environmental Performance Review: Romania, Economic Commission for Europe*. New York: Committee on Environmental Policy, UN Publications.

UNEP (2011). Towards a green economy, pathways to sustainable development and poverty eradication. A synthesis for policy makers. Nairobi, https://sustainabledevelopment.un.org/content/documents/126GER_synthesis_en.pdf [Accessed on 11 August 2017].

World Bank (2012). *Inclusive Green Growth: The Pathway to Sustainable Development*. Washington, DC, World Bank.

6

Overcoming Structural Disadvantages with Local Green Economies?

The Case of Two Maritime Cities

JEREMY MOULTON, WINFRIED OSTHORST, PAULINE DEUTZ, ANDREW JONAS AND RÜDIGER WURZEL

6.1 Introduction

The strong potential for economic growth and job creation, potentially within new techno-industrial regimes, to accompany ecological improvements is underlined by United Nations Environment Program's (UNEP's) Green Economy Initiative (UNEP and ILO, 2008). Cities are recognised as crucial green economy (GE) actors (OECD, 2013) and as spheres of environmental progress (Geels, 2011), as well as actors for sustainability in general (Satterthwaite, 1997). The literature has identified the key role of local governments' agency in cooperation with and independent of other vital societal actors such as businesses and non-governmental organisations (NGOs) (e.g. Broto and Bulkeley, 2013).

Addressing the role of cities for the development of the GE raises a number of questions. Cities are highly diverse with respect to their socio-economic situations, political constellations, problem structures, capacities, and competencies—in turn, these factors impact a city's ability to successfully modify its actions towards environmental sustainability. While many self-identifying 'green cities' in developing countries are struggling with pollution control and the extension of basic urban infrastructures to the poor (OECD, 2013), in OECD countries and some industrialising countries, climate change policies have emerged as a key issue, increasingly framed as urban low-carbon transition or carbon control (While *et al.*, 2010). As Chapter 2 in this collection addresses, understandings of GE vary, yet in cities the characteristics of the GE centre most frequently around renewable energy and resource-efficient technologies (Payton and Kneller, 2009). However, cities are also shaped and positioned in hierarchies by locational competition and global value chains (Krätke, 1995). Therefore, cities, especially small-to-medium-sized ones, can be constrained by their multi-level governance (MLG) context and constrained in their abilities to act (Wurzel *et al.*, 2019). Nonetheless, the geography of maritime cities offers them the opportunity to attract a key component of the contemporary GE—the offshore wind energy (OWE) industry. In this chapter, we compare and contrast the attempts made by two such cities to engage in economic development founded in the GE in order to understand how cities have attempted to use the GE approaches to compensate for their structural disadvantages (e.g. resulting from declining traditional industries and poor infrastructure (Wurzel *et al.*, 2019). Specifically, we ask the extent to which medium-sized cities initiate and maintain innovative processes, and what actors are relevant to their degree of success.

This chapter answers these questions by investigating the GE-oriented strategies of two structurally disadvantaged European cities—Kingston-Upon-Hull (United Kingdom) and Bremerhaven (Germany). Characterised by de-industrialisation, severe social problems and budgetary pressures, both cities are routinely ranked highly in measures of deprivation, such as unemployment and ill-health. Yet, both cities have attempted to benefit from the reorientation of national energy policies towards renewables by becoming centres of the emerging OWE. Whilst the OWE sector represents the roles that cities might play in promoting and working within GE industrialisation, it is not, of course, the only sector where climate impact can be created. The housing sector, one where municipalities can exert much influence, is a highly important part of broader climate policy efforts. The CO_2 reductions created by improvements to housing stock are an important environmental benefit of the GE. Further to this, they are often high-value investments, creating jobs for a range of workers, e.g. builders, electricians and other small and medium-sized enterprises (SMEs). While the two cases are very similar with respect to these and some further dimensions, they differ substantially in other respects, such as the strategy applied, the role of the local government in the two countries and actor constellations.

This chapter starts with a conceptual discussion of the GE and the local dimension. Reviewing the central debates in the literature allows for the identification of core areas of GE relevant to the local level. Further, the differentiation between a narrow economic development approach to GE and a wider approach embracing transformational (more integrated and impactful) elements is relevant. Subsequently, the chapter explains the case cities' main characteristics and positions them in urban hierarchies, thereby identifying both cities as structurally disadvantaged cities. The following case descriptions address the OWE sector and the public housing sector, key aspects of both cities GE.

The comparative assessment argues that even structurally disadvantaged cities are in principle capable of contributing to GE development, and of benefitting from green growth. However, clear limitations result from their lack of capacities and resources. Moreover, the dependence on national policies and the growing role of multinational enterprises in the GE makes them vulnerable to change.

Transition-oriented activities do exist but remain subordinate to activities designed to stimulate economic development.

6.2 Green Economy and the Local Dimension

In the academic literature, approaches to GE range from a focus on broad socio-economic transitions to an emphasis on economic restructuring and from specific sectors or national policies to the global economy (e.g. Ferguson, 2015). Although the areas addressed by GE approaches are diverse, energy production and use ranks particularly high due to its relation to climate change and resource demand in general (Payton and Kneller, 2009). In their focus on growth, innovation and ecological improvements in their response to environmental problems, GE strategies could be understood as cases of ecological modernisation (EM), but with a stronger focus on economic development. Some critics view GE (and EM) as an incoherent analytical (and political) concept, de-politicising distributive aspects in capitalist restructuring (e.g. Brand, 2012). Others, such as Bailey and Caprotti (2014), are interested in differences between different forms of GE. They identify functional domains and drivers of GE strategies, which could lead to contradictions between sectors, localities or even parts of society. Notwithstanding limitations with GE (or EM) as an economic development tool, given the competition between locations inherent in a capitalist economy (Deutz, 2014), the way in which opportunities are interpreted by regional and local governments, businesses and communities becomes relevant (Jonas et al., 2011). As a consequence, the GE is expected to be less a coherent project than a contested arena of practices, which leaves room for conflicting normative interpretations of diverse societal cultures.

The affinity between GE and EM allows for reference to basic distinctions yielded from the older debate on EM. Here, too, economic processes are seen as tools for substantial environmental progress, and as enhancing competitiveness. While some versions of EM identify the economy as an autonomous sphere (e.g. Huber, 1982), the predominant political and social science EM perspective emphasises the leading role of the state (e.g. Jänicke, 1990). Hence, types of innovations, appropriate governance patterns and instruments are of analytical interest (e.g. Mol and Spaargaren, 2000). The initially strong focus on technological progress and industry-state relations was criticised by some as 'weak EM', to be complemented by a stronger orientation towards broad institutional restructuring and societal conflict as the engine of 'strong EM' (Christoff, 1996). Not coincidentally, these tensions between merely technocratic, economistic or efficiency-oriented strategies, and the approaches additionally addressing broader aspects of cultural transformation, including different patterns of consumption, are increasingly mentioned in the debate on urban climate policies (Bulkeley and Betsill, 2013).

Bailey and Caprotti (2014) underline the importance of transitions within socio-technical systems (Raven *et al.* 2012) to understanding the contradictions of the GE. In these studies, large scale interactions at different levels are investigated, e.g. operationalised as landscapes, regimes or niches. Of interest in this context are intentionality, steerability and instruments, as well as conditions for path dependencies and path change (see Geels, 2011). Regarding cities, their potential in creating niches is important (Geels, 2011; Raven *et al.*, 2012). Aiming explicitly at integrating regions and cities into transition perspectives, Truffer and Coenen (2012) emphasise the role of green technology cluster initiatives and sustainable regions and regions/cities as transition 'managers'. Applied to sustainable development cities (SDCs), it is debatable whether cities such as Bremerhaven and Hull have the capacities to function as niches and to contribute to innovations. Underlining the demand for a 'politicised' interpretation of transitions further, Hodson and Marvin (2010) pinpoint the role of low-carbon programs for reinforcing the position of metropoles within urban hierarchies. While economically and politically leading cities modernise their infrastructure and improve their locational qualities through ambitious climate policies, Hodson and Marvin (2010) suggest that there are problematic effects on cities occupying weaker positions in urban hierarchies, e.g. because of a widened gap in locally achieved standards and qualities.

Here, competition between cities and regions within hierarchies is understood as a consequence of global economic and technical transitions. Sassen (1991) identified such hierarchies for different parts of the economy, depending on their world-market integration (Scott *et al.*, 2001), and separately for each of the globally leading economic centres. This results, for example, in a European city system in which leading metropoles function as prime nodes of Europe's world-market integration. At the same time, other cities and regions are positioned in a peripheral and structurally disadvantaged situation (Krätke, 1995). Socio-economic analysis, e.g. for Germany, confirms these arguments by reconstructing severe disparities between clusters of German cities in terms of social structure, wealth, public budgets and institutional capacity (Neu, 2012). Applied to the GE it has to be asked how this form of transition influences the existing hierarchies (and vice versa). Of course, different national forms of carbon regulation may result in contrasting constellations between 'people, places and firms' (While *et al.*, 2010: 89). In the case of the German *Energiewende*, new prospects of peripheral regions in energy production are underlined, leading to a new spatial order of the sector (Gailing *et al.*, 2013). In addition, studies on wind energy industries highlight successes of cluster strategies in peripheral regions in the UK and Germany, similarly situated in de-industrialised coastal areas with a weakened maritime economic profile, and potentially leading to a "Green re-industrialization" despite a peripheral position (Dawley, 2014; Fornahl *et al.*, 2012). The question is if and to what extent peripheral cities are really able to mobilise the cultural, institutional and economic resources necessary to improve their position, and if they can really substantially contribute to stronger versions of EM, beyond symbolic dimensions.

Decisions in cities about the mobilisation of resources and the orientation of strategies depend on bargaining processes and power relations at the local level. Here, carbon-control regimes within cities are seen as a new type of local coalition aiming at the development of locational qualities through new environmental protection politics (NEPUD) (Jonas *et al.*, 2011). Factors such as partisanship, local societal pressures, capacities of NGOs, and committed key individuals, including from within local authorities, are considered relevant for supporting ambitious sustainability-oriented local policies (Bulkeley and Kern, 2006). In European contexts, investigating distinguishable types of regimes as alliances between local actors demands the recognition of, amongst others, the relevance of public–public, as well as public–private, relations (Frank, 2000). Hence, relations between different sectors or functions within municipalities become decisive. Core functions of urban governance structures are *economic development* and *welfare* (Stoker, 2011), which are characterised by distinct mixtures of participants, objectives, normative frames and outcomes (Pierre, 1999).

To analyse the development of the GE at the local level, including in SDCs, and to understand differences or even contradictions within local strategies, it is important to consider developments in more than one core function. With regard to GE development, an emerging industry such as renewable energy could serve as an example for the economic development function. For the welfare function, public housing constitutes an example due to its relevance for the local society, and tensions between its capacity for GE and potential consequences of carbon control measures on weaker parts of the society. For the SDCs analysed here it is thus of interest if actors of these different functions cooperate, or act in isolation and only within the limitations of functional rationales.

The cities chosen as cases, Bremerhaven and Hull, allow further to address consequences of differences in the degree of autonomy municipalities have in different countries. Here, comparative research on local government sees the British type of centralised central-local government relations as a contrast to the decentralised German type of local government (Wollmann, 2004). The scope of action of German municipalities and the high degree of decentralisation result from the federal system, shielding them from the direct regulative influence of the federal government (Bulkeley and Kern, 2006). Although Europeanisation and liberalisation, together with budgetary pressures in both countries reduced local autonomy and have exerted convergence pressures, important differences in the degree of local discretion persist (Wollmann, 2004). It is of interest if and how the development of the GE in SDCs in the UK and Germany in the two sectors addressed is influenced by differences in the degree of local autonomy and actor constellations that are a consequence of the respective political system.

In summation, an investigation of SDCs' GE strategies allows for the analysis of the extent to which peripheral cities can exploit the opportunities provided by green growth. This includes examining the restrictions cities are confronted with, different types of local government systems, and whether the form of EM displayed is weak (reliant on technocratic solutions) or stronger (enforced by policies even where economically restrictive). Finally, it has to be asked if local actors are acting in accord, or if controversies exist, and which impact on the local GE approach.

6.3 Comparing Two European Structurally Disadvantaged Maritime Cities Studies

6.3.1 Bremerhaven and Hull: Similar Cases in Different Urban Systems

As city cases, the chapter utilises Kingston-Upon-Hull (Hull) in the UK and Bremerhaven and in Germany, due to their important similarities in relation to the GE and their shared form of SDC.

The national conditions relevant to the two case cities provide important context for the emergence of ambitious urban climate policies and green growth strategies in fields such as renewable energy technologies. Both countries have developed leading offshore wind industries in parallel. Here, national policies and regional development instruments interacted with local-level initiatives (Dawley, 2014; Fornahl *et al.*, 2012). Whilst their national policy contexts differ, they are offered some consistency in the shared supranational policy framework of the European Union (EU) which has set ambitious renewables targets, for example. At the same time, the urban systems of both countries are characterised by severe disparities, with cities shaped by ageing industries being structurally disadvantaged in terms of locational qualities, social structure, resources, capacities at the local level and infrastructure quality. In terms of urban hierarchies, both have occupied a lowly position in their respective nations. Both Hull (England, East Yorkshire) and Bremerhaven (Northwest Germany, State of Bremen) can be considered SDCs since they were characterised by the decline of long-dominant maritime industries, including shipbuilding and fishing. This led to persistent structural problems, such as population losses and high unemployment (see also Jonas *et al.*, 2017). In 2015, both cities had unemployment rates more than twice the national average. Nevertheless, maritime industries and the port sector continue to be economically central. Moreover, administrative capacities and public resources are scarce. In order to counter the long-term problems, both cities have turned to the GE and the economic potential it offers, resulting in substantial employment increase and improved economic prospects for the respective regions. The turn to the GE has involved the attraction of external businesses to establish facilities in the cities, i.e. original equipment manufacturers (OEMs—those companies that are at the end of the production chain), and the companies that supply them. It has also involved a degree of municipal action, work that has taken place within the city in a bid to produce positive environmental and economic results.

In the following sections, two such elements of the GE-turn in these cities are analysed—the OWE and public housing sectors. These sectors are of particular interest as they respectively cover the energy production and energy use aspects of GE, as well as economic development and welfare functions of urban governance. Whilst they differ in terms of actor constellations and dominating rationales, they both clearly reflect the GE—creating economic activity whilst producing an environmental benefit.

6.3.2 Offshore Wind

Offshore wind activities in Bremerhaven emerged in the early 2000s in an effort to exploit the opportunities of the 1998 coalition between the Social Democratic Party (SPD) and the Greens, which endeavoured to develop renewable energies, including from offshore wind installations in the German Exclusive Economic Zone. The legal parameters for OWE expansion were set by the *Erneuerbare Energien Gesetz* (EEG—Law on Renewable Energies) of 2000. Consequently, in 2002, the state (Land) of Bremen and the city of Bremerhaven identified the emerging OWE industry and, much less significantly, the (existing) onshore equivalent as a potential major growth sector. The local authority decided in 2003 to develop an encompassing strategy, pooling resources and approaches, to turn Bremerhaven into a centre of the new industry (Bremische Bürgerschaft, 2003). Together with other measures, the city and state explicitly sought to stop the decline of Bremerhaven by turning its coastal locational characteristics into an advantage (Bremische Bürgerschaft, 2007b: 10).

In the following years, state and city agencies (including the Bremerhaven Economic Development Company—Bremerhavener Gesellschaft für Investitionsförderung (BIS)) facilitated the creation of enterprises needed for establishing a sectoral value-chain. State-based research programmes supported technological innovations in enterprises' sustainability (Bremische Bürgerschaft, 2007a). Moreover, BIS, city and Senate helped to attract the creation of nationally-funded, prominent, research facilities, established as Fraunhofer Institute for Wind Energy and Energy System Technology (IWES) in 2009. The IWES provides testing facilities for blades, and, since 2011, of complete nacelles (Becker *et al.*, 2013).

Initiated by the BIS, the Wind Energy Agency Bremerhaven/Bremen (WAB) was founded as a business network, gradually becoming a sectoral association at the national level. Further, specialised academic training programmes in the local state-financed University of Applied Sciences Bremerhaven (Hochschule Bremerhaven) and professional training and skill enhancement concepts, based on cooperation between a broad range of public and private sector actors, were created (Bremische Bürgerschaft, 2007a). Additional elements included the state-financed development of specialised industrial areas and first port handling facilities. In 2010, the state decided to build the Offshore Terminal Bremerhaven (OTB) on the Weser River, estimated to cost €180 million and to be financed by commercial investors. As a result of its strategy, in 2012, the city had attracted a number of GE enterprises, covering central positions of the value-chain. Examples include the turbine producers ADWEN and SENVION (onshore), the blade producer POWER BLADES and the foundation fabricator WESERWIND (Becker *et al.*, 2013). At that time, the cluster offered about 3,500 jobs (Interview 2017).

In 2010, Bremerhaven brought together and packaged the emerging OWE industry, climate research centres and climate-linked tourist attractions with the concept *'Kurs Klimastadt'* (course climate city), seeking to re-imagine the city by referring to the new positive developments. As demanded by the local Greens, *Klimastadt* was extended in 2011 into a frame for ambitious strategic carbon management, which included participatory elements (Mederake, 2015: 20 and passim).

However, while until 2012 the development of the OWE industry had been a tremendous success (e.g. in terms of jobs created and OEMs and suppliers attracted), the cluster and the city's strategy experienced some serious setbacks in the following years. In late 2012, the search for an appropriate investor for the OTB failed and the Senate decided to invest public resources (SWAH, 2012). The EEG reforms of 2014 and 2016 reduced both the overall OWE capacity targets, the specific feed-in tariffs, and introduced reduced annual capacity extension quotas as of 2017 (Gawel and Purkus, 2016). As a consequence, uncertainty for investors led to drastically reduced contracts as of 2013, resulting in severe job losses in the city's OWE sector. These losses were driven by the dissolution of WESERWIND (2015) and POWERBLADES (2017) and severe cutbacks at SENVION (which will likely also close in 2020 after completing its last orders) and ADWEN (which now only maintains an operations and maintenance presence in the city).

In parallel, market concentration within the increasingly mature industry became palpable. In 2012 Siemens, already world market leader, supplied 80 per cent of the offshore wind turbines for the North Sea market, while ADWEN held less than 5 per cent of the contracts (Reichhardt and Rogge, 2012). In 2015, Siemens decided to build its turbine factory for the North Sea market, offering about 1000 jobs, in neighbouring Cuxhaven, where a specialised terminal was already under construction, disappointing expectations in Bremerhaven (*Weser-Kurier* 08.10.2016). Subsequently, some regional suppliers relocated their activities. Following this, the environmental NGO BUND legally challenged the OTB due to its effects on ecologically sensitive sites. While BUND argued that the terminal was now neither economically viable nor necessary for the *Energiewende* (Interviews, 2016–2017), the city justified the project with the expansionist strategy of the remaining producer ADWEN. In 2016, a preliminary court decision halted the realisation of the OTB project for several years (Interviews 2016–2017). A further change of conditions occurred when Siemens, as part of a merger aiming to realign other businesses, became the owner of its direct competitor ADWEN with its 1,100 jobs in 2016, and indicated in spring 2017 that it would considerably reduce ADWEN'S market activities (*Weser-Kurier* 07.06.2017). By 2018, ADWEN employed only 211 people in Germany (primarily in Bremerhaven) (ADWEN, 2018). While state and city politicians remain publicly supportive of the OTB, the project has been beset by legal problems and doubts surrounding the potential usefulness of the terminal with the predominant OWE manufacturer, Siemens, located in a neighbouring city (*Weser-Kurier* 07.02.2019). Perhaps signalling a decline in aspirations surrounding the project, in September 2019 the news broke that funds that had been put in reserve to fund the OTB were likely to be used to help supplement a Bremen state's cash-strapped budget (*Weser-Kurier* 11.09.2019). The once-thriving OWE manufacturing industry in Bremerhaven has suffered a terminal decline with no clear path to recovery.

With Hull, there are a number of distinctions from the case of Bremerhaven, despite the two cases inherent similarities. OWE forms only part (albeit a significant one), rather than the totality of the GE in Hull. Hull's turn to the renewables sector has two elements, with the city courting both the OWE and biomass sectors. The curse of the significant sectoral decline, in both the docks and the fishing industries in the city, left Hull with swathes of land that could be used to attract potential GE investors. The notion of the GE being potentially lucrative for Hull first emerged for the local authority in 2006, with the receipt of the report commissioned to assess the city's economic potential. The competitive assessment report, researched and written by external consultants, highlighted the opportunities that lay in the expansion of the biomass industry, with no mention of OWE (IBM, 2006). The local authority unilaterally began to pursue the green economy as a potential source of economic recovery for Hull, by courting potential OEMs and other GE businesses (Interviews 2015–2016).

One impediment to the evolution of the GE in Hull was the impermanence of economic development agencies working on the city's behalf, primarily due to changes of policy at the national level, Hull's economic agencies went through a period of institutional upheaval between 2006 and 2010. A period of continuity began in 2010 with the establishment of Local Enterprise Partnerships (LEPs), regional development agencies, by the Department for Business, Innovation and Skills (Her Majesty's (HM) Government 2010). The Humber LEP, the regional agency in question, set to work on promoting the region as a potential heart of the UK's burgeoning renewable sector, under the branding of *Energy Estuary*. Hull was well placed geographically and in terms of its preparedness to take-up the call to the renewables sector (Deutz, 2014). The realisation of Hull's long-held GE ambitions is embodied in Green Port Hull, an area of the city governed by a Local Development Order (LDO). The LDO, coupled with Enterprise Zone status, set specific financial incentives for the quayside land for businesses working in the renewable or low-carbon sectors (Hull City Council, 2012). As of 2016, the Green Port Hull site included over 500 hectares of land and had already generated a £1 billion programme of investment in Hull (Green Port Hull, 2017). For the UK's third-most deprived city, this is a sum that has the potential to be of monumental impact.

The most significant portion of that investment came with the successful effort to host a major OWE facility in the city. The somewhat delayed development of the GE sector in Hull (compared to Bremerhaven, for example,) meant that when the city was successful in attracting an OWE OEM to the city. That OEM was an established, significant player, and the very same company whose decision to not place a facility in Bremerhaven had been so disastrous to the city's OWE industry—Siemens. The Siemens-Green Port Hull development was the result of £310 million co-founding partnership between the German conglomerate and Associated British Ports (ABP), the private sector company which owns and operates the port site in Hull. The function of the Siemens plant, as well its location within Green Port, began to vary even after a memorandum of understanding was signed between the company and the local authority. In its realised form, which opened in late 2016, the facility was set to produce 600 wind turbine blades annually, as well as readying the components for eventual placement in the North Sea. By early 2017, the plant employed 700 people, 95 per cent of whom came from the city or region (Bounds, 2016). By 2019, that figure had risen to slightly over 1000 jobs. Whilst Siemens-Green Port Hull was the flagship project of Hull's GE turn, it was far from being the only innovation. Other notable GE developments in the city include a 28MW energy-from-waste plant, Energy Works (gasification from the waste facility), a biomass-handling port facility and a £400 million biofuel refinery plant.

The local authority has attempted to fully embrace this GE reindustrialisation with the brand *Energy City* for Hull. *Energy City* became an operating ideal for key players within the city's economic development team, driving forward efforts to further attract GE actors to the city. Interestingly, *Energy City* replaced an earlier bid to brand the city in a more environmentally conscious manner as *Green City*, showing the shift in the balance between environmentalism and economics (Interviews 2015–2016). Despite the wholehearted embracement of GE, there are clouds on the horizon for the sector in Hull. The UK's vote to leave the EU has thrown-up a number of questions relating to trade and costs for the sector which is dependent on an interconnected North Sea energy sphere. This was a particular concern for Siemens and the unknowns have put a pause on the company's expansion plans in the city (Interview 2016). Further to this, the predicted boom in indirect jobs that GE was touted as bringing to the city, which estimates put as high as leading to 10,000 new jobs for the city, has so far not emerged.

6.3.3 Public Housing

In the realm of public housing, Bremerhaven relies on its municipal housing company STÄWOG, which owns just over 5000 apartments with some 8000 tenants. Confronted with substantial vacancies due to the city's population loss, STÄWOG used national funds and subsidies for improving its building stock. Besides energy efficiency programs, it also relied on national programmes supporting municipal housing companies in disadvantaged cities for addressing social problems, such as *'Soziale Stadt'* (Social City). Since 1997, STÄWOG improved the energy efficiency and overall standards of approximately 40 per cent of its apartments. In addition, its subsidiary STÄSERVICE operates some highly-efficient, block-type thermal power and heating stations as well as photovoltaic systems which is able to sell the self-produced electricity to about ten percent of the STÄWOG tenants, making use of respective provisions of the EEG that explicitly aim at supporting municipal utilities (Mederake, 2015). Between 2005 and 2011, a 23 per cent reduction of CO_2 emissions of STÄWOG's apartment stock had been achieved. Measured in CO_2 / m^2, STÄWOG became the most successful regional housing company according to a sectoral study regarding energy efficiency (SUBV, 2016: 29).

With similar ambitions, the city's local facility management company, Seestadt Immobilien, undertakes refurbishment of municipal buildings with the aim of reducing CO_2 emissions, e.g. in schools. Among others, it has built zero-emission buildings for two nurseries (Mederake, 2015). Moreover, both STÄWOG and Seestadt Immobilien became active partners in *Klimastadt* projects and in respective co-operations with further public agencies, societal actors, and administrations. As for motives, a clear public-good orientation towards the city, and an entrepreneurial style, seeing cooperation as central means for improving the quality of housing stock, including investment into buildings and stabilisation of social relations among tenants can be identified. The economic imperative also lies at the heart of the cooperation. Aside from the jobs created by retrofitting,

STÄWOG commissioned research into both climate and economic impact of retrofitting as opposed to the replacement of housing stock. The research found that retrofitting was markedly less expensive and was more likely to provide energy savings (Guratzsch, 2016), thereby bolstering the case for GE housing work to be undertaken. At the same time, however, these activities depend crucially on financial assistance programmes from higher levels of government (Mederake, 2015).

In Hull, the main driver for energy efficiency improvements to public housing is the reduction of fuel poverty. In 2014, the percentage of households suffering from fuel poverty was a third higher in Hull than it was in the rest of England (Hull Data Observatory, 2017). However, by 2017, the last year for which data was available, the figure had dropped to 13 per cent above the national average (ibid), demonstrating that there has been some success in combatting the issue within those three years. Energy conversation in housing is driven by the Home Energy Conservation Act (HECA) from 1995, which empowers local authorities to act on residential properties. In 2012, Hull City Council released a HECA report and action plan that included ambitions on energy efficiency, afforded by the national government's Green Deal – which made explicit links between the economic and environmental benefits of housing improvements (Department of Energy & Climate Change and Huhne, 2010). This ambition included utilising Green Deal funding to insulate 3000 Council properties. However, due to lack of staffing as well as institutional lethargy the local authority was not quick to act on the potential Green Deal opportunities (Interview 2016). In 2015, the Conservative government stopped the Green Deal programme. Plans to develop a district heating scheme that would benefit residential properties similarly failed to gain traction during this time.

Despite the disappointments of the Green Deal, the public housing sector has made some significant GE advances since the 2012 action plan, as jobs have been created, and investment attracted, in the effort to reduce emissions levels in the Council's housing portfolio of 24,300 properties. The installation of solar PVs on 500 Council homes was one flagship project for the city. Further to this, a 10-year, £550 million project (funded by the local authority, the Regional Growth Fund and a number of other national sources) to construct 4000 new homes and retrofit old properties in the city is being undertaken, with an emphasis on energy efficiency. The properties are all to be designed to be rated according to the Standard Assessment Procedure (SAP)—a national energy rating scheme. Elsewhere in the city, the Goodwin Development Trust has drawn attention to the affordability of energy-efficient housing by installing prefabricated, highly efficient housing in a central Hull housing estate. Between 2005 and 2014 Hull made significant improvements to combined public and private household emissions levels, reducing CO_2 emissions by 40 per cent in this time (Department for Business, Energy & Industrial Strategy, 2019).

6.4 Conclusions

The above cases constitute important empirical examples for the assessment of the course and content of the green re-industrialisation one can find when SDCs turn to GE in a bid to overcome some of those disadvantages. Of course, as attention was drawn to in the introduction, whilst expectations of GE-impacts are often high in a city turning to the sector, it is no silver bullet to structural disadvantages. Ambition in Bremerhaven and Hull has, to varying degrees, been frustrated. There are important lessons to be drawn for other SDCs and the wider GE.

Bremerhaven and Hull demonstrate that SDCs, though economically marginalised, can play roles in the GE and contribute to sectoral development, i.e. OWE. Geographical remoteness, something that was a curse for both cities in the years since the decline in their once-dominant maritime industries, is something that can be turned into an opportunity as energy production markedly changes. However, the creation of such opportunities is not and could not be due solely to a local authority's actions. Instead, in both cases, the GE option arose because of national and EU policy direction. Further to this, both cases show the emerged dominance of one multinational in the OWE sector in the North Sea – Siemens. When Bremerhaven turned to OWE in the early 2000s, there were a number of OEMs to court and who came to the city. The contemporary situation is markedly different. The choice of one company can be a critical moment for an SDC trying to embrace GE industrialisation, as Bremerhaven and Hull's differing fates attest to. With Siemens' dominance established and with a more conservative expansion of OWE capacity in the at-least near future, it seems that there will little opportunity for other SDCs to play a role in the sector. This reinforces Krätke's (1995) assertion that whilst cities may undoubtedly improve, if only for a short period, their relative position in hierarchical relations, one city's gain is another's loss. However, as this chapter has focused only on two case study cities, future research should focus on a wider range of cities and countries in order to provide more conclusive empirical evidence for or against Krätke's claim.

The importance of the national framework in enabling city action is repeated in the public housing sector. Both cities were only able to demonstrate any form of GE ambition when funding from higher levels of governance was forthcoming. As the case of Hull and the Green Deal demonstrates, retraction of national-level funding can quickly limit ambition. SDCs have weak resource bases, which are further hit through national austerity programmes (more so than richer counterparts), thus further limiting the capacity for transformational projects, e.g.

Klimastadt. SDCs are able to position themselves to exploit potential opportunities in the GE, but they remain limited by funding shortcomings and changing national policy focus. Therefore, one can identify the GE ecological transitions that SDCs can truly contribute to as, at times, fleetingly symbolic.

Turning to the effects of local government systems on a local government agency, there are some points of contrast. Wollmann's (2004) assertion that German local authorities are able to achieve a greater degree of policy coordination than their British counterparts is shown in this case to bear weight. In Bremerhaven, where *Klimastadt* was able to become a key local concept, STÄWOG adopted ambitious GE methods. In Hull, where there is less institutional room for manoeuvre, energy efficiency was a less forefront aspect of public housing. Ownership of public utilities are, however, becoming private-oriented in Germany, diminishing the opportunity for local authority initiative in the GE (Bulkeley and Kern, 2006). Our two cases support the widely-held view more decentralised local government systems provide more possibilities for supporting ambitious EM. However, more cases need to be examined in relation to this finding.

Lastly, we consider the relevance of inner-urban relations and their impact on 'place-making'. Both cities clearly undertook work in place-making, with efforts to brand their cities to reflect the niches they had worked to create (Geels, 2011; Raven et al., 2012). Periods of success in local GE, in OWE and public housing, were made possible by the public–private and public–public agreement on the issue, a recognised necessity (Franz, 2000). There was institutional unity on the desire to push for OWE in both cases, for example. At the heart of this unity was the shape of the GE in question – undoubtedly growth-oriented, with the balance between economy and the environment tipped noticeably to the latter in most regards. This is especially reflected in the case of Hull's continued embrace of biomass despite the increasing evidence of its negative environmental impact (Clark, 2014). In both cases, the focus of GE reflects SDC needs—with employment being one of the foremost concerns. Likewise, the GE link to public housing was undoubtedly linked to welfare. Thus, two core functions of urban governance structure were satisfied (Stoker, 2011). Interestingly, however, while the jobs case for OWE was highly publicised in both cities, this was not mirrored in the housing sector which focused more on savings and welfare.

In summary, there are conclusions to be drawn in relation to what the GE means for SDCs. These two cities show that any turn to environmentalism is likely to be limited, even when there is a significant degree of ambition (e.g. Bremerhaven). In playing host to green re-industrialisation, cities can play a role in the GE. In terms of EM, this is clearly work that is on the weaker end of the weak-strong typology. Neither city has managed to take the next step that is seen as vital in urban climate policies—cultural transformation (Bulkely and Betsill, 2012). Neither city has effected the path change (Geels, 2011) that might be expected of them by academics and the citizens of Hull and Bremerhaven alike. For these cities, the GE has meant the opportunity to improve living conditions for public housing residents, and to secure more jobs. As is found time and again throughout this collection, the GE has struggled against dominant forces, both political and economic, which treat environmental necessities as, at best, second-order priorities. GE strategies, when they have been employed, have been technocratic rather than transformative. However, as Truffer and Coenen (2012) argue, they have the capacity to be the groundwork for later transformation. Cities are not solely the local authority, they are webs of urban government, local economic development agencies, businesses, and many other actors. For successful transformative strategies to be designed and implemented those actors need to work in a coordinated manner in order to best exploit the opportunities provided, whether they be changes in national policy or when the long-awaited multinational corporation comes to town.

References

ADWEN (2018). Agreement on reconciliation of interests and social plan at ADWEN in Germany. Available online: www.adwenoffshore.com/agreement-on-reconciliation-of-interests-and-social-plan-at-adwen-in-germany/ [Last accessed 14 September 2019].

Bailey, I. and Caprotti, F. (2014). The green economy: functional domains and theoretical directions of enquiry. *Environment and Planning*, 46(8), 1797–1813.

Becker, G., Kellner-Stoll R. and Köpke, R. (2013). *Eine Stadt im Aufwind*. Bremen: Fachverlag NW.

Bounds, A. (2016). Siemens opens £31m turbine blade plant in Hull. Available online: www.ft.com/content/69b68b16-b7da-11e6-ba85-95d1533d9a62?mhq5j=e1 [Last accessed 14 September 2019].

Brand, U. (2012). Green Economy - the Next Oxymoron? *GAIA*, 21(1), 28–32.

Bremische Bürgerschaft (2003). Mitteilung des Senats vom 11. February 2003. On- und Offshore-Windkraft in Bremen und Bremerhaven. Drs. 15/1375, Bremen.

Bremische Bürgerschaft (2007a). Mitteilung des Senats vom 24. April 2007. Offshore-Windenergie – Chance für Bremerhaven. Drs. 16/1385, Bremen.

Bremische Bürgerschaft (2007b). Mitteilung des Senats vom 16. January 2007. Entwicklungsperspektiven für die Seestadt Bremerhaven. Drs. 16/1268 Bremen.

Broto, V. and Bulkeley, H. (2013). A survey of urban climate change experiments in 100 cities. *Global Environmental Change*, 23(1), 92–102.

Bulkeley, H. and Betsill, M. (2013). Revisiting the urban politics of climate change. *Environmental Politics*, 22(1), 136–154.

Bulkeley, H. and Kern, K. (2006). Local government and the governing of climate change in Germany and the UK. *Urban Studies*, 43(12), 2237–2259.

Christoff, P. (1996). Ecological modernisation, ecological modernities. *Environmental Politics*, 5(3), 476–500.

Clark, P. (2014). Biomass report adds to debate on power station subsidies. Available online: www.ft.com/content/18350b14-1273-11e4-a581-00144feabdc0 [Last accessed 14 September 2019].

Dawley, S. (2014). Creating new paths? Offshore wind, policy activism, and peripheral regional development. *Economic Geography*, 90(1), 91–112.

Department of Energy & Climate Change & Huhne, C. (2010). Green Deal to create green jobs. Available online: www.gov.uk/government/news/green-deal-to-create-green-jobs [Last accessed 14 September 2019].

Department for Business, Energy & Industrial Strategy (2016). *2005 to 2017 UK local and regional CO_2 emissions – data tables*. Available online:www.gov.uk/government/statistics/uk-local-authority-and-regional-carbon-dioxide-emissions-national-statistics-2005-to-2017 [Last accessed 14. September 2019].

Deutz, P. (2014). A class-based analysis of sustainable development. *Sustainable Development*, 22(4), 243–252.

Ferguson, P. (2015). The green economy agenda. *Environmental Politics*, 24(1), 17–37.

Fornahl, D., Hassink, R., Klaerding, C., Mossig, I. and Schröder, H. (2012). From the old path of shipbuilding onto the new path of offshore wind energy? *European Planning Studies*, 20(5), 835–855.

Franz, P. (2000). Suburbanization and the clash of urban regimes. *European Urban and Regional Studies*, 7(2), 135–146.

Gailing, L., Hüesker, F., Kern, K. and Röhring, A. (2013). Die räumliche Gestaltung der Energiewende zwischen Zentralität und Dezentralität. *IRS Working Paper*, 51.

Gawel, E., and Purkus, A. (2016). EEG 2017—Mehr Markt bei der Erneuerbare-Energien-Förderung? *Wirtschaftsdienst*, 96(12), 910–915.

Geels, F. (2011). The role of cities in technological transitions, cities and low carbon transitions. In Bulkeley, H., Broto, V., Hodson, M. and Marvin, S. (eds.), *Cities and low carbon transitions*. New York: Routledge, pp. 13–28.

Green Port Hull (2017). About Green Port. Available online: http://greenporthull.co.uk/about-green-port [Last accessed 14 September 2019].

Guratzsch, D. (2016). Verbietet endlich das Bauen neuer Wohnungen! Available online: www.welt.de/kultur/kunst-und-architektur/article151224460/Verbietet-endlich-das-Bauen-neuer-Wohnungen.html [Last accessed 14 September 2019].

HM Government (2010). *Local Growth: Realising Every Place's Potential*. London: The Stationary Office.

Hodson, M. and Marvin, S. (2010). Can cities shape socio-technical transitions and how would we know if they were? *Research Policy*, 39(4), 477–485.

Huber, J (1982). *Die verlorene Unschuld der Ökologie*. Frankfurt am Main, Fischer-Verlag.

Hull City Council (2012). *Port of Hull: Local Development Order: Adopted – May 2012*. Hull.

Hull Data Observatory (2017). *Fuel Poverty*. Available online: http://109.228.11.121/IAS_Live/dataviews/tabular?viewId=21&geoId=5&subsetId= [Last accessed 14 September 2019].

IBM (2006). *Hull Citybuild: Competitive Assessment: IBM-PLI Perspective on Hull.*

Jänicke, M. (1990). *State Failure*. London: Polity Press.

Jonas, E., Gibbs, D. and While, A. (2011). The new urban politics as a politics of carbon control. *Urban Studies*, 48(12), 2537–2554.

Jonas, A. E. G., Wurzel, R., Monaghan, M. and Osthorst, W. (2017). Climate change, the green economy and re-imagining the city. *Die Erde – Journal of the Geographical Society of Berlin*, 148(4), 197–211.

Krätke, S. (1995). Stadt - Raum - Ökonomie - Einführung in aktuelle Problemfelder der Stadtökonomie und Wirtschaftsgeographie, Basel/Boston/Berlin.

Mederake, L. (2015). Opportunities for the local government of Bremerhaven provided by the project "Klimastadt Bremerhaven" in times of limited municipal room for manoeuvre. *GLOKAL Arbeitspapier zur Nachhaltigkeitspolitik*. No.2.

Mol, A. P. J. and Spaargaren, G. (2000). Ecological modernisation theory in debate: a review. *Environmental Politics*, 9(1), 17–49.

Neu, M. (2012). Regionale Disparitäten, Berichterstattung zur sozioökonomischen Entwicklung in Deutschland, 185–200, Wiesbaden, VS Verlag für Sozialwissenschaften.

OECD (2013). *Green Growth in Cities*. Paris: OECD Publishing.

Payton, S. and Kneller, P. (2009). *The future of Cleantech in Europe*. London: Caspian Publishing.

Pierre, J. (1999). Models of urban governance. *Urban Affairs Review*, 34(3), 372–396.

Raven, R., Schot, J., and Berkhout, F. (2012). Space and scale in socio-technical transitions. *Environmental Innovation and Social Transitions*, 4, 63–78.

Sassen, S (1991). *The Global City*. New York: Princeton.

Satterthwaite, D. (1997). Sustainable cities or cities that contribute to sustainable development? *Urban Studies*, 34(10), 1667–1691.

Scott, A. J., Agnew, J., Soja, E. W. and Storper, M. (2001). Global city-regions. In Scott, A. J. eds., *Global City-Regions*. Oxford: Oxford University Press, pp. 11–30.

Stoker, G. (2011). Was local governance such a good idea? *Public Administration*, 89(1), 15–31.

SUBV [Der Senator für Umwelt, Bau und Verkehr] (2016). *Fortschreibung des Klimaschutz- und Energieprogramms (KEP) 2020*. Anlage C:Entwurf (Stand: 27.01.2016).

SWAH [Der Senator für Wirtschaft, Arbeit und Häfen] (2012). *Bremens Kraftanstrengung für Energiewende und Arbeitsplätze*. Pressemitteilung 4 December 2012. Bremen.

Truffer, B. and Coenen, L. (2012). Environmental innovation and sustainability transitions in regional studies. *Regional Studies*, 46(1), 1–21.

UNEP and ILO (2008). *Green Jobs: Towards Decent Work in a Sustainable, low-Carbon World*. Washington: Worldwatch Institute.

Weser-Kurier (2016, 8 October). Das Ringen der Seestädte Cuxhaven und Bremerhaven.

Weser-Kurier (2017, 7 June). Zittern in Bremerhaven.

Weser-Kurier (2019, 7 February). Offshore-Terminal Bremerhaven darf vorerst nicht gebaut werden.

Weser-Kurier (2019, 11 September). Haushaltslose Zeit wird lang.

While, A., Jonas, A. and Gibbs, D. (2010). From sustainable development to carbon control, *Transactions of the Institute of British Geographers*, 35(1), 76–93.

Wollmann, H. (2004). Local government reforms in Great Britain, Sweden, Germany and France. *Local Government Studies*, 30(4), 639–665.

Wurzel, R., Moulton, J., Osthorst, W., Mederake, L., Deutz, P., and Jonas, A. E. G. (2019). Climate pioneership and leadership in structurally disadvantaged maritime port cities. *Environmental Politics*, 28(1), 146–166.

7

Shifting Models of Energy Companies towards Green Economy in Europe

ROSA MARIA FERNANDEZ

7.1 Introduction

The international economic crisis of 2007–2008 was considered to be a good opportunity to change macroeconomic patterns and lead the world (particularly Western countries) into a green economy and a green growth path. After the launch of the Green Economy Initiative in 2008 and the call for a 'Global Green New Deal' in 2009 (UNEP, 2009a, 2009b) however, there seems to be no coordinated effort at international level to reach the targets that a green economy should aim for, and each country is adopting differing measures based on their own local or national priorities.

This chapter contributes to this edited volume by focusing on the role of European energy companies in the transition to a green economy as the private actors taking part in public policy making. It uses the notion of governance as set out by Heritier and Rhodes (2011), Jordan and Schout (2006) or Kohler-Koch and Eising (1999) among many others. Bearing in mind the European Union (EU) context used for the analysis, the chapter also builds on the notion of multi-level governance as suggested by Conzelmann and Smith (2008) or Fairbrass and Jordan (2004). The chapter begins with the clarification of the definition of the green economy that will be used throughout. In addition, it will particularly address the following research questions: What role can businesses play (particularly energy businesses) in engendering a 'green economy'? What changes should they undertake in pursuing this overarching goal? What type of political and economic environments are required to encourage business organisations to assist in the construction of a 'green economy'? And what lessons can be drawn for policy-making in this area? It will do so by analysing the development that energy companies have experienced in the European Union setting particularly in the last couple of decades, their interaction with policymakers and their adaptation to changing regulatory frameworks and competition from third countries. This way it will be possible to identify gaps in business strategies and dysfunctionalities in governance interactions that may act as barriers in the process of reaching the 'green economy' goal.

Having said this, it makes sense to begin with the concept of 'green economy'. Definitions of 'green economy' seem to proliferate, with at least eight identified coming from different international institutions or forums (United Nations' Department of Economic and Social Affairs (UNDESA), 2012), which does not contribute to the clarification of suitable courses of action even if they have many elements in common. This would reinforce the arguments of those who call for a more radical approach in the way that policymakers respond to crises, with a new economy that would give the environmental base and global environmental justice the priority in the policy discourse (Bina and La Camera, 2011).

For the purpose of this chapter we will use the definition that the United Nations Environment Programme (UNEP) formalised in 2011 and that has been widely repeated ever since that a:

> *...green economy is the one that results in improved human well-being and social equity, while significantly reducing environmental risks and ecological scarcities.*
>
> *(UNEP, 2011)*

The concept suggests that we adopt a holistic approach, encompassing the three dimensions of sustainable development as used by the United Nations for decades (economic, social and environmental) (UNDESA et al., 2012). In addition, the chapter will build on the inclusive notion of governance, which relies on the interaction of public and private actors to engage in policy formulation (Heritier, 2002) to see if that interaction is leading the European energy sector towards the green economy.

The main aspect that this chapter cover relates to energy companies (i.e. business private actors) to analyse if and how they have adapted to the new discourse coming from public sector bodies and demands from the citizenship. According to the Global Green New Deal, the economic stimulus to get out of the crisis should focus on areas that in many cases are linked to the energy sector: Energy efficiency in old and new buildings; Renewable energy technologies; Sustainable transport technologies; planet's ecological infrastructure; and Sustainable agriculture (UNEP, 2009b). The question is then: are traditional energy companies shifting their business model to adapt to the new environment or not?

Within the European Union, the Europe 2020 Strategy, particularly through the 'Resource Efficient Europe' flagship initiative (Commission of the European Communities (CEC), 2011), builds on this approach, and the agreement: '*...to stimulate the transition to a green economy and to strive towards an absolute decoupling of economic growth and environmental degradation*' has been formalised in the Seventh Environment Action Programme to 2020 (Official Journal of the European Union (OJEU), 2013). The problem for the EU is the implementation of measures at Member State level and the lack of a unified position in key policy areas, which keeps slowing down the progress in issues such as sustainability or climate change (Fernandez, 2012), in which energy plays a central role. So, the chapter will also look at the government actors and their role within the governance framework, bearing in mind that in the EU context the term normally used is multi-level governance (Conzelmann, 2008).

One of the measures that green economy supporters advocate involves fiscal stimulus so that green investments and innovation can take place, as well as the elimination of harmful subsidies. In the energy sector, this translates into incentives to green energy sources (renewables) and the elimination of existing subsidies to fossil fuels, particularly coal. One would expect European energy companies to take the necessary steps to adapt themselves to the new scenarios and regulations in order to keep their competitiveness and avoid losing market share against potential new entrants, particularly in a globalised economy. This chapter will try to clarify whether or not they are doing so, and whether the institutional framework supports change or undermines it through confusing or contradictory regulation. It will also analyse in which way business actors try to influence the outcome of regulatory measures approval as part of the normal governance interaction process.

The chapter will continue with an overview of the situation of traditional energy markets in Europe to focus then on the new actors entering these markets from third countries (Section 7.2). It will be followed by the analysis of the change in regulatory frameworks and political discourses in Europe so that the role of the public bodies in the energy governance framework can be understood (Section 7.3). Section 7.4 will present different types of strategies that energy companies are adopting as a response to the changes in the governance setting (new business actors and changing public actors discourse) so that issues can be identified. The chapter will end with a conclusion section in which answers to the research questions posed will be provided, based on the analysis undertaken in the preceding sections.

7.2 New Actors in the European Energy Markets

7.2.1 Traditional Energy Markets Structure

The European energy sector has been traditionally difficult to regulate, as proved by repeated modifications of the gas and electricity directives in an attempt to increase liberalisation and competition (see for instance, for the electricity market,

Directive 96/92/EC replaced by Directive 2003/54/EC (OJEU, 2003) subsequently replaced by Directive 2009/72/EC (OJEU, 2009)). It cannot be said that these attempts have been successful and in most European member States energy providers still act as a monopoly or oligopoly (International Competition Network (ICN), 2011). Very few examples indicate a competitive number of companies, as shown in the electricity sector by the market share of the largest generator (Eurostat, 2019a).

Some countries are more open to competition than others. In Poland, no electricity provider has more than 18% of the market share, while both in Malta and Cyprus, one single company dominates the market (with a change in Malta only in 2017). The general trend points out towards more open markets, as shown by the decrease in market shares over time in countries such as Belgium, Portugal, Italy, Czechia or Lithuania, the latter quite remarkably. Conversely, there are cases where more concentration is happening, such as Germany, the UK or Hungary. In other Member States , the situation has not changed much (France or Sweden), which in itself is indicative of the lack of effective progress in the liberalisation of the internal electricity market. The overall picture then is mixed.

7.2.2 New Participants in the Market

The lack of clear direction in the European energy market has created opportunities for companies from countries such as China and Russia to access European energy (and other) assets, taking advantage of the weakened financial position of many companies during the last crisis (Vladimirov and Stefanov, 2016). Examples of this are a 21% participation by the Chinese Three Gorges Project Corporation in Energias de Portugal (Ma and Kowsmann, 2011), the main shareholder of Hidroelectrica del Cantabrico in Spain (La Nueva España, 2013), or a 25% stake in the Portuguese electricity network (De Clercq, 2015).

In terms of which countries 'own' the main energy companies the situation nowadays has changed compared to how it was in past decades, and the big EU based companies are not the only ones and certainly not the best positioned in the global market, with a raising presence of companies from the BRIC (Brazil-Russia-India-China) countries (Lopez, 2011). While fifteen or twenty years ago the Global 500 Fortune list was dominated by North-American based companies, with Gazprom and a few EU giants keeping a stable presence in the Energy area of the list, since then China, Turkey, Brazil and South Korea are consolidating their presence (Fortune, n.d.). In the petroleum refinery area, the dominant companies are still renowned Western names (Exxon, BP, Shell) but Chinese companies appear also quite high on the list (Fortune, n.d.). With regard to oil and gas, the big public companies that are on top of the rankings are from Russia and the United

States, the latter due to the increase in the production of shale oil (Rapier, 2016). In fact, the situation moves quite quickly, as can be observed in Table 7.1.

If we compare the situation between 2014 and 2016, it can be argued that these traditional energy companies (understood here as those focused on fossil fuels and with long-standing presence and market experience) have not had the best of times and rank lower in terms of revenues (see Table 7.1). It is worth noting at this point that renewable energy is not a significant part of the business portfolio for any of these companies.

The relevance of energy companies for EU economies is still unquestionable. They are key contributors to employment creation and value addition (Eurostat, 2019b). But, it is also clear that this importance is uneven among the different Member States and it appears quite polarised in a reduced number of countries (Figure 7.1).

Table 7.1 showed how worldwide companies from out of Europe, particularly China, are taking a stake within the energy sector. Investments from China in Europe's energy sector are considered quite small (Voss, 2013), but the 21.35% stake of China Three Gorges in EDP (Energias de Portugal) (EDP, 2014) indicates the direction of travel. Russia's attempts to increase its presence in the European market is more persistent and visible and has political roots. Lukoil and Gazprom tried to acquire part of the Spanish Repsol in 2008 (Tremlett, 2008), through the shares owned by the heavily indebted construction company Sacyr. Intense negotiations with Zapatero's government had among others, the purpose of smoothing the path for Russian firms to buy stakes in Spanish energy companies (Shchedrow and Harding, 2009). Gazprom also signed agreements with the German E.ON for long-term gas supplies (E.ON, 2012), in an attempt to ensure dependence from Russian gas. Both countries, China and Russia, have different approaches and different reasons for their interest in the EU energy sector. At the moment, partly due to the Ukrainian crisis, it seems there is more room for an increase of the Chinese presence within European borders (Gippner and Nitoiu, 2015).

At the same time, the regulatory framework up until recently favoured the promotion of renewable energies has proven extremely successful, particularly the feed-in-tariffs systems implemented in many Member States. Capacity installed has grown steadily in the last decade (Eurostat, 2017), with an increase in primary renewable energy production between 2006 and 2016 of 66.5% (Eurostat, 2018). This framework has contributed to the creation of new companies focused on the renewable energy business, which has had a positive impact over employment in several member States (as shown in Figure 7.1b and Eurostat, 2019b), and still has the potential to create up to 1.5 million additional posts by 2050 (Duscha et al., 2014). But it has also involved the loss of market share for the traditional energy companies, forced now to search for new business models as demand is shifting from oil and gas to renewables and it seems some of them have not been able to

Table 7.1. *Energy Companies in the Global 500 Fortune list 2014–2016*

2014				2016			
Company Name	**Country**	**Ranking Global 500**	**Type of Ownership**	**Company Name**	**Country**	**Ranking Global 500**	**Type of Ownership**
Glencore	Switzerland	10	Private	E.ON	Germany	32	Private
Gazprom	Russia	17	Government owned	Gazprom	Russia	56	Government owned
E.ON	Germany	18	Private	Engie (previously GDF Suez)	France	89	Partly public
GDF Suez	France	44	Partly public	China Huaneng Group	China	217	Government owned
RWE	Germany	130	Private	CEFC China Energy	China	229	Private
China Huaneng Group	China	221	Government owned	State Power Investment	China	342	Government owned
China Goudian	China	297	Government owned	China Guodian	China	345	Government owned
Jinneng Group	China	309	Government owned	Gas Natural Fenosa	Spain	365	Private
Korea Gas	Korea	340	Government owned	China Datang	China	406	Government owned
Koc Holding	Turkey	341	Private	Koc Holding	Turkey	419	Private
CEFC China Energy	China	349	Private	Korea Gas	Korea	464	Government owned
Gas Natural Fenosa	Spain	360	Private	Ultrapar Holdings	Brazil	474	Private
GasTerra	Netherlands	373	Government owned	Greenergy Fuels Holdings	UK	477	Private
China Datang	China	396	Government owned				
Ultrapar Holdings	Brazil	430	Private				
AntarChile	Chile	488	Private				

Source: Fortune (www.fortune.com, as extracted on 7 July 2015 and 11 May 2017

Note: Oil refining, mining and utilities (gas and electricity) are classified separately. The only companies that appear listed in other categories are Gazprom and GDF Suez

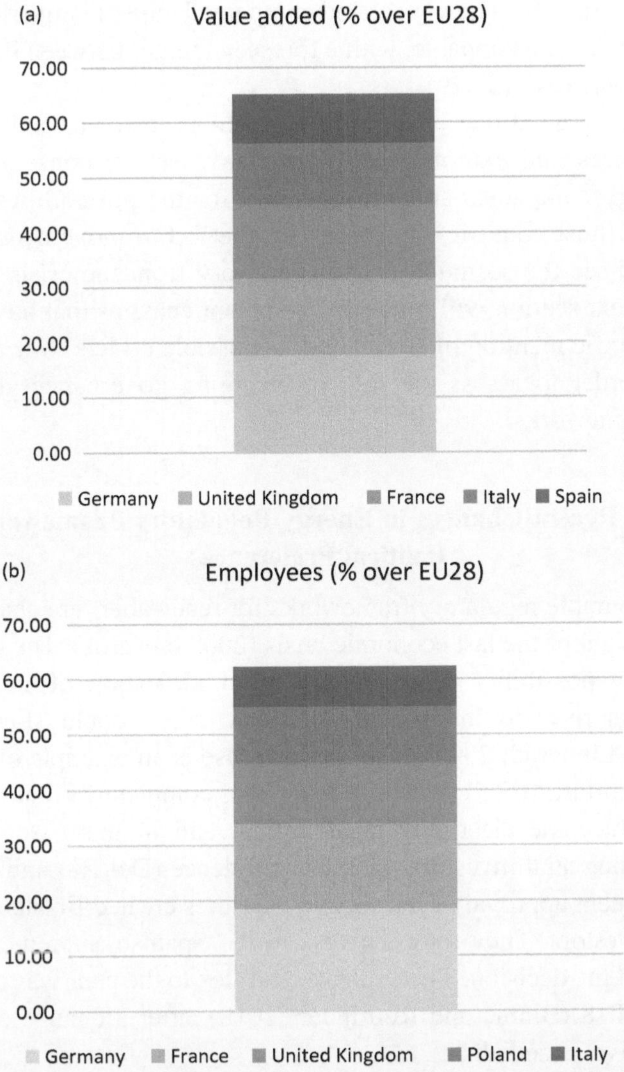

Figure 7.1 (a and b). Concentration of value added and employment. Electricity, gas, steam and air conditioning supply. (Cumulative share of the five principal member states as a % of the EU28). 2016.
Source: Eurostat (Structural Business Statistics overview, extracted 25 June 2019)
Note: Data for Malta not available.

adapt (Pfeifer, 2013; The Economist, 2013). A good example of this trend is the case of E.ON, who established plans to shut down a good number of its European nuclear reactors, affected by the shift from nuclear power to renewables in Germany and other countries and the subsequent fall in electricity prices (Patel, 2015). In fact, it has split the business to focus on renewables, with the fossil fuel assets being absorbed by a newly created company, Uniper (Timperley, 2016). The move in the sector is unstoppable, with a foreseen merger between RWE and E.ON on the cards (Durakovic, 2019).

It can then be argued that changes in regulations, market conditions, shifts in policy preferences and external factors can have severe consequences for the future of energy companies and subsequently for the possibilities of economic growth of their host countries. Focusing on the EU, a movement in the wrong direction could see the so much desired recovery from the crisis interrupted or delayed. The next section will focus on the recent changes that have been taking place, with specific mention of Brexit and its possible effects over a green energy transition, in order to assess the role of changing governance and multi-level governance frameworks.

7.3 The Recent Changes in Energy Regulatory Frameworks and Political Preferences

Previously favourable regulatory frameworks for renewables are changing rapidly, particularly in light of the last economic crisis (2008 onwards). The effects are still unclear, but the possibility of elimination or modification of support schemes generally brings risks to investment decisions and it could slow them down (Boomsma and Linnerud, 2015). The Spanish case is an example of a 180-degree shift. The feed-in-tariff (FIT) system in Spain was completely eliminated under the pressure to reduce the electricity tariff deficit, and in this case the move got translated into potential investors' lack of confidence (Del Rio and Mir Artigues, 2014). Government approval of retroactive measures created financial problems to the existing investors. They took the case to the Spanish Supreme Court (Roca, 2014) to contest the decision. The controversial 'tax to the sun' was only abolished at the end of 2018 (Binnie and Rodriguez, 2018), after a change of government from conservative to socialist.

However, Spain is not the only country where the FIT system has suffered modifications or suspensions. Financial restrictions linked to the austerity programmes approved for several member States who were bailed out during the crisis played an important role. Portugal had to approve similar measures to Spain in light of the bailout by the International Monetary Fund (IMF) (Cascao and Luis de Sousa, 2014), subsidies for heating have also disappeared, and FITs will not be applicable to new installations (RES-Legal, 2019). Ireland and Greece, also bailed out, suspended their FIT systems too, though later, and so did Czechia. A good number of Member States have started using, in combination with (Germany) or instead of (Netherlands) the FIT system, a feed-in premium or premium tariff, which is a price-based mechanism linked to market prices.

The lack of available financial resources created by the crisis has not been the only driver for change. Despite the apparent wish to promote renewables and meet the targets set for 2020, and the aim to become a low carbon economy by 2050, the discourse of the European Commission seems to have shifted from 'sustainable, smart and inclusive growth' to a focus on the security of supply and market competition. The move from fixed tariff rates to feed-in premiums in 2016 was outlined already in 2013 (CEC, 2013), considering wind and solar technologies mature enough to face market competition. On the opposite side of the spectrum, some reports (Whitley et al., 2017) confirm the continuing support for fossil fuels, particularly coal, in at least 10 member states, which would be contrary to a green economy approach. According to the Commission plans (CEC, 2013), subsidies for fossil fuels should disappear by 2020, but in 2016 it was approved to allow coal subsidies to continue for another 8 years (Hope, 2016). This could suggest a change in priorities in the public bodies of the multi-level governance framework at the EU level, affecting the regulatory framework of the Member States (public bodies too), which consequently is having an impact on the investment decisions of the private actors (energy companies). The shift in the discourse can create confusion in investors, as there is a clear contradiction between supporting a transition to a green economy and at the same time allowing subsidies to fossil fuels to continue. In some countries, contradictions may emerge due to differences in the government preferences at local, regional and national levels (Spain), and tensions can appear between actors at the same level, with unions, for instance, concerned about employment effects in fossil fuel regions (Campos-Martin et al., 2020), while citizens would voice their climate and environmental priorities (Greta Thunberg – Bryant, 2019; Extinction Rebellion – Calder, 2019).

Something similar happened initially with the energy efficiency (and renewables) targets for 2030. After multiple rounds of negotiations, the potential gains that could come from the promotion of energy efficiency were outweighed by the fears of negative impacts on the European Emissions Trading Scheme (ETS). The Commission called for a 30% target but the Council opted for a conservative goal of 27%, to be reviewed in 2020 (CEC, 2015a). This was an indicative and not a binding target, which left Member States without individual targets, weakening the possible outcomes. This has just recently changed, with the target for renewables being raised to 32%, making it binding instead of indicative (Vaughan, 2018). Though this change points towards the right direction, it also indicates frequent changes in the regulatory framework, which again affect investment decisions.

It is likely that this change has been influenced by the momentum created by the entry into force of the Paris Agreement, on 4 November 2016, following the Paris Summit in 2015 (UN, 2016). It was perceived as a success for the EU (Arias Cañete, 2016) insofar it managed to present a unified position (CEC, 2016a) in comparison to the lack of EU unity shown in Copenhagen 2009. The Paris Agreement also constitutes an opportunity for the EU to reinforce its commitment towards a 'clean energy transition', with specific mention of the 'investment and innovation in renewable energy' (CEC, 2016a). In line with a green economy approach, the EU view of the Paris Agreement focuses on 'economic transformation' with fundamental shifts required in several sectors, including energy. Within this context, the EU considers itself ready for a transition to a low carbon economy through the priorities set up by its Energy Union project (CEC, 2015b), even if a big part of such project is centred around the security of supply, and the recognition that in reality there are twenty-eight regulatory frameworks to manage. For these reasons the Commission launched a public consultation process on a new energy market design (CEC, 2015c), but no specific actions seem to have been taken as a result of such consultation at the time of writing this chapter.

The aims set up in the Energy Union package may be conditioned by the environment of uncertainty created by the Brexit vote (23 June 2016) which will see the number of EU member states reduced to twenty-seven. With one fewer country involved in the decision-making process, there is potential for future agreements to be reached more quickly, even if a move from twenty-eight to twenty-seven is not such a significant change numerically. It is clear that the number of votes (in the Parliament, for instance) will be altered considerably given the status of the UK as a 'big' country, so proportions for majorities could become more complex. The fact that the UK participated in the recent European Elections (May 2019) but was scheduled to leave the EU by 31 October 2019 (now January 2020), makes matters more confusing. If the UK decides to scrap some of the targets it is bound to by European regulations, green investments in the country could be adversely affected. Effects are likely to be different by sector, and though it is expected that not that many changes will affect energy, due to the UK's own commitments to reduce emissions, clean air and recycling could see negative outcomes, with differentiated effects for England, Scotland and Wales in the latter case (Gosden, 2017). Others argue that the effects in the renewable energy sector will be bigger, given the fact that the UK has been the biggest beneficiary of funding from the European Investment Bank (EIB)—24% since 2007 on this area (Kreivi, 2016), and out of the EU the possibilities of receiving funding will be reduced (Mongoose Energy, 2016). On the other side of the story, there are also arguments saying that the EU will improve its renewable energy outlook without the UK since the country is far behind its targets for 2020 while other member states are making significant progress (Lycetts, 2017).

In sum, what we are finding at the moment is shifts in political preferences and policy priorities both within the EU institutions and Member States, some of them contradictory in goals, with so far uncertain consequences for the progression towards a green economy in Europe. Interestingly though, the EU seems to have acknowledged the need for clarity and it has proposed a regulation of the governance of the Energy Union (CEC, 2016b) to provide better coordination between EU and national actors and reduce administrative burdens. One could wonder, however, if this would be enough, given the necessary role that cities and regions have to play in the success of the green energy transition (E3G, 2015). Recent surge on citizens' movement in favour of more climate-friendly policies also poses questions over the adequacy of the existing multi-level governance framework, hinting that a bottom-up approach may be required, or at least a better balance between bottom-up and top-down initiatives.

7.4 Different Energy Company Strategies

Whether at the national or at EU level, continuous changes in regulations and targets create an uncertain environment for investors, which does not help them develop long-term strategies. This becomes particularly important when companies are trapped in a crisis situation, as it has been recently the case, and need to find alternative solutions to keep themselves in the market. Given the relevance of the energy sector in the European (and international) economy, energy companies will not be different from others in their search for profitability and market survival. But, there are differing approaches to the way in which each type of company deals with the challenges of changing environments, and there can be several strategies being implemented simultaneously.

This section will present examples of those strategies or behaviours, in order to distinguish to which extent they are following or not a green economy approach. It will do so using concepts from corporate social responsibility (Carroll, 1979; Clarkson, 1995) and business strategy (Reeves et al., 2012; Campagne et al., 1995) literature. From corporate social responsibility (CSR) literature we mainly find a classification of companies' approach in four types: reactive, defensive, accommodative and proactive. From business strategy and management literature, we can find classifications of business strategies as: classical, adaptive, shaping and visionary or simply as proactive and reactive, or preventive and corrective.

One type of strategy adopted mostly by the big traditional energy companies can be defined as preventive or reactive, in trying to lobby governments at the national level, or the European institutions, so that regulations and measures are approved or modified according to their interests. In this case, they would be trying to prevent the change from happening (Thammatucharee, 2013), i.e. an unfavourable regulation to be approved, instead of having to correct the situation once the change has taken place. The oil industry has been classified in this regard also as 'classical' (Reeves et al., 2012) in so far the environment it has to work in is relatively predictable but change would be costly to adopt if required.

We have seen a boost of these lobbying activities (Warleigh and Fairbrass, 2002; Fairbrass, 2003; Hauser, 2011) in the last years, through individual companies or their representative interest groups, pushing for lenient targets on renewable energy use, favourable conditions of the ETS, or the promotion of non-conventional fossil fuels (shale oil and gas). This has been particularly visible during the negotiations for the 2030 targets (Tolbaru, 2012; Lipton and Hakim, 2013). The shape of the final agreement (see the previous section) suggests initial successful lobbying by established fossil fuel focused energy companies, with renewable (green) energy business as the losers of the battle. It is difficult to consider this type of strategy though, from the governance perspective, as cooperation between private and public actors (Heritier, 2002). It could be read as a competition between private actors defending their own interests and public actors concerned about the 'greater good' (a greener, low-carbon economy). The issue in this respect is that the EU, due to the increasing number of policy areas in which it has competencies, including energy, does not have sufficient resources nor expertise to evaluate the pros and cons of different courses of action. Instead, it increasingly relies on expertise and information provided by interest groups (Hauser, 2011). If all types of energy companies, traditional and renewable, had the same financial and institutional resources to gain access to European authorities, this would not be an issue, but we have seen in previous sections that traditional energy companies are bigger in size and as such, they have greater access to resources. This leaves newer smaller companies at a disadvantageous situation, thus the information base for EU decision-making institutions could be distorted. If only business elites have access to the political institutions and the provision of information is asymmetrical (Hauser, 2011), the legitimacy of the governance framework can be compromised. Lobbying in this context takes a negative connotation (Warleigh and Fairbrass, 2002). In the same context, it could be argued that if the dialogue only takes place between governments and certain companies, citizens' voice is not truly heard, which again shows imbalances in the multi-level governance framework.

The other type of strategy companies can take is an adaptation (Reeves et al., 2012) through flexible and quick decision-making processes. In these cases, renewable energy companies seem to be doing better. In fact, if the revenue of the big traditional companies has been declining significantly in the last years (See for instance E.ON or RWE—Chazan, 2016, which explains their recent move to merge), it seems to be mostly due to their failure to adapt to new market conditions and wider demand for non-polluting energy sources. In this case, the worst affected companies are those with a non-diversified portfolio (Dallos, 2014). Within the adaptation process, one of the possible paths that companies can follow is the internationalization of the business (Fernandez, 2013). This has been one of the main options chosen by companies in Spain, and not only for those belonging to the energy sector (Cinco Dias, 2010).

Iberdrola is a good example of adaptation. Given the turbulent environment in Spain and the negative regulation towards renewables at the domestic level, it directed its attention to countries inside and beyond Europe (Quilter, 2013), and now focuses its research and development activities on the offshore wind (Smith, 2014). Such a move put the company, international leader on wind energy, ahead of regulatory changes, as, for instance, the UK government announced shortly afterwards Iberdrola's decision to focus on offshore wind, the withdrawal of support for onshore wind farms (Nelsen, 2015). This type of strategy can be classified also as proactive (Campagne et al., 1995) or preventative (Thammatucharee, 2013), but this time in a positive way as opposed to the lobbying activity. Acciona, another Spanish company well known for its renewable focus, has also taken action to strengthen its international activities, and its partnership with KKR, an investment group, is expected to create one of the largest operating international renewable energy portfolios worldwide, with assets outside Spain including in the US, Mexico, Italy, Portugal, Australia and South Africa (KKR, 2014).

In Germany, the phase-out of nuclear power stations scheduled for 2022 has also forced companies to react. Bearing in mind the losses in the traditional sectors, E.ON is not only closing or selling part of its traditional business but is expanding its presence in the renewables market through a partnership with the United States' solar power company Sungevity (Nicola, 2015). Operations in the solar sector have expanded from Germany and the Netherlands to the UK (Sungevity, 2015).

Another example of the recent changes observed and the forced adaptation to the new 'renewables friendly' scenario by the traditional energy companies can be found in France. Engie, previously known as GDF Suez, not only changed the name, but is shifting its business from natural gas and nuclear into renewables. It acquired Solairedirect SA in 2015, as part of its plan to double renewable-power capacity in Europe over ten years, but also aiming to expand operations into countries such as India and Chile (Patel and Nicola, 2015).

Energy companies, as any others, require stable regulatory frameworks in order to make investment decisions. They require unequivocal messages about the path that energy policy is going to take from both the national and EU public actors. Currently, the preference for security of supply, which would benefit traditional fossil fuel energies and companies, and the preference for decarbonisation and greener economy, area in which renewable energy companies would have the advantage (as they can directly contribute to greenhouse gas emissions reduction) are themes proving to have contradictory messages. This dichotomy of messages results in the private actors, energy companies, choosing a variety of strategies in order to keep or strengthen their position in the market. Traditional energy companies have been trying to influence the decision-making process through lobbying activities in the European institutions in order to prevent unfavourable regulations to be adopted. It has become apparent that they have had some level of success. However, this has not been enough to prevent new actors entering the market, from third countries but also from around the EU, focused on the renewable energy business. In order to survive they have started to diversify their activities and in some cases shut down nuclear and fossil fuel parts of their business. On the other side of the table, renewable energy companies, smaller and more flexible, have adapted to situations in which the preference for renewables could appear unclear on the side of the public actors, by opening themselves to other markets both within and outside the EU.

7.5 Conclusions

In answering the first research question posed by this chapter, it would be fair to say that energy companies have a big role to play in the transition of Europe into a green economy, as providers of different energy sources that enable economies to grow but also if fossil fuels are the main sources used, as contributors to the increase on global greenhouse gas emissions. It is renewable energies in this regard (wind, solar, photovoltaic, concentrated-solar-power, biomass, tidal, etc.) the ones that would contribute to 'improve human well-being' and 'reduce environmental risks' (UNEP, 2011). So, investments and support of the governance framework should be directed towards renewable technologies (UNEP, 2009b), contributing to the creation of job opportunities. It is worth noting though, that this role of energy companies in the green economy transition is likely to be concentrated in a reduced number of Member States, but due to their size and influence in the EU as a whole (Germany, France, Italy, Spain) it is foreseeable that such role will be substantial. It could be overshadowed by the role played by other energy-related sectors where interventions are being planned, in particular the ones over energy efficiency of buildings.

The energy sector has experienced numerous regulatory changes in recent decades, at EU level and also at country level, with influences over the decision-making process coming from political events and political preferences (such as the Russia-Ukraine crisis or more recently Brexit), international commitments to reduce greenhouse emissions and fight against climate change (the Paris Agreement), or pressures from private sectors reluctant to change.

It has been observed though, that whether voluntarily or not, traditional energy companies have started shifting their business models towards greener sectors, i.e., renewables, conscious that otherwise, they would keep on losing market share against new companies specifically dedicated to the renewable energies area.

These new companies are usually smaller in size (number of employees, revenues) but that makes them more flexible and easier to adapt when variations in the regulatory framework occur. So, in answering the second research question posed at the beginning: 'What changes should energy companies undertake in order to contribute to a green economy?', it seems clear that they need to be proactive instead of reluctant to change, shift towards the renewable sector if they have not done so yet, and internationalise their business beyond the European frontiers. The latter strategy can be also a response to the increasing presence of non-European companies in the EU market.

The answer to the third research question (what type of political and economic environments are required to encourage business organisations to assist in the construction of a 'green economy'?) is more complex. In order for the transition to take place, the regulatory and governance framework needs to be transparent (CEC, 2016b) and stable, and explicitly geared towards a greener economy, which has not been the case over recent times. The effects of the Brexit vote are still quite unpredictable. It is yet to be seen what the UK will do with regard to environmental and energy-related commitments after it leaves the EU; it is yet to be seen if funds the UK has been benefitting from for the investment in renewables through the EIB will be made available for other Member States; and it is yet to be seen if the change in the distribution of votes in the European institutions will involve or not a more powerful position to countries that traditionally have not shown good green credentials, such as the case of Poland (Martewicz, 2017). The political arena across Europe, with recent examples of populist and Eurosceptic trends showing in some member states, can only complicate decision-making in every policy. There is also uncertainty over how the new energy market design is going to look like, with specific questions about the role of ACER (Agency for the Cooperation of Energy Regulators) and ENTSO-E (European Network of Transmission System Operators for Electricity). In the case of ENTSO-E, some stakeholders (particularly businesses) mention a possible conflict of interest due to the fact that at the same time it is an association which supposedly represents the public interest and a lobby organisation with its own commercial interests (CEC, n.d.). This poses questions about the future governance of energy markets and reinforces the need for transparency.

All this could lead to a lack of trust in a true movement towards a green economy transition, so with regard to the political environment, in particular, it could be said that transparency and stability are the main elements required, and based on some of the issues identified, it could be argued that there is a need for change in the governance framework, quite possibly with wider participation of citizenship and non-traditional lobby groups, as well as the establishment of the necessary settings for all interest groups to have equal opportunities to access the political institutions.

In terms of the lessons to be learnt by policymakers (last research question), it is important to highlight the public demand for change voiced by citizens in different forums, which should make policymakers reflect on the way forward. This should happen, in light of recent mass demonstrations, without ignoring citizens' priorities. Activism by the younger generations is growing and should not be bypassed either by governments or energy companies or any other stakeholders.

References

Arias Cañete, M. (2016). How will the Paris agreement impact EU climate and energy policies? Brussels, European Commission. 2 August 2016. Speech/16/264.

Bina, O. and La Camera, F. (2011). Promise and shortcomings of a green turn in recent policy responses to the "double crisis". *Ecological Economics*, 70, 2308–2316.

Binnie, I. and Rodriguez, J. E. (2018). Spain scraps 'sun tax' in measure to cool electricity prices. *Reuters*, 5 October 2018. Extracted on 25 June 2019 from https://www.reuters.com/article/us-spain-politics-electricity/spain-scraps-sun-tax-in-measures-to-cool-electricity-prices-idUSKCN1MF1T0

Boonsma, T. K. and Linnerud, K. (2015). Market and policy risk under different renewable electricity support schemes. *Energy*, (89), 435–448.

Bryant, M. (2019). Hundreds of young people join Greta Thunberg in climate protest outside UN. *The Guardian*, 30 August. Extracted on 12 September 2019 from https://www.theguardian.com/environment/2019/aug/30/greta-thunberg-un-climate-protest-new-york

Campos-Martin, J.M., Crespo, C. and Fernandez, R.M. (2020). Energy Governance in Spain. In M. Knodt and J. Kemmerzell, eds., *Handbook of Energy Governance in Europe*. Cham: Springer.

Calder, S. (2019). Extinction Rebellion to blockade Dover port later this month. *The Independent*, 11 September. Extracted on 12 September 2019 from https://www.independent.co.uk/travel/news-and-advice/dover-extinction-rebellion-port-closure-heathrow-airport-pause-closed-ferry-calais-a9100416.html

Cascao, V. and Luis de Sousa, A. (2014). *Electricity regulation in Portugal: An overview*. Practical law. Multi-jurisdictional guide 2014. Energy and Natural Resources.

Carroll, A. B. (1979). A three-dimensional conceptual model of corporate social performance. *Academy of Management Review*, 4(4), 497–505.

Campagne, J.P., Jacot, J.H., Frein, Y. and Vitry, G. (1995). A framework to specify a reactive and proactive management system. Conference proceedings. INRIA/IEEE Symposium, (3), 251–259.

CEC. (n.d.). Preliminary results from the public consultation on Electricity Market Design. Extracted on 16 May 2017 from https://ec.europa.eu/energy/en/consultations/public-consultation-new-energy-market-design

CEC. (2011). *Roadmap to a Resource Efficient Europe*. Brussels, 20 September 2011. COM(2011) 571 final.

CEC. (2013). *Communication from the Commission. Delivering the internal electricity market and making the most of public intervention*. Brussels, 5 November 2013. C (2013) 7243 final.

CEC. (2015a). *2030 framework for climate and energy policies*. Climate Action, extracted on 13 July 2015 from http://ec.europa.eu/clima/policies/2030/index_en.htm

CEC. (2015b). *Energy Union Package. A Framework Strategy for a Resilient Energy Union with a Forward-Looking Climate Change Policy*. Brussels, 25 February 2015. COM(2015) 80 final.

CEC. (2015c). *Launching the public consultation process on a new energy market design*. Brussels, 15 July 2015. COM(2015) 340 final.

CEC. (2016a). *The Road from Paris: assessing the implications of the Paris Agreement and accompanying the proposal for a Council decision on the signing, on behalf of the European Union, of the Paris agreement adopted under the United Nations Framework Convention on Climate Change*. Brussels, 2 March 2016. COM(2016) 110 final.

CEC. (2016b). *Proposal for a Regulation of the European Parliament and of the Council on the Governance of the Energy Union*. Brussels, 30 November 2016. COM(2016) 759 final.

Chazan, G. (2016). E.ON reports largest loss after coal and gas writedowns. *Financial Times*. 9 March 2016. Extracted on 28 November 2017 from https://www.ft.com/content/b5fffac6-e5c5-11e5-ac45-5c039e797d1c

Cinco Dias (2010). Las grandes empresas invierten en el exterior el doble que en España. 27 November 2010. Extracted on 14 July 2015 from http://cincodias.com/cincodias/2010/11/27/empresas/1290868779_850215.html

Clarkson, M. B. E. (1995). A stakeholder framework for analysing and evaluating corporate social performance. *Academy of Management Review*, 20(1), 92–117.

Conzelmann, T. (2008). Towards a new concept of multi-level governance? MLG Atelier. 10 September 2008. Extracted on 11 May 2017 from European Committee of the Regions: http://cor.europa.eu/en/activities/governance/Documents/Conzelmann.pdf

Conzelmann, T. and Smith, R., eds. (2008). *Multi-level Governance in the European Union: Taking Stock and Looking Ahead*. Baden Baden: Nomos.

Dallos, G. (2014). *Locked in the past. Why Europe's big energy companies fear change*. Greenpeace report.

De Clercq, G. (2015) Portugal's EDP springboard for China Three Gorges investment abroad. *Reuters*. 18 June 2015. Extracted don 12 May 2017 from http://www.reuters.com/article/us-edp-china-three-gorges-idUSKBN0OY1HU20150618

Del Rio, P. and Mir-Artigues, P. (2014). A cautionary tale: Spain's Solar PV Investment Bubble. International Institute for Sustainable Development. February 2014.

Durakovic, A. (2019). Renewables deliver for E.ON as RWE deal stays on track. *Offshorewind.biz* 13 May 2019. Extracted on 25 June 2019 from https://www.offshorewind.biz/2019/05/13/renewables-deliver-for-e-on-as-rwe-deal-stays-on-track/

Duscha, V., Ragwitz, M., Breitschopf, B., Schade, W., Walz, R., Pfaff, M., de Visser, E., Resch, G., Nathani, C., Zagame, P., Fougeyrollas, A., and Boitier, B. (2014). *Employment and growth effects of sustainable energies in the European Union*. Final Report. Contract no.: ENER/C1/428-2012.

E3G (2015). *Energy Union & Governance: The role of local actors*. Briefing paper. October 2015.

EDP. (2014). *Energy that makes a difference*. Annual Report 2014.

E.ON. (2012). E.ON reaches settlement with Gazprom on long-term gas supply contracts and raises Group outlook for 2012. Press Release 7 March 2012.

Eurostat. (2017). *Smarter, greener, more inclusive? Indicators to support the Europe 2020 Strategy*. 2017 edition. Eurostat Statistical Books. Luxembourg: Publications Office of the European Union.

Eurostat. (2018). *Energy, transport and environment indicators*. 2018 edition. Eurostat Statistical Books. Luxembourg: Publications Office of the European Union.

Eurostat. (2019a). Market share of the largest generator in the electricity market. Extracted on 24 June 2019 from http://ec.europa.eu/eurostat/web/energy/data/main-tables

Eurostat. (2019b). *Structural Business Statistics Overview*. Key indicators for EU electricity, gas, steam and air conditioning supply sectors (2016). Extracted 25 June 2019.

Fairbrass, J. (2003). The Europeanization of Business Interest Representation: UK and French Firms Compared. *Comparative European Politics*, 1(3), 313–334.

Fairbrass, J. and Jordan, A. (2004). *Multi-level governance and environmental policy*. In I. Bache and M. Flinders, eds., *Multi-level Governance*. Oxford: Oxford University Press, pp. 147–164.

Fernandez, R. M. (2012). The European Union and International Negotiations on Climate Change. A limited role to play. *Journal of Contemporary European Research*, 8(2), 192–209.

Fernandez, R. M. (2013). Internationalisation, crisis and sustainability: opportunities to reinforce corporate social responsibility strategies. *International Journal of Human Rights and Constitutional Studies*, 1(3), 267–277.

Fortune (n.d.). Global 500. Available at: http://www.fortune.com/global500

Gippner, O. and Nitoiu, C. (2015). China is outflanking Russia in the struggle to woo Europe. *The Conversation*, 19 June. Extracted on 8 July 2015 from http://theconversation.com/china-is-outflanking-russia-in-the-struggle-to-woo-europe-43031

Gosden, E. (2017). What will Brexit mean for the environment and Britain's green targets? *The Telegraph*. 10 March 2017. Extracted on 16 May 2017 from http://www.telegraph.co.uk/news/0/what-would-brexit-mean-for-britains-green-targets/?WT.mc_id=tmg_share_em

Hauser, H. (2011). European Union lobbying post-Lisbon: An economic analysis. *Berkeley Journal of International Law*, 29(20), 680–709.

Heritier, A. (2002). New modes of governance in Europe: Policy making without legislating? *IHS Political Science Series*: 2002, No. 81. [Working Paper]

Heritier, A. and Rhodes, M. (2011). *New Modes of Governance in Europe: Governing in the Shadow of Hierarchy*. Basingstoke: Palgrave Macmillan.

Hope, M. (2016). Fossil Fuel Lobby Celebrates as EU Gives Coal Subsidies a Lifeline. *DeSmog UK*. 30 November 2016. Extracted on 10 July 2017 from https://www.desmog.uk/2016/11/30/fossil-fuel-lobby-celebrates-eu-gives-coal-subsidies-lifeline

ICN. (2011). Abuse of dominance in the energy sector – A European perspective. ICN Unilateral Conduct Working Group Seminar. 8 November 2011. Extracted on 22 November 2017 from http://www.internationalcompetitionnetwork.org/uploads/library/doc768.pdf

Jordan, A. and Schout, A. (2006). *The Coordination of the European Union: Exploring the Capacities of Networked Governance*. Oxford: Oxford University Press.

KKR. (2014). KKR and Acciona partner in global renewable energy business. Press Release 24 June 2014.

Kohler-Koch, B. and Eising, R., eds. (1999). *The Transformation of Governance in the European Union*. London: Routledge.

Kreivi, E. (2016). *Green Bond Market Development and EIB*. European Investement Bank. Climate Awareness Bonds. Extracted on 28 November 2017 from http://www.eib.org/attachments/green-bond-market-development-and-eib.pdf

La Nueva España (2013). De HC a EDP. 14 March 2013. Accessed on 23 October 2015 from http://www.lne.es/asturama/2013/03/13/hc-edp/1381858.html

Lipton, E. and Hakim, D. (2013). Lobbying bonanza as firms try to influence European Union. *The New York Times*, 18 October 2013.

Lycetts (2017). Renewable energy in the EU: Better off Brexit? *Energy Digital*, 3 February 2017. Extracted on 16 May 2017 from http://www.energydigital.com/renewable-energy/renewable-energy-eu-better-brexit

Lopez, L. (2011). The 15 biggest energy companies in the world. *BusinessInsider*. 25 October 2011. Extracted on 24 November 2017 from http://www.businessinsider.com/the-15-biggest-energy-comapnies-in-the-world-2011-10?IR=T

Ma, W. and Kowsmann, P. (2011). China Gets Stake in Portugal's EDP. *The Wall Street Journal*. 23 December 2011. Extracted on 12 May 2017 from http://www.wsj.com/articles/SB10001424052970204464404577114471370252452

Martewicz, M. (2017). Poland faces harsh EU reality in push for coal exemptions. *Bloomberg*. 16 May 2017. Extracted on 10 July 2017 from https://www.bloomberg.com/news/articles/2017-05-16/poland-faces-harsh-eu-reality-in-its-push-for-coal-exemptions

Mongoose Energy. (2016). What would Brexit mean for UK renewables? Extracted on 16 May 2017 from http://mongoose.energy/what-would-brexit-mean-for-uk-renewables-2/

Nelsen, A. (2015). Wind power generates 140% of Denmark's electricity demand. *The Guardian*, 10 July 2015. Extracted on 13 July 2015 from http://www.theguardian.com/environment/2015/jul/10/denmark-wind-windfarm-power-exceed-electricity-demand

Nicola, S. (2015). EON to Expand Solar Sales in Germany in Tie-Up with Sungevity. *Bloomberg*. 12 May 2015. Extracted on 17 July 2017 from https://www.bloomberg.com/news/articles/2015-05-12/eon-to-expand-solar-sales-in-germany-in-tie-up-with-sungevity

OJEU. (2003). Directive 2003/54/EC of the European Parliament and of the Council of 26 June 2003 concerning common rules for the internal market in electricity and repealing Directive 96/92/EC. 15 July 2003.

OJEU. (2009). Directive 2009/72/EC of the European Parliament and of the Council of 13 July 2009 concerning common rules for the internal market in electricity and repealing Directive 2003/54/EC. 14 August 2009.

OJEU. (2013). Decision No 1386/2013/EU of the European Parliament and of the Council of 20 November 2012 on a General Union Environment Action Programme to 2020 'Living well, within the limits of our planet'. 28 December 2013.

Patel, S. (2015). More nuclear plants deemed unprofitable in Sweden, Germany. *Power*. 08 January 2015. Extracted on 15 May 2017 from http://www.powermag.com/more nuclear-plants-deemed-unprofitable-in-sweden-germany/

Patel, T. and Nicola, S. (2015). Engie buys Solairedirect for $222 million in renewables push. *Bloomberg*. 1 July 2015. Extracted on 11 May 2017 from https://www.bloomberg.com/news/articles/2015-07-01/engie-buys-solairedirect-for-222-million-in-renewables push

Pfeifer, S. (2013). Europe's utility groups forced to find new business models. *Financial Times*. 5 August 2013.

Quilter, J. (2013). Iberdrola signals 2015 plans. WindPower Monthly. 21 February 2013. Extracted on 14 July 2015 from http://www.windpowermonthly.com/article/1171814/iberdrola-signals-2015-plans

Rapier, R. (2016). The 25 biggest oil and gas companies in the world. Forbes. 30 March 2016. Extracted on 24 November 2017 from https://www.forbes.com/sites/rrapier/2016/03/30/the-worlds-largest-public-oil-and-gas-companies/#6ddd91f73173

Reeves, M., Love, C. and Tillmanns, P. (2012). Your strategy needs a strategy. *Harvard Business Review* (9). Extracted on 28 November 2017 from https://hbr.org/2012/09/your-strategy-needs-a-strategy

RES-Legal. (2019). Legal sources on renewable energy. Available at http://www.res-legal.eu

Roca, M. (2014). Spain caps earnings from renewables in subsidy overhaul. *Bloomberg*. 6 June 2014.

Shchedrov, O. and Harding, B. (2009). Update 3 – Russia, Spain sign energy deal, smoothing investments. *Reuters* 3 March 2009. Extracted on 8 July 2015 from http://uk.reuters.com/article/2009/03/03/gazprom-repsol-idUKL357888920090303

Smith, P. (2014). Iberdrola shifts R&D investment to offshore wind. WindPower Offshore. 24 February 2014. Extracted on 14 July 2015 from http://www.windpoweroffshore.com/article/1282073/iberdrola-shifts-r-d-investment-offshore-wind

Sungevity (2015). E.ON and Sungevity launch UK collaboration. Press Release. 28 July 2015. Extracted on 17 May 2017 from http://www.sungevity.com/article/?Id=a6MU00000004DexMAE

Thammatucharee, Y. (2013). Preventive vs corrective approaches in management. *Nationmultimedia*. 14 March 2013. Extracted on 28 November 2017 from http://www.nationmultimedia.com/business/Preventive-vs-corrective-approaches-in-management-30201909.html

The Economist. (2013). European utilities. How to lose half a trillion euros. Europe's electricity providers face an existential threat. 13 October 2013.

Timperley, J. (2016). E.ON completes split of fossil fuel and renewable operations. *The Guardian*, 4 January 2016. Extracted on 25 June 2019 from https://www.theguardian.com/environment/2016/jan/04/eon-completes-split-of-fossil-fuel-and-renewable-operations

Tolbaru, A. M. (2012). Lobbyists brace for new battle over EU energy efficiency. *EurActiv* 18 July 2012.

Tremlett, G. (2008). Concerns over rising power of Russian energy firms as Lukoil targets Spanish oil group. The Guardian, 22 November. Extracted on 8 July 2015 from http://www.theguardian.com/environment/2008/nov/22/energy-russia-lukoil-repsol-gazprom

United Nations. (2016). Paris Agreement Entry into Force. Depositary Notification. C.N.735.2016.TREATIES-XXVII.7.d, 5 October 2016. New York.

UNEP. (2009a). *Global Green New Deal. Policy Brief.* March 2009.

UNEP. (2009b). *Global Green New Deal. An Update for the G20 Pittsburgh Summit.* September 2009.

UNEP. (2011). *Towards a Green Economy: Pathways to Sustainable Development and Poverty Eradication.*

UNDESA. (2012). *A guidebook to the Green Economy. Issue 1: Green Economy, Green Growth, and Low-Carbon Development – history, definitions and a guide to recent publications.* Division for Sustainable Development.

UNDESA, UNEP and UNCTAD. (2012). *The Transition to a Green Economy: Benefits, Challenges and Risks from a Sustainable Development Perspective.* Report by a Panel of Experts to Second Preparatory Committee Meeting for United Nations Conference on Sustainable Development.

Vaughan, A. (2018). EU raises renewable energy targets to 32% by 2030. *The Guardian*, 14 June 2018. Extracted on 25 June 2019 from https://www.theguardian.com/business/2018/jun/14/eu-raises-renewable-energy-targets-to-32-by-2030

Vladimirov, M. and Stefanov, R. (2016). The Kremlin's Economic Grip on Europe. Foreign Policy. 23 December 2016. Extracted on 24 November 2017 from http://foreignpolicy.com/2016/12/23/the-kremlins-economic-grip-on-europe/

Voss, H. (2013). Chinese Investments into the EU Energy Sector. Short term Policy Brief 71. Europe China Research and Advice Network (ECRAN), IS91. 2010/256-524. February 2013.

Warleigh, A. and Fairbrass, J., eds. (2002). *Influence and Interests in the European Union: The New Politics of Persuasion and Advocacy.* London, UK: Europa Publications.

Whitley, S., van der Burg, L., Worrall, L., and Patel, S. (2017). *Cutting Europe's lifelines to coal. Tracking subsidies in 10 countries.* Overseas Development Institute (ODI) Policy briefing, May 2017.

8

Carbon Calculation and the Urban Green Economic Opportunity

WILL EADSON AND AIDAN WHILE

8.1 Introduction

Contributions to this book each focus on critical research questions relating to governance and multi-level governance of the green economy. The aim of the following chapter is to examine how the wider context of multi-level governance (MLG) influences possibilities for green economic activity at the local or urban scale. In so doing, the chapter responds explicitly to the research question set out in Chapter 1: How is the green economy being defined in an MLG context? It also speaks to questions about the political/economic environments required to encourage business organisations to assist in the construction of a green economy; and how businesses, government and civil society organisations relate to one another in seeking to establish a vibrant green economy. What follows is rooted in theories of governance and MLG (see e.g. Bache and Flinders, 2004) and in particular deploys the notion of multi-level meta governance (Jessop, 2004) to capture how definitions of the green economy are shaped by and seek to shape norms and discourses of economic development.

This chapter focuses on the visibility of the urban green economy and especially on attempts to make the economic and employment case for low carbon initiatives. It centres on an examination of studies in five cities that develop potentially challenging visions of future urban economies, most notably through 'Mini-Stern' reports that seek to consider the economic costs and opportunities of carbon reduction and energy security pressures across the entire urban economy. These studies followed the 2006 Stern report on the economics of climate change, whose calculations about the global economic impacts of climate change acted as a successful MLG device (Du Gay et al., 2012) to set the context for international, national and local decision-making. Focusing on carbon implies a narrower definition than considerations of a broader set of issues relating to the green economy but carbon is a central component of contemporary policies for greening the economy (Bulkeley et al., 2010; Hodson and Marvin, 2010; While et al., 2010). The chapter also speaks to work on the relationship between changing carbon and energy calculations and new economies of value and worth around *'agents, spaces, relations and objects'* (Lohmann, 2009: 499) in cities. It aims to expand existing conceptualisations of the politics of calculation to illuminate how calculations (re)present a range of assumptions about territory, the way people live and the nature of place and society in the present and the future. Understanding the methods and practices of these calculations are as politically important as the 'social' elements of negotiation and implementation: as MacKenzie (2009: 442) states, *'the specifics ... matter'*.

We start, immediately below, by considering the studies and techniques that might be used to make the green economy visible and politically legible, focusing on their role as governance devices that appeal to different interest groups. This is developed with specific reference to calculations and accounting techniques. Of special interest is the dual translation of 'economising carbon' and 'carbonising economies' in representing places as sites of the green economy. The empirical sections focus on how future green economies are being represented by cities in England, and how these potentially lead to seeing urban economies differently. These sections draw on case studies in five English cities, looking at the development of strategic documents that sought to calculate the economic costs and benefits of moving to green urban economies. We conclude by reflecting on what kind of city is being represented in these studies and asking broader questions about the nature of such representations in relation to hegemonic representations of capitalism and their ability to visualise a future that encompasses the notion of the green economy as pro-poor as well as pro-growth. Our concern with understanding how the green economy is being defined leads us to ask what kind of city is produced in these calculative constructions; what kind of green economy is constructed; and what do they tell us about cities as multi-level objects within MLG systems?

8.2 Visibility, Calculation and the Green Economy

The chapter starts with the premise that although environmental restructuring is gathering pace, the arguments for investment in green economic development have to be made visible.

8.2.1 A Governable Object

The ability to govern is predicated on constructing a governable object: 'Before one can seek to manage a domain such as a city, it is first necessary to conceptualize and represent the processes and relations that define it *qua* city' (Lapsley et al., 2010: 309). This includes dealing with uncertainty in casting forwards and generating stabilised visions of the future. This is a political process, requiring the enrolment of different actors across different ecologies of practice through the use of 'governance devices',

> *... crucial for the success of a certain form of rationality and the organisational arrangements it seeks to materialise*
>
> *(du Gay* et al., *2012: 1085).*

In particular, a crucial element of contemporary governance is the role of policy-makers at different levels to instil particular narratives, norms or 'rules of the game' within societal and governance systems in order to achieve state goals: forms of (multi-level) metagovernance (Haughton et al., 2008; Jessop, 2004).

In order to develop links across different ecologies, there is a need to create 'hinges': 'connections through which benefits in one realm are translated to meaningful benefits in another' (Du Gay et al., 2012). Du Gay and colleagues' notion of rendering governance liquid highlights the important work required to justify potential returns on change relative to the status quo, and relative to other governance and intervention options. This is not solely about a narrow fiscal calculus, though that will be important. It is also about how fiscal arguments play out alongside other costs and benefits. Indeed, for transformative proposals, intervention is likely to involve a range of interconnected changes that need to be presented and accepted as a coherent package.

However, in order to do things differently (or keep doing them the same), future possibilities have to be made visible through strategies, plans, studies or visualisations. They have to present alternative ways of seeing and generate new modalities that create a stabilised set of logics that give more concrete form to abstract discursive hinges. This is redolent of how cities, bound to multi-level metagovernance norms of place-based entrepreneurialism have:

> *... come to mimic large corporations, as they engage in various kinds of exercise aimed at projecting and visualising the city as it should become, and how it should transform itself to get there ... [S]trategic plans and 'visions' of the city, as forms of entrepreneurial displays, have come to be construed as vital elements in acquiring the investment needed for restructuring and regeneration*
>
> *(Lapsley* et al., *2010: 307).*

This raises questions about the performative power of such projects: how arguments are presented, the selectivity of the information, the chosen audience, and so on:

> *... the big picture is an aesthetic phenomenon that is more effective if strategists can convince their audience with an impressive performance ... the strategist speaks with the authority of science while simultaneously mobilizing people, galvanizing their support for a transformed reality*
>
> *(Kornberger, 2013: 105).*

The construction of the urban green economy is therefore performative: constructing narratives to visualise future possibilities; acting as seductive governing technologies to enrol other actors; and providing decision-making tools. Within an MLG context, a wide range of actors within and beyond the state, and within and beyond individual cities need to be enrolled into programmes for change (Fairbrass and Jordan, 2004). In their own reflections on the Leeds City Region Mini Stern, Gouldson and Wesselink (2014) frame these issues around the role of artefacts in producing *ideas*, *arguments* and *data*. This is used to explore the report's policy impacts in the Leeds city-region. We take an alternative approach to interrogate: what formulations are being promoted through such artefacts, and what they mean for understanding the urban green economy; what medium is used; what assumptions underpin visualisations and what they mean for how the urban green economy is conceived; and what is and is not represented within visualisations. This includes considering what shapes these interventions within an MLG context (van Stigt et al., 2015), and the implications this might have. We are concerned with representation as a means of intervention (Lapsley et al., 2010).

8.2.2 The Selectivity of Making Visible: The Role of Calculations

The process of visioning and representing tends to airbrush conflict (Lapsley et al., *ibid.*). However, the calculation process can bring conflicts and trade-offs into focus as different elements are made comparable. This includes considerations of what is and is not made visible, and what previously visible properties might disappear from view in a new urban calculus. Calculative practices matter (Miller, 2001). As Lövbrand and Stripple (2011:189) note, 'the ways in which we *represent* reality are intimately linked to the ways in which it is acted upon and governed'. Calculative practices shape spatial imaginaries and 'delineate the space in which "true" statements about the city can be made' (Kornberger and Carter, 2010: 325).

Calculating cities using a particular set of properties requires a number of translations, including the following: constructing a calculative currency; constructing a calculable object; implementing calculations on the object; and implementing calculations within the object. In this chapter, we are largely concerned with the first and second of these programmes. This involves creating a currency of equivalence (what are the 'essential' properties of the space in calculative terms?) and scalar and territorial decisions about the boundaries to the city, alongside questions about the powers that may be exercised by the city governments and the aimed for a level of change. Cities are multi-level and multi-spatial objects, in terms of governance arrangements that determine what is possible (Katagawa, 2013), and the spatial relations between actors within cities (Allen, 2009).

Calculations are also an important tool in equivalising different spaces to render visible competitive fields (Kornberger and Carter, 2010). In order to compete effectively against others, the competition must be made visible and rendered legible in the same terms as the self. Constructing benchmarks and rankings allows comparison of competitive strengths and weaknesses between places and, accordingly, strategy development. Economisation and benchmarking both allow for visualisation of different properties of places to assert the importance of these properties to different actors in ways that other means might not: what is measured is what matters. The literature on calculative practices tends to focus on the 'darker edge' of their role in producing reductive, neoliberal governmentalities (Stripple and Bulkeley, 2014). However, while calculations are a means of ordering space, they are not always reductive. Rather, rendering different properties visible can create new complexities of governing and create new possibilities of action by reproducing the properties of spaces. In other words, calculative practices can be about opening-up as well as closing-down:

> *. . .every mode of calculation produces a certain form of visibility which creates unique possibilities for intervention while displacing others*
>
> *(Mennicken* et al., *2008: in While, 2010: 51).*

The next section takes these points forward to consider how performative calculations can and are playing an important role in the MLG of the green economy, and is emerging as a key mode of urban green economic governance.

8.3 Seeing Territory Differently as a Space of Carbon Flows: The Battle for Low Carbon Transitions

The last decade has seen moves to challenge existing modes of carbon capitalism. Challenges include pressure from social movements and environmental organisations to frame capitalism as the key problem in producing a low carbon society. More influential voices within and closer to policy circles have, however, sought instead a reinvention of carbon capitalism: capitalism based on the commoditised exchange value of carbon stocks and flows rather than the use-value of carbon inputs (Bumpus and Liverman, 2008; Paterson and Stripple, 2011). The notion of the green economy in itself might be seen as an overarching governance device to promote environmental concerns through appeal to more financially-driven ecologies of practice. This is an era in which future uncertainties and competing ideas of what a low carbon society will or should look like are being fought out, with future studies and calculative policy practices important tools in this battle.

Central to this new carbon economics is the idea that how things are valued, and therefore the value of things is altered by re-pricing fossil fuels inputs and by valuing choices that reduce or replace fossil fuels. To redeploy a refrain made famous by a particularly recalcitrant carbon capitalist of the old kind, that process of revaluation involves relative 'known knowns, known unknowns and unknown unknowns'. Low-carbon transition involves hedging against future value structures, in a context where intervention may influence the nature of those future value structures.

Visualising the urban green economy involves a politics of sense-making, of seeing the urban in a way that is politically legible, and opening up different policy possibilities (While, 2010). This is partly about rendering possibilities visible and a central element of this is the politics of calculation: about the practices that are utilised and developed to produce altered urban cartography based on a revised set of calculative logic. Calculations hold a particular power and are central to defining the value of ideas (Mueller and Whittle, 2010). Numbers can render complex phenomena easily legible, concisely.

This discursive contest is taking place alongside and is enabled by, wider governmental calculative practices. For example, Lövbrand and Stripple (2011) make reference to different ways that carbon is being rendered governable through the construction of different carbon accounting techniques. These include methods that underpin the economisation carbon, for instance through the creation of 'carbon credits', the creation of national 'carbon sinks' and individualised carbon budgets. We could also consider different ways that new carbon economies are developed and applied to different scales and territories of governing. These include commodification through market mechanisms as well as financialisation as a function of commodification (carbon rendered as an investible asset), but also fiscal measures such as taxation and subsidies for high/low carbon activities. In the UK, carbon shadow pricing has also been used as a policy evaluation tool for a number of years (Department for Business, Energy and Industrial Strategy (BEIS), 2017).

Calculative visions of the urban green economy are also an increasingly common feature of urban governance. Alongside confluence of energy and carbon emissions goals (Lovell et al., 2009), rising energy costs, cost implications of increased carbon reduction pressures and the potential economic opportunities for low-carbon and energy transitions are leading to greater attention among urban governments to the economics of green economic restructuring. While (2010) writes of the emergence of a spatial carbon calculus, with a focus on the creation of new forms of calculation that seek to cost or value carbon through monitoring, targets or the formation of new markets; the aim being to encourage territorial units to be seen as spaces of carbon flows. The emergent emphasis on carbon as a mode of accounting or basis for a logic of control involves re-configuration of existing spatial imaginaries. This potentially creates new relations, connections and disjunctures between spatial elements, akin to the technique described by Bridge (2010) as:

*... **a cartography** of resources, reserves, fluxes, sinks and dumps that territorializes and fixes carbon in space while at the same time throwing spaces into new forms of relation, creating an imaginative gazetteer of enclosure and connection*

(Bridge, 2010: 2).

As noted above this involves a range of political decisions, including about what elements the city consists of, and how these can be measured. For instance, in their exposition of the carbon calculus in Portland (USA) Rutland and Aylett (2008) show how political concerns regarding the role of local government shaped how 'local' carbon emissions were constructed: the local carbon governance object became 'what local government felt they could influence'. Rules, routines and accepted norms about policy design and implementation were crucial, including paradigms set by national and international actors. The techniques of calculation and the limits to data also matter. Eadson (2012) argues that methods used to measure carbon emissions in England led to a reductive notion of the 'carbon city', consisting only of individual data points rather than uncovering a city made up of energy systems and carbon flows. These issues are potentially amplified when carrying the 'double translation' involved in rendering visible the urban green economy: economising carbon (e.g. carbon pricing) and carbonising the economy (applying pricing/calculation to economic mapping). Thinking about the urban green economy means recasting the urban using a different economic calculus, with potential impacts on the calculative potential of different sites, assets and connections. This potentially leads to a reshaped ontology of spaces; seeing the urban differently through a carbon-economic lens.

In this context the currency of equivalence is important. The construction of carbon spaces involves the equivalisation of different greenhouse gases (GHGs) as 'carbon dioxide equivalent' values. This is helpful to visualise the city as a space of carbon stocks and flows. The calculation of costed carbon stocks and flows opens up carbon as a more legible governable object within the existing urban political calculus. The hegemonic status and ultra-fungibility of money makes it convenient for both conceptualising and performing visions of the carbon city. Economising nature allows the creation of a hinge to link different ecologies of practice.

At the broadest level, these calculations allow illumination of whether places are comparatively highly exposed or well placed to respond to economic pressures relating to carbon reduction. This might be through analysis of the entire urban economy's relative exposure to future economic and regulatory pressures, or of its relative economic strength in 'green' economic sectors. More fundamentally, it might involve reconsidering the urban realm as a set of exposed, high potential or undervalued assets. This might include revaluing the material fabric of the city according to a green economic calculus, but also the selective omission of assets that are incalculable or politically difficult to approach.

Calculations might manifest themselves in a range of different ways, leading to different visualisations of different carbon-economic properties. This includes both the subject of calculations and the methods used. Examples include:

- Applying a shadow price to energy or carbon flows at city or sector level
- Calculating actual energy costs at a city or sector level
- Extrapolating potential impacts by measuring historical economic performance against historical emissions
- Calculating the costs and benefits of carbon abatement
- Calculating economic benefits of low carbon economic activity
- Calculating the potential of existing urban assets as renewable energy sites

An important factor is how other governmental calculative practices shape how urban carbon-economic calculations are made. For example, the use of different types of carbon pricing methodologies by central government might make significant differences to the overall valuation of urban carbon-economic properties.

In the following sections, we apply the concepts of rendering visible through calculation as a form of metagovernance device to analyse how studies in UK cities have used calculative devices such as those listed above to envisage future scenarios for the urban green economy, with specific reference to the calculation of carbon emissions and flows. We begin with an overview of the case studies and key documents involved before moving on to analyse how the documents were used to define the urban green economy, to more broadly reconfigure understanding of urban assets through the trope of the green economy and finally as governance devices to enrol different governance actors, most notably economic development professionals and local businesses.

8.4 Positioning Low Carbon in Five English Cities

The publication of the Stern report on *The Economics of Climate Change* in 2006 (Stern, 2006) was a pivotal moment in the governance of climate change. The report translated challenges posed by climate change into economic calculations, acting as an effective and influential governance device by creating a hinge that appealed to a wide range of policy actors. Climate change was rendered visible and therefore governable in economic development terms. In the UK, the Stern report was influential in the adoption of ambitious carbon reduction targets in the 2008 Climate Change Act as well as the integration of carbon shadow pricing into the policy decision matrix for national government departments. It also helped catalyse sub-national policy discussion, most notably through the development of 'Mini-Stern' reports in some cities and regions, and growing emphasis on economic opportunities in green economic sectors such as renewable energy technologies.

Following these developments, this chapter analyses the content and impacts of Mini-Stern reports and similar studies to calculate the economic implications of an urban green economy. The material presented below is based on documentary analysis and 30 in-depth qualitative interviews with key stakeholders in the cities of Bristol, Leeds, Leicester, Liverpool and Manchester, each of which produced a number of calculative reports and studies in the period 2007–2015.[1] These studies evidenced different ways cities have sought to map out the potential of the green economy to influence policy: in doing so seeking to (re)present the urban differently. Interviews were professionally transcribed, then coded and analysed alongside the studies using qualitative data analysis software.

In this section, we look at a number of these studies, including three Mini-Stern reports and local Low Carbon and Environmental Goods and Services (LCEGS) sector estimates and projections. In Bristol, we look at a study focusing on prospects for a post-oil future. While each study focused on calculative methods of carbonising urban economies, they also sought to represent the green economy in different ways. The studies and key calculative devices are outlined in Table 8.1, followed by a brief description of each study. Common to each of the studies was the use of calculations to define the green economy (albeit in different ways), the revaluation of urban assets using a green economic calculus, and the utilisation of texts as performative governance devices to enrol a variety of different actors: these themes form the basis of the analysis presented following the descriptions of each study.

8.4.1 Mini-Stern for Manchester

In 2008, a study of the impacts of EU and UK climate legislation on the Manchester city-region economy was published by Deloitte, commissioned by the New Economy commission of the Association of Greater Manchester Authorities (AGMA). The study emphasises the cost of inaction on climate change to the city's economy, alongside the potential economic opportunities for taking a proactive stance on carbon reduction and developing green economic sectors. This involved three calculative devices. The first of these is a 'sectoral risk profile', which scores existing economic sectors in the city region according to a set of criteria relating to energy/emissions intensity and size of the sector in the city region. The second calculation focused on the ability of different sectors to greatly reduce their energy and emissions without affecting economic growth. This was explored by mapping the historical relationship between sectoral gross value added (GVA) and

[1] Empirical research was conducted as part of the Carbon Value Change and Policy Choices in Local Governance project (British Academy grant SG111169).

Table 8.1. *Examples of calculative studies of the urban green economy*

Document	Commissioning Body	City	Key calculation(s)
Gouldson et al. (2011) *The economics of low carbon cities: a Mini-Stern for Leeds City Region*	Leeds City Region	Leeds City Region, (replicated for Sheffield and Hull City Regions and for Hong Kong)	Present and future city-regional energy costs Marginal Abatement Cost Curve (MACC) of mitigation measures
Deloitte (2008) *'Mini-Stern' for Manchester: assessing the economic impact of EU and UK climate change legislation on Manchester City Region and the North West.*	New Economy Manchester/ Association of Greater Manchester Authorities	Greater Manchester	Extrapolation of historic GVA-emissions relationship at city and sector level Sectoral risk profile based on emissions/ energy intensity and employment levels
Regeneris and Quantum Consulting (2009) *The economic impact of EU and UK climate change legislation on Liverpool and the Liverpool City Region.*	The Mersey Parnership	Liverpool City Region	Application of carbon tax to commercial and industrial emissions Identification of 'at risk' jobs as a result of energy-carbon legislation
CRESR (2014) *Low carbon Leicester and Leicestershire*	Leicester and Leicestershire Enterprise Partnership	Leicester and Leicestershire	Calculation of size/ growth of LCEGS sector—Department for Business Innovation and Skills methodology
Bristol Green Capital (2009) *Building a positive future for Bristol after peak oil*	Bristol Green Capital	Bristol	Application of peak oil assumptions to Bristol's economy

Source: Authors

emissions. The final calculation addresses a 'failure to adapt' scenario, forecasting the cost of inaction on carbon reduction against existing and future policy and price pressures across the Manchester economy as a whole. This is based on applying emissions reduction in line with UK emissions targets to GVA forecasts by assuming a continuation of existing relationships between GVA and emissions.

8.4.2 Mini-Stern for Liverpool

The Mini-Stern for Liverpool (Regeneris and Quantum, 2009), commissioned by Liverpool City Region's Merseyside Partnership, takes a broadly similar approach to the Manchester Mini-Stern. The Liverpool study takes an approach aligned to the original Stern Report by using the Social Cost of Carbon (SCC) to measure the potential cost of carbon emissions to the city-region's economy. The Social Cost of Carbon was used by Stern and was used by the Department for Environment, Food and Rural Affairs (DEFRA) between 2002 and 2007 to calculate financial values for carbon emissions in policy-making.[2] The social cost of carbon is not directly related to GVA impacts, but instead to a range of economic and (monetised) social costs. The report also considers the green economic opportunities for the City Region. For example, it outlines the potential of the area's natural assets to provide economic growth, with particular emphasis on its coastal position to provide opportunities in tidal energy, as well as on-shore and offshore wind energy. There is also consideration of low carbon energy generation through new energy from waste plants and biomass, with a discussion of the potential value of the Mersey Forest in this regard.

8.4.3 Mini-Stern for Leeds

Academics in the Centre for Low Carbon Futures at the University of Leeds were commissioned by Leeds City Region to conduct a Mini-Stern Review, which was published in early 2012 (Gouldson et al., 2012). The Leeds Mini-Stern weighs up the potential investment opportunities to cost-effectively reduce energy use and emissions across the City Region. This is framed within a calculative devise based on the increasing energy costs that represent economic leakage from the City Region. Investing in carbon reduction measures offers both a means of reducing this level of leakage and a means of producing economic benefits to the City Region through direct and indirect income generation. The more detailed analysis in the study uses marginal abatement cost curves derived from the analysis by the Committee for Climate Change to develop a list of potential carbon reduction measures that could theoretically be applied without incurring any cost: they would pay for themselves through energy savings over time. Based on this analysis, Gouldson et al (*ibid.*) generate a scenario that would see the creation of almost 10,000 jobs and an increase in GVA by £440 million per year by 2022.

[2] There is, however, some opaqueness in the Liverpool MS regarding this: although they talk about the SCC in the report, they give a link to the Shadow Price of Carbon (adopted from 2007–2009).

8.4.4 Bristol Peak Oil study

Building a positive future for Bristol after Peak Oil (2011) was commissioned through the Bristol Partnership, a local strategic body bringing together business, the public sector, local communities, voluntary sector, higher and further education. The calculative framing for the study focuses on continuing social and economic security in the context of predictions of increasingly scarce oil reserves over the coming century. The report is less overtly performative in its use of calculative techniques. Instead, the overarching implications of a post-oil society are used as a backdrop for narrative devices. This includes the use of 'flashbacks' to previous oil crises and vignettes from citizens of an imagined future Bristol where a successful transition had been made. The focus is on societal functions rather than a narrower concern for high-GVA economic sectors: social and economic opportunities in relation to transport, food, healthcare, industry, public services and utilities are presented.

8.4.5 City LCEGS Sector Studies

A number of cities have produced sector studies that seek to capture the size, composition and potential growth of economic activity based on the opportunities of the green economy. In general terms, this has involved the calculative construction of a new economic sector: LCEGS. An important element of this is that the sector has been calculatively produced at a national level, with data available at regional, city-regional and local levels. In this way, cities are able to understand the economic value of their own LCEGS sector as well as benchmark and rank this against 'competitor' cities. Examples include studies for Leicester and Leicestershire (CRESR, 2014); Manchester (Enworks, 2013); and Sheffield (Enworks, 2013). In this chapter, we focus on the Leicester and Leicestershire study.

Having briefly outlined the five key urban green economy studies under consideration the chapter now turns to analysis of three themes to emerge from the research. The analysis shows: how these studies sought to define the green economy; how thinking about the city in terms of the green economy led to the reconsideration of urban assets; and how successful these visions were at influencing and mobilising actors in the governance of the green economy.

8.5 Defining the Green Economy: Economising Carbon, Carbonising Economies

Defining the green economy through a calculative lens leads to particular conceptualisations, deployed to particular ends. A central focus of the different studies analysed for this chapter is to define local economies in relation to future carbon value change. This unfolds differently across the studies but a dominant position has been to persuade a new constituency of actors to take the green economy seriously; in particular, economic development professionals, businesses and business networks. A monetised figure is used to create a hinge between the world of environmental policy and that of economic development. This was felt to be critical to advancing low carbon goals, in particular for the green economy to become a central part of future economic development rather than a threat or adjunct to core policy concerns:

For me the Mini-Stern was always there as a piece of evidence that would allow us to talk about low carbon within an economic setting rather than as an environmental issue

(Policy Manager, Leeds City Region).

Within this logic, the green economy was framed in most instances through the trope of entrepreneurial urbanism (Harvey, 1989): a point of potential competitive advantage for generating endogenous growth, attracting grants and investment. This framing was particularly strong in Manchester, a city in many ways synonymous with notions of the entrepreneurial city (Ward, 2003). Here the Mini-Stern study was framed around Manchester's level of economic exposure (measured by GVA) to low carbon legislation and rising carbon/energy costs. The green economy is defined therefore not as a discrete sector but as a necessary end-state for the city's economy as a whole, with attendant risks to its future economic development. The advent of the green economy is as much a risk as an opportunity, but nonetheless must be addressed.

A central theme of much of this work is the double translation of economising carbon and then carbonising economies, achieved through various means. For example, the Manchester Mini-Stern took its lead from an understanding that,

...the climate change agenda is altering market conditions and the underlying assumptions previously used to determine trends and establish the economic priorities for the Manchester City Region

(Deloitte, 2008: 5).

The study sets out an agenda focused on maintaining Manchester's economic competitiveness in this context, with a central emphasis on 'gaining the support and confidence of the business and investment community by creating economic opportunity and reducing market uncertainty' as a 'prerequisite for success' (Deloitte, 2008: 5). This was a key focus of the document: rendering carbon reduction imperatives legible for those involved in economic policy development and the business community within the Manchester City Region. Despite asking challenging questions about the future of urban economies, the calculative logic might be argued as calculating out social and political dimensions of sustainability. Such a view chimes with portraits of the green economy as a "passive revolution" based on obfuscating contradictions between economic and ecological sustainability' (Wanner, 2015: 23).

To a certain extent, these studies, therefore, perform a function that aligns with the broader multi-level metagovernance (Jessop, 2004) of climate change policy and sub-national economic policy. The logic of international (UN and OECD), European Union (EU) and national governance centres on the economic case for change with the original Stern report a central 'device'. These studies took this logic as a starting point and combined it with the existing local economic development logic to produce a narrative around jobs and investment.

Despite the overarching concern for investment and attracting capital, the calculative activities do begin to consider some human challenges and possibilities of the green economy as relating to financial costs and jobs for people as well as GVA for capital. Each of the studies provides some indication of job impacts. For instance, Gouldson et al. (2012) estimate up to 4,400 jobs can be created over 10 years through the implementation of cost-effective carbon reduction measures in Leeds. Importantly studies such as Liverpool's Mini-Stern (Regeneris and Quantum, 2009) focus not only on job creation through the transition to a green economy, but also on jobs put at risk by a UK-wide transition. This flipside to analysis of the green economy is critical to a rounded view of the possibilities and challenges a move to a green economy brings about. This is more central to the Northern Mini-Sterns (Liverpool, Manchester, Leeds) where the effects of previous rounds of economic restructuring are still keenly felt. Here, the rhetoric is as much about economic exposure and vulnerability as a possibility and hope. For instance, the Liverpool Mini-Stern emphasises that,

> *... there are of the order of 99,000 jobs currently in the Liverpool City Region in sectors that could be significantly adversely affected in the future by climate change regulation and regulation*
>
> *(Regeneris and Quantum, 2009 p32).*

Calculative devices can create potential for more fundamentally different ways of seeing the urban economy and hints at different potential framings of the green economy also come through in some of the studies. In Leeds the focus again was on monetizing the costs and benefits of intervention on low carbon, but also opening up questions around private sector, state and civil society investment in low carbon transition as well as the social benefits of a more energy-efficient housing stock and transport system. In Leeds and in Leicester, there was also a concern for ensuring that local investment in low carbon benefit local businesses and residents: a feeling that given the right steer, a move towards a green economy could in turn help to localise economic flows. This was made explicit through the Leeds study (Gouldson et al,. 2012) which viewed a low carbon transition as a means of redirecting economic flows to multi-national energy firms into the local economy. The report focused on energy costs for the City Region as a whole, translated as economic leakage that impacts on local GVA:

£5.2 billion in energy costs going out of the city, £54 billion total economy in Leeds City Region, so we're almost in fuel poverty when you look at it like that!

(Policy Manager, Leeds).

The Bristol study (Bristol Green Capital, 2009), in many ways at odds with the other reports, takes this further, using a potential for a post-oil future to re-examine economic activity as commonly approached in economic development circles. Rather than focus on GVA and employment, the study recognises the potential for a more diverse localised economy to take root, focused on a circular economy as much led by civil society and informal economic activity as by investment from the state and large firms. There are clear nods to de-growth discourses (Fournier, 2008), and the green economy is interpreted as an opportunity to fundamentally reshape economic activity. There are, therefore, hints at how carbon-economic calculative devices can in turn open up space for considering the overarching economic paradigm for cities.

8.6 Rethinking Urban Assets through Green Economic Calculation

In many respects, the green economy is about creating new economic opportunities as markets are created for new environmental goods and services. Some of those opportunities will be about the location of sites for the management and production of goods and services, for example, the location of factories and research and development (R & D) facilities for renewable energy and low carbon products. However, low carbon value change also raises prospects for creating green economic opportunities through revaluing and mobilising existing urban assets. Indeed, one element of low-carbon restructuring—and therefore its politics of calculation—is the need to render visible processes of ontological value change. This is essential for low carbon alternatives because the ability to realise (and capture) the benefit of low-carbon restructuring opened up by MLG processes lies in seeing resources and resource flows differently. For example, the things that make up the urban (roofs, green spaces, derelict land, air flows) potentially take on new value as resources for renewable energy generation, energy security or carbon sequestration.

Each of the studies explored in this chapter includes proposals for creating economic and employment value from aspects of the existing urban infrastructure not previously valued in that way. As noted above the growing prominence of the green economy has led to the creation of new accounting practices that capture economic activity in this area: this in itself represents a new way of calculating the city economy and of rendering visible previously incalculable activities. Accounting for the LCEGS sector cuts across traditional economic classifications (such as the Standard Industrial Classification (SIC) index used in the UK), instead classifying activities according to their position within the whole 'green' supply chain. Thus, for example, plumbers are recast as key economic agents in the new green economy (see CRESR, 2014) due to their role in implementing a wide range of low carbon technologies. Accounting for LCEGS also acts as a ranking device, squarely positioning the urban green economy as a locus of competition between places.

The 'green' revaluation of economic assets also extends to natural and physical urban assets. The Liverpool Mini-Stern, for example, highlights the possibilities for wind and tidal energy opened-up by its coastal position, and the potential to tap into the Mersey Forest as a biomass producer, while the Bristol Peak Oil study explores the potential for urban food production. The implications of the Leeds Mini-Stern include revaluing the built environment as both a drain on economic resources through inefficient use of energy and a potential source of economic opportunity through the use of roof space for solar energy production. As the Leeds Mini-Stern makes clear, rendering green economic assets visible creates the potential to leverage those assets through financialisation that can allow for upfront investment needed to capitalise on the underused and undervalued urban potential. For example, the potential for solar energy generation can only be realised if solar panels are installed and linked effectively to local or national energy grids.

The calculations represented across the various studies, therefore, start to present an altered image of the urban that identifies the potential of urban assets to generate not only revenue but to provide the basis for local employment (and pathways to employment) in the installation, maintenance and management of low carbon infrastructures. Most of all perhaps those calculative practices generate discussion about local management frameworks that can take forward the overlapping benefits of CO_2 reduction, local infrastructure upgrade and locally meaningful employment. The idea of locally meaningful employment and pathways to employment is particularly significant in the context of ever more precarious work in UK cities. Realising the potential of urban assets such as roofs is also about making visible the opportunities for property interests who need to be enrolled into new assemblages of new green/low carbon infrastructure. This is clearly evident in the mapping work undertaken by the Bristol solar power study that presents the solar generation potential for each individual house.

Inevitably, visions for capitalising on seemingly undervalued urban assets are selective in their representations. For example, carbon sinks also remain unvalued as potential assets. Similarly, the territorial bounding of the studies leads to little consideration of changing ways in the material and economic relations between places as different assets are revalued. The requirement for cities to rely on their regional hinterlands for energy sources, food or carbon sequestration in a low carbon society may lead to different political-economic relations between cities and their peripheries, including new points of political tension.

8.7 Calculation as Enrolment Device

As performative texts, it was important that the reports successfully enroled and mobilised different interest groups to accept and then act on the findings. The evidence and recommendations within reports and policy prescriptions were difficult to implement directly because they were looking to a societal mode of green regulation that was not yet in place. As argued above, the studies were about making the case for (and de-risking) local action in advance of broader national and international changes:

The Mini-Stern was crucially important to doing that because for the first time it set out figures in terms of jobs and in terms of cost for acting, but also failing to act. All these pieces of work are based on our best understanding of the economy, of the cost of low-carbon technology, of the speed of development of that technology, so all of them date very quickly ... But in terms of being a corralling point to get local authorities, to get private businesses to see the benefits of co-ordinated action to scale up activity at a GM level it was important... The Mini Stern helped bring about the Low Carbon Economic Area and the Low Carbon Economic Area helped bring about engagement particularly around particular strands such as the housing retrofit, which is really beginning to gain momentum

(City Region Policy Manager, Manchester, March 2012).

The quotation above also shows how the report had been an important catalyst for a series of other policy initiatives in the Manchester City Region. Similarly, the Mini-Stern for Leeds was part of an expanded local debate about climate change action in the city, changing the lexicon of carbon reduction and in turn, opening up policy debates about green investment:

It's provided a platform and some really clear headline figures that can just be taken as snapshots to help make the argument for what we're trying to do. It's making an impact and bringing low carbon more into the mainstream economic thinking now. Which is absolutely what we wanted it to do

(LA Policy Manager, Leeds, April 2014).

The idea of wanting to talk about what an investment portfolio would look like and therefore going for pots of money to develop specific projects has all come out of the fact that we did that strong piece of evidence work, so from my point of view it's succeeded

(City Region Policy Manager, Leeds, April 2014).

Type I and II MLG processes (Hooghe and Marks, 2004) combined with local policy networks were working to ensure that carbon-economic investment was a policy agenda for these cities, and the Mini-Sterns were one way of helping to further the case for investment. The Mini-Sterns also diffused across different English localities. The Manchester Mini-Stern was the catalyst for both the Liverpool and Leeds reports; and in turn, the Leeds Mini-Stern has been influential across England, as a number of other local authorities and city regions have commissioned the authors to replicate the study for their localities, including Sheffield, Hull and Birmingham.

8.8 Conclusions: Seeing Cities Differently Amid Multi-level Lock-ins

This chapter set out to explore how arguments are being made for the development of an urban green economy through studies that highlight the economic and employment impacts of low carbon policy. The empirical examples above show how calculative governance devices have been used to define the green economy in different ways across England. These range from those directly following a mainstream weak ecological modernisation perspective (Gibbs, 2000), focusing on a reconfigured economy working to similar economic 'rules', to transformational visions which foreground possibilities for reimagined localised, 'convivial' economies (North, 2010).

The studies outlined show how such representations can be potentially transformative in revaluing urban economies, potentially extending to altered conceptions of the properties of cities. Yet this opening-up of possibilities is always selective. Representing a 'green' future is part of a political struggle and it can be difficult to overcome existing norms, and in particular to overcome the challenges of calculating the unknown. Such conceptualisations of the urban green economy take place within the strictures of existing modes of governance, unable to fully represent the possibility of a non-correspondence between the changes needed to transition and existing logics. The Bristol Peak Oil study demonstrates an example where this is partially achieved, however, by employing alongside calculative devices a wider range of narrative devices, including citizens' imagined future life stories.

It is important within this context to note that the different studies are products of differing political and economic circumstances in each city. Bristol, used here as an example of how urban economies could be fundamentally reimagined, has a historically prominent green movement, active civil society and strong links between local government and voluntary organisations. This is reflected in the fact that the Peak Oil study was commissioned by Bristol Green Capital, an organisation initially convened by the city council but led by a partnership of civil society organisations. By 2015, it had 800 members. Bristol is also a relatively wealthy city (notwithstanding pockets of deprivation) and its economic challenges are more concerned with managing the impacts of growth which perhaps more readily opens up questions about the value of growth in and of itself. Manchester, Liverpool, Sheffield and Leicester on the other hand still bear the significant scars of previous rounds of economic restructuring and the green economy must be framed in terms of economic growth (or risks to economic growth) for local politicians to accept its legitimacy as a mainstream cause. Equally, however, these studies were commissioned with a particular audience in mind, businesses and economic development professionals, and as a result critical issues for these cities relating to poverty and 'just' green jobs are left relatively unattended. The future is viewed in terms of high skilled, high pay industries rather than as a means for potentially providing high levels of employment across different sectors (see for example the Trade Union-led '1 million climate jobs' campaign (www.climate-change-jobs.org). The broader political climate in these cities is more typically corporatist with traditionally close ties between local authority and local industries, in recent times seen as necessary to ensure continued investment in these cities.

These studies also highlight limits to urban scale action even within the formal territory of a particular place. The city cannot be understood solely as a container of activity: cities are porous, multi-level, multi-scale phenomena. For example, cities import and export services, goods, energy, people, waste (and so on). They also provide the site for multi-scalar objects: people and organisations, which operate at different scales often simultaneously. In addition, the city is a multi-level governance object in itself: people and organisations regulated at different scales of governance. This alters the scope of action. For instance, the Mini-Sterns largely ignore large emitters in their midst such as fossil-fuelled power stations because they are 'disembodied'; regulated by national and international governance arrangements and organised by multi-national firms. The Leeds and Bristol studies attempt something more transformational in terms of reducing the influence of and reliance on outside bodies.

The overall story is that green economic futures need to become visible and tangible to alter the trajectory of existing policy frames. The task is to justify, de-risk and legitimise what might be seen as more experimental or risky policy options especially if they involve longer-term commitments in uncertain multi-level contexts. It is to be expected that the need for such studies will diminish over time as what are now considered alternatives become mainstream.

References

Allen, J. (2009). Three spaces of power: territory, networks, plus a topological twist in the tale of domination and authority. *Power*, 2(2), 197–212.

BEIS (2017). *Carbon valuation*. Online source, accessed 3 January 2018: https://www.gov.uk/government/collections/carbon-valuation–2

Bridge, G. (2010). Resource geographies 1: making carbon economies, old and new. *Progress in Human Geography*, 35, 6.

Bulkeley, H., Castán Broto, V., Hodson, M. and Marvin, S. (2010). *Cities and Low Carbon Transitions*. London: Routledge.

Bumpus, A. and Liverman, D. (2008). Accumulation by decarbonization and the governance of carbon offsets. *Economic Geography*, 84(2), 127–155.

Du Gay, P., Millo, Y. and Tuck, P. (2012). Making government liquid: shifts in governance using financialisation as a political device. *Environment and Planning C: Government and Policy*, 30(6), 1083–1099.

Eadson, W. (2011) Constructions of the carbon city. In J. Flint and M. Raco, eds., *The Future of Sustainable Cities*. Bristol: Policy Press.

Enworks (2013). The economic potential of low carbon and environmental goods and services (LCEGS) sector in Greater Manchester. http://enworks.com/resources/Economic%20potential%20of%20LCEGS%20Sector%20in%20Greater%20Manchester_1.pdf

Fournier, V. (2008). Escaping from the economy: the politics of degrowth, *International Journal of Sociology and Social Policy*, 28(11/12), 528–545.

Gibbs, D. (2000) Ecological modernisation, regional economic development and regional development agencies. *Geoforum*, 31(3) 299–313.

Gouldson, A., Kerr, N., Topi, C., Dawkins, E., Kuylenstierna, J. and Pearce, R. (2012). *The Economics of Low Carbon Cities A Mini-Stern Review for the Leeds City Region*. Leeds: University of Leeds.

Harvey, D. (1989). From managerialism to entrepreneurialism: The transformation of urban governance in late capitalism *Geographiska Annaler*, 71B, 3–17.

Haughton, G., Counsell, D. and Vigar, G. (2008). Sustainable development in post-devolution UK and Ireland, *Regional Studies*, 42(9), 1223–1236.

Hodson, M. and Marvin, S. (2010). Can cities shape socio-technical transitions and how would we know if they were? *Research Policy*, 39(4), 377–485.

Hooghe, L. and Marks, G. (2004) Contrasting visions of multi-level governance. In I. Bache and M. Flinders, eds., *Multi-Level Governance*. Oxford: Oxford University Press.

Jessop, B. (2000). The crisis of the national spatio-temporal fix and the ecological dominance of globalizing, *International Journal of Urban and Regional Research*, 24, 323–360.

Jessop, B. (2004). Multi-level governance and multi-level meta-governance. In I. Bache and M. Flinders, eds., *Multi-Level Governance*. Oxford: Oxford University Press, pp.49–74.

Katagawa, F. (2013). City-regions, universities and innovation: the evolution and transformation of UK urban governance institutions. In Philip Cooke, ed., *Re-framing regional development: evolution, innovation and transition*. Abingdon: Routledge.

Kornberger, M. (2013). Disciplining the future: On studying the politics of strategy. *Scandinavian Journal of Management*, 29(1), 104–107.

Kornberger, M. and Carter, C. (2010). Manufacturing competition: how accounting practices shape strategy making in cities. *Accounting, Auditing & Accountability Journal*, 23(3), 325–349.

Lapsley, I., Miller, P. and Panozzo, F. (2010). Accounting for the city. *Accounting, Auditing & Accountability Journal*, 23(3), 305–324.

Lohmann, L. (2009). Toward a different debate in environmental accounting: The cases of carbon and cost–benefit. *Accounting, Organizations and Society*, 34, 499–534.

Lövbrand, E. and Stripple, J. (2011). Making climate change governable: accounting for carbon as sinks, credits and personal budgets, *Critical Policy Studies*, 5(2), 187–200.

Lovell, H., Bulkeley, H. and Owens, S. (2009). Converging agendas: Energy and climate change policies in the UK. *Environment and Planning C*, 27(1), 97–109.

Mackenzie, D. (2009). Making things the same: Gases emissions rights and the politics of carbon markets. *Accounting, Organizations and Society*, 34, 440–455.

Miller, P. (2001). Governing by numbers: why calculative practices matter. *Social Research*, 68(2), 379–396.

North, P. (2010). Eco-localisation as a progressive response to peak oil and climate change – A sympathetic critique. *Geoforum*, 41(4), 585–594.

Rutland, T. and Aylett, A. (2008). The work of policy: actor networks, governmentality, and local action on climate change in Portland, Oregon, *Environment and Planning D: Society and Space*, 26, 627–646.

van Stigt, R., Driessen, P. P. J. and Spit, T. J. M. (2013). Compact city development and the challenge of environmental policy integration: a multi-level governance perspective. *Environmental Policy and Governance*, 23, 221–233.

Stern, N. (2006). *The Economics of Climate Change*. London: HM Treasury.

Stripple, J. and Bulkeley, H. (2014). *Governing the climate: new approaches to rationality, power and politics*. Cambridge: Cambridge University Press.

Wanner, T. (2015). The New 'Passive Revolution' of the Green Economy and Growth Discourse: Maintaining the 'Sustainable Development' of Neoliberal Capitalism, *New Political Economy*, 20(1), 21–41.

Ward, K. (2003). Entrepreneurial urbanism, state restructuring and civilizing 'New' East Manchester. *Area*, 35, 116–127.

Wesselink, A. and Gouldson, A. (2014). Pathways to impact in local government: the mini-Stern review as evidence in policy making in the Leeds City Region. *Policy Sciences*, 47, 407–433.

While, A. (2010). The carbon calculus and transitions in urban politics and urban political theory. In H. Bulkeley, M. Hodson and S. Marvin, eds., *Cities and Low Carbon Transitions*. London: RoutlTcdgc.

Whittle, A. and Mueller, F. (2010). Strategy, enrolment and accounting: the politics of strategic ideas, Accounting. *Auditing & Accountability Journal*, 23(5), 626–646.

9

The Green Economy

Key Lessons and the Way Forward

NICHOLAS VASILAKOS AND JENNY M. FAIRBRASS

9.1 An Overview

As first outlined in Chapter 1, the introduction to this edited collection, the work undertaken and presented in this volume has been assembled as the result of inter-disciplinary and multi-disciplinary research collaboration completed over the course of 12 or more years. During that period, a number of groups of scholars, located primarily in the disciplines of EU studies and Political Science have combined their work with those hailing from economics, environmental science, history, sociology and geography. The academics (and practitioners) who have contributed to the scholarship in this collection have sought to reveal, explain, and evaluate the emerging governance and multi-level governance (MLG) associated with the 'greening' of the European economy (Commission, of the European Communities (CEC), 2019). Those research objectives have, by necessity, demanded an examination of processes and actors involved in any discerned shifts towards a 'green' or 'greener' European economy.

Acknowledging and building on this background, this chapter now proceeds by returning to the underpinning conceptual frameworks (i.e. governance and MLG) and common research questions initially outlined in Chapter 1, then summarises the findings of the case study chapters, reflects on the key results and what they reveal about the 'greening' of the European economy, discusses the limitations of the research conducted and presented, and closes by outlining some ideas for further research.

9.2 Conceptual Framework(s) Adopted and Research Questions

Recall that the contributing case study authors were all asked to adopt and utilise common conceptual framework(s) in order to provide coherence and a shared approach for the volume. The notions of 'governance' and 'MLG' were chosen (as regards 'governance' literature, for seminal works see Heritier and Rhodes 2011; Jordan Schout 2006; Kohler-Koch and Eising 1999; Kohler-Koch and Rittberger, 2006. For key MLG texts, consult Bache and Flinders 2004; Conzelmann and Smith 2008; Fairbrass and Jordan 2004; Hooghe and Marks 2001, 2003; Jessop 2004; Jordan 2001; Knill and Tosun 2008; Kohler-Koch Larat 2009; Marks 1993, 1996; Marks and Hooghe 2004; Peters and Pierre 2004; Piattoni 2009; Rosenau 2004).

Based on the body of the literature above, a number of core research questions were derived (see Chapter 1 for details). All of the contributing authors were tasked to consider those questions and to respond to them using their particular case study to provide empirical data, insights and some conclusions. This chapter now turns to a summary of the main contributions and key findings drawn from each of the case study chapters, employing this literature and reflecting on the core research questions.

9.3 Summary of Discussions and Findings

The seven chapters that form the core of this volume (excluding the Introduction and the Conclusions) were all selected because they highlight or spotlight particular issues relating to the 'greening' of the European Economy. Chapter 2 sets out the terms of the debate about 'greening' an economy and highlights the practical policy issues and obstacles. Chapter 3 adopts a more overtly theoretical stance and addresses key questions about the vital role(s) played by key governance actors such as governments in seeking to create a 'green' economy. The first three chapters provide the context and tone for the chapters that follow.

Other contributions (Chapters 4, 5, 6, 7 and 8) were chosen because they offer fresh empirical data and focus on particular national contexts in 'older' European Union (EU) member states such as the UK and Germany (in the case of the Moulton et al chapter) or on 'newer' EU member states such as Romania (as is the case with the Davidescu chapter). Additionally, the chapters proffered here were selected because they highlight the significant (potential or actual) role of the energy sector in helping (or hindering) the transition to low carbon or 'green' European economy. In effect, evidence about the role played by the energy sector is one of the central themes or topics that lend coherence and commonality to the volume. Moreover, given that all of the chapters utilise certain shared underpinning frameworks and concepts (i.e. 'governance' and 'MLG'), all of the chapters grapple with the issue of the role played by a range of governance actors, at EU, national and sub-national or local level in the private, public and voluntary sectors in 'greening' the European economy. This again provides consistency and cohesion to the collection.

In further detail, Chapter 2 starts with a discussion of the definition of 'green' economies and how this has changed over time. In particular, Benson, Fairbrass, Lorenzoni, O'Riordan and Russel discuss the origins of the term 'green economy', and how this concept re-emerged over a decade ago in discussions across the globe amongst politicians, civil servants, business, non-governmental organisations (NGOs), community interest groups, the media and academics. The authors argue that the notion of a green economy remains elusive and is deeply disputed, often poorly understood and unevenly applied. Their analysis traces the development of the concept, not only in Europe but beyond, in order to provide context for the deliberations in Europe. The chapter also outlines contemporary debates and identifies emerging themes in order to argue that the idea of a green economy, as currently practiced, requires urgent re-thinking and application.

In Chapter 3, Rozema, Fairbrass and Vasilakos consider the ways in which policy actors may advance the notion of a 'green economy' by making it compatible with 'good governance'. As one way of shaping order in advanced industrialised societies, the idea of green economy translates into a discourse propagated by the government and non-state actors where it is conceived as 'the right thing to do', thereby fitting current economic activity into governance arrangements which are also tailored to meet environmental objectives. The authors reflect on current theoretical debates about a 'green economy' in the EU as a conception of 'good governance', the latter being an umbrella concept encompassing principles of legitimate public policy-making such as accountability, transparency, public engagement or institutional reform. They conclude that a European green economy can be achieved as a product of 'good governance', whilst also simultaneously considered as 'the right thing to do'. This theoretical reflection reinvigorates interest in normative power and the will to govern as productive forces for governance, through its capacity to instil affinity with a particular rendition of economic ordering.

In Chapter 4, Hoerber, Agafonow and Akhabbar propose a change in the ownership structure of energy utilities through the introduction of social enterprises. This seems to be a pertinent approach because, in parallel to the EU 2020 strategy, the EU has introduced a Social Business Initiative (SBI). The authors of this chapter believe that the combination of both policies can change the ground rules of energy production and provision within the EU. To explain this, the authors use a theoretical model that draws on a MLG framework, which enables the analysis to take into account the effects and interdependencies of governance on various actors of the energy sector, namely national governments and energy producers. Their analysis shows that although using social enterprises in the renewable energy sector will foster the emergence of greener communities, it is also more likely to benefit well-off estate owners than less affluent tenants. This effect could be reversed with the design of a regulatory framework that requires social enterprises to use a pricing policy that discriminates clients by their tenure status, charging more affordable prices to tenants only.

Davidescu in Chapter 5 discusses the experience of Romania in transitioning towards a green economy. As the author explains, until recently Romania had limited credentials with regard to ambitious environmental policy and a difficult transition to the market economy and democracy. However, the country has surprisingly experienced the emergence of a green economy discourse separate from sustainable development and a range of green economy initiatives in niche sectors and across different levels of government, with a peak of activity in 2016–2017. The chapter links this to the agenda of a technocratic caretaker government, as well as the emergence of sub-national actors from the environmental movement and local and regional level, who were able to successfully engage in green economy initiatives, bypassing the national government level. Using the example of the renewable energy sector, this chapter shows that significant growth in this area usually associated with the green economy does not necessarily ensure either sustained or green practices.

Chapter 6 assesses the attempts of maritime port cities to use the green economy in a bid to overcome long-term structural disadvantages. Moulton, Osthorst, Deutz, Jonas and Wurzel argue that these cities perceive climate change not only as a threat but also as an opportunity for 'green' growth in the form of new technologies and industries (such as the renewable energy industry). However, the emerging literature on the green economy underlines the dangers of uneven chances to exploit economic opportunities, reinforced locational competition, and the prevalence of technocratic, instead of transformative, strategies. The chapter uses as a case study Bremerhaven (Germany) and Hull (UK); two coastal cities that suffered major economic setbacks as a result of severe declines in local maritime industries (e.g. fisheries and shipbuilding). Albeit with differing strategies, both cities have turned to renewables, especially offshore wind, and the 'green' improvement of public housing as a source of jobs and growth. The analysis that is presented in this chapter shows how local green economies can develop, and what impact they may have on local economies. The cases also exhibit the challenges that cities can face in trying to maintain their role as centres for the green economy, including through financial restrictions (a hallmark of structurally disadvantaged cities exacerbated by austerity), regional competition and changing national policy contexts.

The changing role of energy companies in the context of European green economies is examined by Fernandez in Chapter 7. As the author explains, the traditional model of European energy company has been characterised by big entities that usually play a relatively important role as national champions in terms of market share, assets value, vertical integration, political influence and employment volumes, among other factors. However, the last decade has seen these big firms losing market power to new entrants. This chapter uses the framework of green economy as the one that approaches macroeconomic issues through innovative ways, promoting green investments through the most adequate regulatory measures, and considering green energy as one of the sectors where these investments should be focused. The chapter goes on to point out the important role of energy companies in the transition of Europe into a green economy. The chapter also highlights the barriers that energy companies impose themselves through old fashioned strategies that do not take into consideration the wider demands from a much larger group of stakeholders in a changing society, and argues for the importance of embracing a business model that is proactive and in favour of change, rather than try to maintain the status quo.

In Chapter 8, Eadson and While examine how definitions of the green economy are shaped by and seek to shape norms and discourses of economic development. The authors draw on MLG theories alongside literature from critical accounting to investigate ways that urban policy actors have sought to make the case for investment in the green economy. In doing so the chapter expands existing conceptualisations of the politics of calculation (in a MLG context) to illuminate how calculations represent a range of assumptions about territory, the way people live and the nature of place and society in the present and the future. Empirically the chapter focuses on a series of 'Mini-Stern' reports commissioned by urban governments in England which took as inspiration Nicholas Stern's influential 2006 report on the economics of climate change. The authors analyse how these reports use various calculative devices relating to carbon reduction in order to justify, de-risk and legitimise what might be seen as experimental or risky policy options; and the implications for how cities are represented as a result.

9.4 Key Findings, Challenges and Limitations: Ideas for Further Research

9.4.1 Key Findings

We now turn to consider the key findings generated by the preceding case study chapters. Returning to our overriding research objective, the main outcomes arising from the research are as follows. First, that a number of labels have currency alongside 'green economy', and that while the term 'green economy' tends to be more fashionable (and as widely used) than 'sustainable development' or even 'sustainability', it seems that all of these terms may have been superseded or displaced by the words 'circular economy'. For the moment, at least, the latter term has gained currency amongst a range of actors including the EU (CEC, 2019).

In conclusion, however, despite the use of multiple terms, ultimately the debate is still focused on issues concerning climate change, energy, food production, the environment, biodiversity and eco-systems. But, because a range of terms are in use and there are multiple interpretations, the word and the idea are still contested and disputed and we continue to face the challenge of more widely and effectively implementing the 'green economy'. What is striking is that more recent iterations of the idea appear to place greater weighting on social justice and fairness (CEC, 2019). Second, what also emerges clearly from the research reported in the case study chapters is that 'greening' an economy is not a domain confined to governments but needs the buy-in of business and other societal actors if it is ever to be implemented effectively. In a number of the case studies (see Chapters 4, 5, 6, 7 and 8), the involvement and support of city councils, local government, small and big business, and other societal groups such as civil society organisations has helped to drive towards a greener economy. Third, moreover, the focus on energy as a route towards a green or greener economy is also revealed by the case study chapters and is justified by the evidence collected both in theoretical and practical terms. Clearly, energy transitions are one of the central components of a green economy: essential to creating or establishing a green economy.

Turning to examine some of the individual research questions and the data gathered we find a number of significant patterns. See Table 9.1 for details.

9.4.2 Limitations of the Present Volume and Future Research

In common with all forms of research, there are some limitations to the work undertaken. First, this research is geographically bounded, confined to European case studies, and in a sense even more limited to three countries (the UK, Germany and Romania). Moreover, the research conducted and reported has concentrated primarily on energy-based case studies.

Given these limitations, it would be advisable to both extend the geographical boundaries to include other parts of the world where strides are being taken to 'green' the economy. As discussed in Chapter 2, countries such as New Zealand and South Korea would provide interesting data and offer some further lessons about the topic. But, equally, a focus on places or countries that might be considered more laggard with respect to this issue also warrant an investigation. The USA, for example, also mentioned briefly in Chapter 2 could provide a useful and informative case study. In addition, to extending the geographical boundaries, future research should widen its policy range to encompass research into other aspects of a 'green economy' such as food production, transport, and climate change.

Table 9.1. *Summary of research questions and answers*

Research Questions	Evidence and responses
How is the term 'green economy' being defined?	A range of definitions are in use but most align with the EU's definition in its 2019 'The New Green Deal' paper.
What role can businesses play in engendering a 'green economy'	Case studies reveal that businesses can and do play a pivotal role. They are important gate-keepers. See Chapters 4, 5, 6, 7 and 8 for details.
What changes can/should businesses undertake with regard to the following in their endeavours to create or help build a 'green economy'?	Businesses can/should amend their actions to play a leading or supporting role in combination with other actors. See Chapters 4, 5, 6, 7 and 8 for details.
What incentives or opportunities do businesses require to encourage them to innovate to help develop a 'green economy'	Some case studies reveal the significance of finance and investment and the role of government as a facilitator or partner. Some case studies highlight the importance of the regulatory environment. See Chapters 4 and 8 in particular.
What sort of funding structures/sources and types of capital would assist businesses to shift towards a 'green economy'?	Could be public or private investment or a combination of the two. See Chapter 8 as an example.
What types of political/economic environments are required to 'encourage' business organisations to assist in the construction of a 'green economy'?	May require a particular regulatory environment to bring about the transition to a green economy.
What forms of business organisation might be most effective in addressing the shift towards a 'green economy' (e.g. social enterprise, large multi-national, community based)?	Case studies show that businesses of different types (e.g. social enterprise) and size can play a major role. See Chapters 4 and 7.
How might the form of business adopted affect or assist in creating 'green local communities'?	Social enterprises in particular could assist. See Chapter 4.
How and to what extent might businesses help to eradicate poverty via their efforts with regard to the construction of a 'green economy' (locally, nationally, and internationally)?	Through the provision of 'green jobs'. See Chapter 6.
How do businesses, governmental and civil society organisations relate to one another in seeking to establish a vibrant 'green economy'?	Active partnership may be the most effective form of interaction.
To what extent and how can 'green jobs' contribute to the construction of the wider 'green economy'?	See above and Chapter 6 in particular.

Source: Authors

9.5 Closing Reflections

Over the course of a dozen or more years, a great deal of primary, empirical research has been conducted by the scholars who have contributed to this volume. Their work has sought to illuminate the subject of greening an economy, wrestling with the various terms and meanings in use, attempting to clearly identify examples of a 'green' economy in action, explaining and evaluating the developments and trends that they have found. Quite clearly the task that they have begun to undertake is vast and so too is the practical application of the ideas surrounding the topic. We admit that this volume only scratches the surface of the subject. Much more work, both academic and practitioner, remains to be undertaken and completed before we are in a better position to attain a green global economy, let alone a European one. However, at the time of writing there are hopeful signs. Populations around the world are beginning to recognise and appreciate how important a green economy is and will be in the future, not least because they have suffered ill-effects (such as flooding or drought) that can be linked back to a lack of a 'green economy'. What is particularly encouraging is that the youth of the world has been sparked into action. We may yet live to see a genuinely 'green' economy in Europe and across the globe if individuals, communities, local authorities, national governments, businesses and international organisations such as the EU and the United Nations are and remain determined to see this project through to the end and bring about a truly 'green' economy.

References

Bache, I. and Flinders, M., eds. (2004). *Multi-level Governance*. Oxford: Oxford University Press.

Conzelmann, T. and Smith, R., eds. (2008). *Multi-level Governance in the European Union: Taking Stock and Looking Ahead*. Baden Baden: Nomos.

CEC (2019). *Communication from the Commission to the European Parliament, the European Council, the Council, the European Economic and Social Committee and the Committee of the Regions. The European Green Deal*. COM(2019) 640 final. Brussels: European Commission.

Fairbrass, J. and Jordan, A. (2004). Multi-level governance and environmental policy. In I. Bache and M. Flinders. eds. *Multi-level Governance*. Oxford: Oxford University Press, pp. 147–164.

Heritier, A. and Rhodes, M. (2011). *New Modes of Governance in Europe: Governing in the Shadow of Hierarchy*. Basingstoke: Palgrave Macmillan.

Hooghe, L. and Marks, G. (2001). *Multi-level Governance and European Integration*. Lanham, MD: Rowman and Littlefield.

Hooghe, L. and Marks, G. (2003). Unraveling the central state, but how? Types of multi-level governance. *American Political Science Review*, 97(2), 233–243.

Jessop, B. (2004). Multi-level governance and multi-level metagovernance. In I. Bache and M. Flinders, eds. *Multi-level Governance*. Oxford: Oxford University Press, pp. 49–74.

Jordan, A. (2001). The European Union: an evolving system of multi-level governance ... or government? *Policy and Politics*, 29(2), 193–208.

Jordan, A. and Schout, A. (2006). *The Coordination of the European Union: Exploring the Capacities of Networked Governance*. Oxford: Oxford University Press.

Knill, C. and Tosun, J. (2008). Emerging patterns of multi-level governance in EU Environmental Policy. In T. Conzelmann and R. Smith, eds. *Multi-level Governance in the European Union: Taking Stock and Looking Ahead*. Baden Baden: Nomos, pp. 145–162.

Kohler-Koch, B. and Eising, R. eds. (1999). *The Transformation of Governance in the European Union*. London: Routledge.

Kohler-Koch, B. and Larat, F. eds. (2009). *European Multi-level Governance: Contrasting Images in National Research*. Cheltenham: Edward Elgar.

Marks, G. (1993). Structural policy and multi-level governance in the EC. In A. Cafruny and G. Rosenthal, eds. *The State of the European Community: The Maastricht Debate and Beyond*. Boulder, CO: Lynne Rienner, pp. 391–411.

Marks, G. (1996). An actor-centred approach to multi-level governance. *Regional and Federal Studies*, 6(2), 20–38.

Marks, G. and Hooghe, L. (2004). Contrasting visions of multi-level governance. In I. Bache and M. Flinders, eds. *Multi-level Governance*. Oxford: Oxford University Press, pp. 15–30.

Peters, B. and Pierre, J. (2004). Multi-level governance and democracy: a Faustian bargain? In I. Bache and M. Flinders, Eds. *Multi-level Governance*. Oxford: Oxford University Press, pp. 75–89.

Piattoni, S. (2009). Multi-level governance: a historical and conceptual analysis. *Journal of European Public Policy*, 31(2), 163–80.

Rosenau, J. (2004). Contrasting visions of multi-level governance. In. Bache and M. Flinders, eds., *Multi-level Governance*. Oxford: Oxford University Press, pp. 31–48.

Index